The Study of International Politics

The Study of International Politics

*A Guide to the Sources
for the Student, Teacher, and Researcher*

Dorothy F. LaBarr and J. David Singer

CLIO BOOKS

Santa Barbara, California • Oxford, England

Library of Congress Cataloging in Publication Data

LaBarr, Dorothy F
　　The study of international politics.

　　Bibliography: p.
　　Includes index.
　　1.　International relations—Bibliography.
　　2.　International relations—Study and teaching—
　　Bibliography.　I.　Singer, Joel David, 1925–
　　joint author.　II.　Title.
　　Z6461.S56　[JX1391]　　　　016.327　　　　76-12545
　　ISBN 0-87436-233-4

American Bibliographical Center—Clio Press, Inc.
2040 Alameda Padre Serra
Santa Barbara, California

European Bibliographical Center—Clio Press
Woodside House, Hinksey Hill
Oxford OX1 5 BE, England

Manufactured in the United States of America

Acknowledgments

We express our appreciation to Andrea Sperlbaum, Mental Health Research Institute librarian, and her assistant Naomi Litzenblatt, for their tireless efforts in helping us track down various elusive materials for this book. Also, we extend our gratitude to Melvin Small, Hugh Wheeler, and Charles Gochman for their suggestions and critiques during the final stages of manuscript preparation. Alan Levy's technical advice and his critiques were invaluable, and we thank him not only for his assistance but also for the cheerfulness with which it was offered. Finally, we acknowledge with warmest thanks the support of the University of Michigan's Mental Health Research Institute and the Department of Political Science.

Contents

Introduction

In a recent bibliography for political science students, the compiler (Clifton Brock, 1969, p. 8) suggests that "the best place to begin a literature search is not in the library at all, but in the office of whatever professor specializes in the subject. . . ." Having been the victims of that sort of advice all too often, we thought there must be a better way. This volume is the result, but before getting into its content and organization, let us say a word about its rationale.

At the beginning of their careers, young instructors tend to welcome students who come to them for guidance into the literature of a given social science problem, and often enjoy being known as "walking bibliographies." But that strategy can eat into one's time in a severe way, and thus become increasingly inefficient for both faculty and students. It also seems inadequate from a *pedagogical* viewpoint, in that the student gets started the easy way and may never develop a capacity for independent library research. That realization leads, in turn, to suggesting greater reliance on the existing bibliographies, such as those listed in Section VIII of this volume.

Bibliographies in our field fall into one of two groups. First, and more numerous, are the highly specialized ones, organized around a specific topic, problem, or theme: war and peace, imperialism, international organization, disarmament, etc. Second are the more general ones, intended to provide an overview of the entire field, but with no claim to depth in any of the sub-field corners. This one is very much of this second type, yet quite unlike other general bibliographies in international politics. What are some of the differences?

First, this volume proceeds from a clear epistemological premise: that international politics can be studied from a scientific point of view; the past 15 years have shown that this is no pipe dream. Thus, even though we include here numerous books, anthologies, and articles that are non-scientific as well as anti-scientific in tone, we do so quite explicitly, and in several places we go so far as to clearly differentiate the more rigorous and scientific works from the others. Second, as working researchers in the international politics field, we not only know of, but actually use, many of the materials listed here. Among these are a good many fugitive items—papers, reports, and monographs that are not "published" in the conventional sense, but which nevertheless are valuable to the student, teacher, or researcher.

A third difference is that we go beyond the mere listing of titles—whether they be the conventionally published books and articles or the more elusive items—and often list their contents. Thus, we provide here the author and title of each paper found in several types of anthologies and journals. A final difference is the organizational one. We think that the orderly arrangement and precise labeling of the sections and sub-sections will make this more usable and efficient than most bibliographies. In that vein, rather than require you to search back and forth between and among a table of contents, an index, and the descriptions found at the beginning of each section in most such volumes, we spell out the basic arrangement pattern right here at the beginning. If you take the few minutes necessary to read that section, you'll know where to look for everything from the start.

In sum, we think this will turn out to be one of the most useful bibliographies in the international politics field. It will help the teacher decide how to organize the course, and will suggest what to include in the reading lists and what to read in preparation for class meetings. It will help the introductory student to gain a sense of the international politics field and to find his/her way into the several sectors of the literature. And for the advanced student, it should lead to a more comprehensive overview of the field and aid in filling the gaps that seem inevitably to remain, regardless of how much formal training has been completed. Even the researcher should benefit from this volume, as a device for "reality testing" and assurance that some critical piece of work is not overlooked. Worth noting, too, is that a volume such as this can be an aid to more efficient writing. That is, in addition to helping you *find* all sorts of materials, it will help you to *cite* them later on when you're preparing a course outline or writing a paper or book. It is one thing to remember that Jones wrote a book about theory building in international politics in the mid-1960s, and quite another to have the full citation at your fingertips.

Scope: Inclusions and Exclusions

Let us now turn from the advertisements and the platitudes as to why this may be a more useful bibliography than others, and get down to specifics. That is, what is *ex*cluded, what is *in*cluded, and where will you find it? Perhaps we should begin with a reiteration of what we do *not* include, given the general notion that almost *everything* falls under the rubric of international (or world) politics, relations, or affairs.

As noted above, you will not find much on any specific problem or topic (except "conflict" in its general sense), but there are (in Section

VIII) bibliographies and bibliographic articles that *do* deal with a wide variety of subjects. Similarly, we steer clear of two highly specialized sub-fields within the international politics realm: international law and international organization. Without for a moment giving aid and comfort to those who think that such a body of law is either non-existent or irrelevant, or who consider international organization so ineffectual as to merit no serious attention, we would be naive to think we can venture into those sub-fields and make a useful contribution. Again, however, there will be several bibliographies on this subject in Section VIII.

Another exclusion that should be made explicit is that of *cross-national politics*. While it is true that the phenomena of inter-national and cross-national politics have considerable overlap, and that some scholars think of anything foreign (i.e., outside their own nations) as international, there *is* a reasonable distinction. That is, political science (like the other macro-social sciences) has a field usually called comparative politics (or sociology or economics) and its concern is with the cross-national comparison of phenomena that occur largely *within* the many national societies that make up the international system. In this bibliography, we attend to phenomena that occur *within* nations only to the extent that they seem to bear directly upon those nations' foreign policies. More specifically, we include only studies that are addressed to either the policies of nations vis-à-vis others or the processes by which domestic and foreign stimuli impinge upon and shape those policies. Two examples typifying this exclusion of cross-national literature are the excellent and extensive work of Gisbert Flanz and Albert Blaustein, *Constitutions of the Countries of the World*, Dobbs Ferry, N.Y.: Oceana (1972), and Amos Peaslee, *Constitutions of Nations*, New York: Justice (1956).

Finally, we admit with some embarrassment to a linguistic provincialism, and a word about that shortcoming is in order. In a field such as ours, it is especially important to go beyond one's own geographical and conceptual borders in the search for ideas and knowledge. But three considerations—none of them reassuring for the field of international politics—led us to remain with English-language materials only. First, only a small (and apparently decreasing) fraction of English-speaking students, teachers, and researchers in our field are able to understand a second language. Second, as one examines the literature on international politics in languages other than English, one is struck by the absence of rigor. For example, almost every nation in the world today has one or several journals of international affairs, yet almost all of them are filled mainly with pre-scientific analyses of current events. The primary difference between them and their English-language counterparts is that *their* articles proceed from a slightly different set of ideological or strategic assumptions; the qualitative differences tend to be negligible. (The only exception we have uncovered is *Études Polemologiques*—formerly *Guerre et Paix*—published by Gaston Bouthoul and his peace research colleagues in Paris.) A third consideration is that many of their books and articles deal not with *inter-national* affairs, but with *foreign* affairs. And since all the 140-odd other nations in today's system are foreign to the one at hand, there is no shortage of material. Thus, to include even the names—not to mention the contents—of all these journals (the number is probably close to 1000) would have taken a great deal of time and space, with only marginal rewards to the users of this volume.

Organization and Description of Contents

I. Approaches to the Study and Teaching of International Politics

In every field of inquiry, it is essential to be self-conscious as to what we're doing and why we're doing it. The international politics field is no exception, and during the past decade or so there has been not only a major increase in such self-consciousness, but a number of sharp challenges to the old ways of studying and teaching the subject. The most important of these challenges is likely to be the methodological one. That is, we have seen the *scope* of the field defined and re-defined on several occasions, and have experienced recurrent revisions of the *policy orientations* and *ethical assumptions* that guide the teacher and researcher, but these tend to come and go in a cyclical fashion. On the other hand, the challenge to the dominant—and essentially pre-scientific—*methodology*, begun in the late 1950s, is likely to be both irreversible and profound in its effects. While the relationship between astrology and astronomy or between alchemy and chemistry may be too strong a comparison, the analogy seems appropriate. Having discovered that the stuff of international politics is quite amenable to the more rigorous types of observation and analysis associated with scientific method, we are unlikely to fall back into the purely poetic and impressionistic modes of an earlier epoch.

This challenge to older methodologies and to their underlying epistemologies has led to many books, articles, and anthologies of articles, and they are well represented in Section I. But you will also find, especially for the past 5 years, a fair amount of literature that calls for a reversal of this so-called behavioral trend; some of it is even labeled "peace research." The central argument in that literature is that only the more trivial questions yield to the demands of rigorous method, and that as long as researchers concentrate on such marginalia, the reactionary establishments (especially in the major powers) will remain unexamined and thus free to practice their imperialistic foreign policies unhindered.

Despite our enthusiasm for the modern methodologies (and explicit rejection of the above argument), we do not include books or articles that are exclusively methodological in focus. These are of two basic types. The first are quite technical, detailed, and statistical, seldom dealing with international politics alone, but usually with the problems of an entire discipline, such as economics, psychology, sociology, and, of course, political science. But they tend to be misleading, and often focus on only one type of method within each discipline; those in political science and sociology, for example, are usually strong on demographic analyses or opinion surveys, and those in psychology are usually strong on laboratory experiment. The second are much more general in that they are written not by scientists or statisticians but by philosophers, historians, and professors of English. They tend to tell us "how to do research," beginning with platitudes about framing questions carefully, then describing a library reference room, and often ending with some pre-scientific sermon regarding the dangers of quantification. The libraries of the world are chock-full of such volumes and you won't need our help to find them.

In this opening section of the book, there are four sub-sections. First, in I-A there are the standard volumes authored by a single scholar, a pair, or perhaps several scholars; also found here are those volumes composed solely of the author's/editor's own articles (i.e., auto-anthologies). The more conventional readers are found in Section I-B, and under these we list the authors and articles that are included in each such anthology. (Here, and elsewhere, when such a collection has been published in more than one edition, we give all the dates, but list the contents for only the most recent edition.) In I-C are representative journal articles on alternative approaches to our subject, but if they are found under the tables of contents of the edited volumes, they are not listed again here. A few of the more readily available compilations of course outlines are in Section I-D.

II. Texts and General Treatises on International Politics

Here we find either textbooks or general "theories" that seek to make sense out of the substantive phenomena of international politics. While most of these efforts will include a chapter or so on approach and orientation, they are less preoccupied with "packing their conceptual bags" than with getting on with the trip. And because one can reasonably expect to write an *article* on how to *approach* our subject but would need a full *book* to describe and interpret the dominant regularities in the international arena, article-length works will appear in Section I, but not here in Section II or in Section III.

And, as before, the tables of contents of edited collections are included. The reasons are two. First, many of us find it desirable to use a varied collection of readings in our courses, to supplement the textbook(s) and to give the student a more diverse set of orientations; having the contents of most of them all together and in front of you should make the choice of such a collection considerably less haphazard. Second, for many of us, these anthologies provide a parsimonious substitute for a full library of the more traditional writings. Having their detailed contents conveniently at hand adds to the efficient preparation of our lectures and articles.

In addition to separate sub-sections for authored books (II-A) and for edited ones (II-B), we include here a third category (II-C)— Propositional Inventories. It is here that we deviate slightly from our inclusions of published works only and list two *un*published dissertations that are obtainable, however, through microfilm at many universities. One may think of the compilations of these inventories as highly condensed textbooks, and indeed two of those listed (Coplin, 1971; and Scott, 1967) are found within the covers of textbooks and are thus listed in both places in this volume. That is, they attempt to summarize in unadorned language the more interesting assertions about international politics that are found in the literature. These assertions may be in the form of empirical generalizations or statements of imputed causality, and they may rest on very solid evidence or be so untested as to qualify only as plausible hypotheses. Unfortunately, given the sparse knowledge base that we now have in international politics, most of them will—or should—fall into the latter category.

III. American and Comparative Foreign Policy

Here we shift our level of analysis from that of the international system to that of specific nations, or perhaps pairs of nations. That is, many writers on international politics will focus on the system as a whole, or at least attempt to generalize about a region, while subordinating the roles of the specific nations; they generally try to achieve a *bird's*-eye view rather than a *worm's*-eye view. But there can be some real progress in our understanding of the general phenomena of international politics if we also drop down to the national level and examine the substance of the separate nations' foreign policies and the way they are made and executed. While we make no pretense of covering all the literature on the foreign policies of past and contemporary nations, and admit to a rather heavy emphasis on U.S. foreign policy, we have canvassed much of the English literature in order to achieve a fairly broad and comparative spread. We emphasize that this is a limited listing, with virtually no attention to specific cases or issues, or to such specific topics as the impact of public opinion and domestic politics on foreign policy, or the ways in which such problems as arms control or trade might be handled. Nor, it should be added, do we claim to have found the clear and sharp boundaries between foreign policy and either international politics or diplomatic history. Again, no effort is made to list the endless number of articles in the various journals, but we do offer book titles under each of the familiar rubrics of Authored (III-A) and Edited (III-B) Volumes.

IV. Journals and Annuals in International Politics

The scholarly journal is, in principle, the major vehicle of communication among researchers, and between researchers and students or teachers. Because it tends to be focused on a fairly specialized sector of the discipline, and *can* be assembled, printed, and distributed quickly—even though it often is not—it should enhance and accelerate both the conduct of research and the dissemination of research findings. But as most of you can appreciate, journals contain many articles that do not report research, or even lead to or build from research. This is particularly true in the international politics field, where scientific method has yet to become an accepted part of the culture. Recognizing this lack, as well as the fact that journal articles have other functions, we have made a brave—if not fully operational—effort to classify our journals into three groups.

In the first group are those few journals that are essentially scientific; that is, the bulk of their articles seek, report on, or assume some degree of reproducible evidence. (Interestingly enough, most of the journals in this category reflect the preoccupation with ultimate policy applications that characterizes the peace research movement.) The tables of contents of each of *these* journals since their inception are included here; and, incidentally, many of these articles are abstracted in *Beyond Conjecture in International Politics* (Jones and Singer, 1972).

In the second group are the more traditional journals. While their articles are generally devoid of hard evidence or attentiveness to method, they often contain a fair amount of historical fact, suggestive interpretation, and innovative conceptual schemes. In the third group are those journals whose concern is less with the *acquisition* of knowledge than its short-run *application*; the policy-oriented ones. We reproduce here the tables of contents of neither the speculative nor the policy journals. Because they are very numerous and have been "in business" for many years, the list would be extraordinarily long, and because they rest more on rather time-bound and space-bound assumptions than on reproducible evidence, their earlier contents are—with some notable and exciting exceptions—not likely to be of great value to students of contemporary affairs in the 1970s.

For all the journals, we show the address of the editorial office, as this is the intellectual base of the journal and the place to which manuscripts are usually submitted. While a subscription order will normally be accepted there or else forwarded to the business office or publishing house, we also supply the latter information when available. As to the general focus and contents of journals, we have—as indicated above—made a rough three-way grouping, but beyond that, we are not prepared to go. Thus, the journal's description reflects not our judgment or impression, but either a quotation or paraphrase from the journal itself.

After some indecision, we decided to subsume annuals (and biannuals) under the journal rubric, given their essential similarity. There are differences, of course. Not only do these appear much less often than four, six, or twelve times per year, but they often tend to encompass a wider domain than journals. Despite that wider net, we do list those annuals, etc. that regularly carry a few articles of direct interest to the student of international politics, but we do not—given the range—list the tables of contents of even the more scientific annuals. We should also note here the difference between this type of annual or yearbook, and those that have the same name while serving more as an annual report of facts, survey of conditions, or chronique of events; these latter are listed in Section VII.

V. Special Series in International Politics

Scholars set down their ideas and findings not only in books or in journal articles but also in single papers; these may, however, be too long, too unorthodox, or even of a quality unacceptable for the regular journals. But because they can nevertheless be quite useful and important, some enterprising scholar, bureaucrat, or publisher will often arrange to bring them together under a general title. Whereas articles are usually typeset, printed, and then bound with a dozen or so other articles to make a single issue of a given journal, these papers are not always "published" in the conventional sense. Rather, the editor of the special series will often seek out manuscripts, or receive them unsolicited, and if found acceptable, a few hundred are run off, enclosed in a distinctive paper cover, and then either sold or given away to specialists in that field. The trouble with such series, however, is that most scholars know only a few of the papers in one or two of the series, and this is unfortunate. We have explored the offerings rather widely, and while we purposely excluded series of a highly specialized nature, we think that this listing will introduce you to some valuable papers that might otherwise be overlooked. For each of the series, we give the dates of inception and termination, the name and address of the editor, and—when obtainable—information on costs and availability of the publications.

VI. Abstracts and Book Reviews

Very often, merely knowing what articles will be found in which journals, annuals, or anthologies will be helpful to you. But authors and journal editors are not particularly careful about the accuracy of titles, and they can therefore be quite misleading. Further, even with careful attention, you may need more information than is conveyed by the title, but less than is found in the article itself. In such cases, it would be useful to have something in between—namely, an abstract.

However, abstracts in the social sciences vary in their usefulness, largely because we have not yet begun to take them or their role seriously. Many of them are written (a) by the author, (b) without a checklist of points to be covered, and (c) on articles that may not even permit or merit abstracting. Despite our reservations, we list a variety of abstracts collections, most of which are published several times per year. And even though several of these are not devoted exclusively or even largely to international politics, we nevertheless think them useful enough to be included here.

Just as abstracts may tell us quite a bit about an article, *reviews* may tell us something about a book. But tracking down one or more reviews of a given work is not easy; they appear in a wide variety of journals and over a wide span of time. While the number of journals devoted exclusively to book reviews in the social sciences is increasing, the bulk of the reviews of books on international politics continues to be found in the major journals listed in Section IV. To find them quickly, there are several guides to and summaries of reviews. In this section, then, you will find the titles of those periodicals or one-shot volumes that bring us abstracts of articles and reviews of books.

VII. Data Sources and Handbooks

As our earlier comments should make clear, we are strongly committed to the scientific mode, and thus to the importance of data-based models and propositions. But, unlike such fields as labor economics or electoral behavior, our field does not get much of its data from governmental or commercial agencies, ready-made for scientific analysis. At best, we must convert into comparable figures the isolated sets of numbers provided by a national government or international organization, and at worst, we must actually "make" our data from weak traces left by ambiguous events and shifting conditions. The purpose of this section is to ease the data-gathering and data-making burden by identifying those limited sources that might be of use to the student of international politics.

We begin—under Approaches (VII-A)—with a few books and articles that examine the availability and quality of certain types of data sets as well as procedures by which to gather, evaluate, or construct one's own data base. Next, we list some of the books and reports that include so-called aggregate data. This is a label used by political and social behavioralists in order to distinguish individual responses to opinion surveys or individual voting patterns from data that describe such large "aggregations" as the precinct, the province, or the nation. We consider this an unfortunate label and prefer to differentiate data sets as to whether they describe the *behavior* of an actor (from an individual to an international organization) or the *attributes* of such an actor. Thus, we list our source titles under Attribute Data, which may also be thought of as Ecological Phenomena; and Diplomatic, Political, and Military Events Data, also labeled as Behavioral Phenomena. Needless to say, we do not list data sources for specific nations (there are often hundreds of sources for the nearly 200 nations appearing in the international system over the past century or so), but only those that cover a fair number of nations and a fair number of observations across time. Finally, we include a very truncated list of document collections, serving only to give the user a rough idea of what is available. Again, we emphasize that the list is almost exclusively Anglo-American in focus.

Another major source of social science data is in the computerized archives found at an increasing number of universities. While these data collections are too numerous and fast-changing to list here, and some fraction of their holdings may be very tentative and low-quality estimates, they can be extremely useful. Among the guides to such collections are: A Guide to Resources and Services, ICPSR, Ann Arbor, Institute for Social Research; annually since 1970–71, and SS Data: Newsletter of Social Science Archival Acquisitions, Iowa City, Laboratory for Social Research; quarterly since 1971.

Some other sources worth noting, and falling into the category of "fugitive materials," are governmental and diplomatic documents that remain unpublished. Happily, an increasing amount of material in that category can be traced and located, thanks to microfilming and related techniques. Many U.S. documents, for example, are found in Laurence Schmeckebier and Roy Eastin, Government Publications and Their Use, Washington, D.C.: Brookings Institution (1961; 1969).

VIII. Bibliographies of International Politics

Finally, Section VIII is devoted to our competition: other bibliographies. Actually, only a few of those listed can be thought of as competitors: those that seek the general coverage offered here. The bulk of them are, however, much more specialized, while a few of them are less specialized and very general. We have included bibliographies on a wide variety of substantive problems or topics in the international politics field, with one exception: the "area studies" bibliography, restricted to a single nation or region. Not only are these very numerous, but, as noted earlier, they usually fall much closer to cross-national and comparative than to inter-national politics.

A number of bibliographies in the social sciences will contain, along with the titles of related bibliographies, lists of the more useful archives. In the world politics field, the range and variety of such archives would be massive, embracing collections of official government documents, intragovernmental memos, memoirs, personal correspondence, unpublished court briefs, draft treaty proposals, and the like. There still seems to be a need for an exhaustive and annotated list of archives, but it is well beyond our reach here. Still another archival area to be explored, but again too extensive (and elusive) to be included in any very helpful fashion, is the one of peace research and history; for example, there is the Bibliography of Resources on the History of Pacifism and Conscientious Objection in the Michigan Historical Collections, William McNitt (Dec. 1973).

To conclude our overview of this section of the book, we call to your attention two diverse sources of information that are worth noting, although omitted from the contents here. They are *Microcard Editions*, a contemporary source of dissertation titles; and *ABC Pol Sci (Advance Bibliography of Contents)*, which covers a wider range than international politics alone, but provides the tables of contents of the articles found each month in many political science journals. And, last, we are not including bibliographical articles or the bibliographies found regularly in specialized journals, since these appear in almost every issue and we assume that students of a given field will be familiar with the articles and with the bibliographies in any given journal.

I. Approaches to the Study and Teaching of International Politics

A. Authored Volumes

Arbatov, Georgi. *The War of Ideas in Contemporary International Relations*, Moscow: Progress Publishers (1973).

Bailey, S. H. *International Studies in Great Britain*, London: Royal Institute (1937).

Bernard, Jessie, et al. [in collaboration with the International Sociological Association]. *The Nature of Conflict: Studies on the Sociological Aspects of International Tensions*, Belgium: UNESCO (1957).

Boasson, Charles. *A Prologue to Peace Research*, Jerusalem: Israel Universities Press (1971).

Bobrow, Davis. *International Relations: New Approaches*, New York: Free Press (1972).

Brookings Institution Report on a Conference on the Teaching of International Relations, Washington, D.C.: International Studies Group (1950).

Dedring, Juergen. *Recent Advances in Peace and Conflict Research: A Critical Survey*, Beverly Hills, Ca.: Sage (1976).

DeRivera, Joseph. *The Psychological Dimension of Foreign Policy*, Columbus, Ohio: Merrill (1968).

Deutsch, Karl W. *Political Community at the International Level: Problems of Definition and Measurement*, Garden City, N.Y.: Doubleday (1954).

Dougherty, James E., and Robert L. Pfaltzgraff, Jr. *Contending Theories of International Relations*, Philadelphia: Lippincott (1971).

Dunn, Frederick S. *War and the Minds of Men*, New York: Harper (1950).

1

Fox, William T. R. *The American Study of International Relations,* Columbia: Institute of International Studies, University of South Carolina (1968).

Fuller, C. Dale. *Training of Specialists in International Relations,* Washington, D.C.: American Council on Education (1957).

Gamboa, Melquiades J. *A Dictionary of International Law and Diplomacy,* Dobbs Ferry, N.Y.: Oceana (1973).

Gange, John. *University Research in World Affairs,* Washington, D.C.: American Council on Education (1958).

Haensch, Gunther. *Dictionary of International Relations and Politics,* Amsterdam: Elsevier (1965).

Handelman, John R., et al. *Introduction to International Relations Theory: Case Studies,* Chicago: Markham (1974).

Hoffmann, Stanley. *The State of War: Essays in the Theory and Practice of International Politics,* New York: Praeger (1965).

Hyamson, Albert M. *A Dictionary of World Affairs,* Washington, D.C.: Public Affairs Press (1947).

Kirk, Grayson. *The Study of International Relations in American Colleges and Universities,* New York: Council on Foreign Relations (1947).

Klineberg, Otto. *The Human Dimension in International Relations,* New York: Holt, Rinehart & Winston (1964).

Lasswell, Harold. *World Politics and Personal Insecurity,* New York: McGraw-Hill (1935).

Lentz, Theo. F. *Towards a Science of Peace,* New York: Bookman Associates (1955).

_____. *Towards a Technology of Peace,* St. Louis: Peace Research Laboratory (1972).

Lieber, Robert J. *Theory and World Politics,* Cambridge, Mass.: Winthrop (1972).

Manning, Charles A. W. *The University Teaching of Social Sciences—International Relations,* Paris: UNESCO (1954).

Mathisen, Trygve. *Methodology in the Study of International Relations,* New York: Macmillan (1959).

McClelland, Charles. *College Teaching of International Relations: Problems of Organization and Collaboration,* San Francisco: Institute for Research on International Behavior (1962).

_____. *Theory and the International System,* New York: Macmillan (1966).

Moon, Parker Thomas. *Syllabus on International Relations*, New York: Macmillan (1925).

Morgan, Patrick M. *Theories and Approaches to International Politics: What Are We to Think?* San Ramon, Ca.: Consensus (1972).

Newcombe, Hanna, and Alan Newcombe. *Peace Research around the World*, Oakville, Ontario: Canadian Peace Research Institute (1969).

O'Leary, Michael, and William Coplin. *Quantitative Techniques in Foreign Policy Analysis and Forecasting*, New York: Praeger (1975).

Plano, Jack, and Roy Olton. *The International Relations Dictionary*, New York: Holt, Rinehart & Winston (1969).

Platig, E. Raymond. *International Relations Research: Problems of Evaluation and Advancement*, Santa Barbara: ABC–Clio (1967).

Reynolds, Charles V. *Theory and Explanation in International Politics*, New York: Barnes & Noble (1974).

Rosenau, James N. *The Scientific Study of Foreign Policy*, New York: Free Press (1971).

––––––. *International Studies and the Social Sciences: Problems, Priorities, Prospects in the U.S.*, Beverly Hills, Ca.: Sage (1973).

Russell, Frank M. *Theories of International Relations*, New York: Appleton-Century (1936).

Singer, J. David. *The Scientific Study of Politics: An Approach to Foreign Policy Analysis*, New York: General Learning (1972).

Stagner, Ross. *Psychological Aspects of International Conflict*, Belmont, Ca.: Brooks-Cole (1967).

Theimer, Walter. *An Encyclopedia of Modern World Politics*, New York: Rinehart (1950).

Vincent, Jack. *A Handbook of International Relations*, New York: Barron's (1969).

Waltz, Kenneth N. *Man, the State, and War: A Theoretical Analysis*, New York and London: Columbia University Press (1959).

Ware, Edith E. *The Study of International Relations in the U.S.*, New York: Carnegie Endowment (1939).

Webster, C. K. *The Study of International Politics*, London: H. Milford (1923).

Weltman, John Jay. *Systems Theory in International Relations: A Study in Metaphoric Hypertrophy*, Lexington, Mass.: Lexington Books (1973).

Wilson, Howard E. *Universities and World Affairs*, New York: Carnegie Endowment (1952).

Woodward, Sir Ernest L. *The Study of International Relations at a University*, Oxford: Oxford University Press (1945).

Wright, Quincy. *The Study of International Relations*, New York: Appleton-Century (1955).

Young, George. *The Pendulum of Progress: An Essay in Political Science ad Scientific Politics*, London: Oxford University Press (1931).

Zimmerman, William. *Soviet Perspectives on International Relations, 1956-1967*, Princeton, N.J.: Princeton University Press (1969; 1973).

Zinnes, Dina. *Contemporary Research in International Relations: A Perspective and Critical Appraisal*, New York: Free Press (1976).

B. Edited Volumes

Butterfield, Herbert, and Martin Wight (eds.). *Diplomatic Investigations: Essays in the Theory of International Politics*, Cambridge, Mass.: Harvard University Press (1966; 1968).
   Martin Wight, Why is there no International Theory?
   Hedley Bull, Society and Anarchy in International Relations
   Hedley Bull, The Grotian Conception of International Society
   D. Mackinnon, Natural Law
   Martin Wight, Western Values in International Relations
   Herbert Butterfield, The Balance of Power
   Martin Wight, The Balance of Power
   G. F. Hudson, Collective Security and Military Alliances
   Herbert Butterfield, The New Diplomacy and Historical Diplomacy
   Michael Howard, War as an Instrument of Policy
   G. F. Hudson, Threats of Force in International Relations
   Michael Howard, Problems of a Disarmed World

DeReuck, Anthony, and Julie Knight (eds.). *Conflict in Society*, London: Churchill (1966).
   S. L. Washburn, Conflict in Primate Society
   M. R. A. Chance, Resolution of Social Conflict in Animals and Man
   Role of Conflict in Human Evolution (Discussion)
   George DeVos, Conflict, Dominance and Exploitation in Human Systems of Social Segregation
   H. V. Dicks, Intra-personal Conflict and the Authoritarian Character
   The Authoritarian Character in War (Discussion)
   J. A. A. van Doorn, Conflict in Formal Organizations
   Patterns of Conflict in Social Groups (Discussion)

Ruth Glass, Conflict in Cities
Role of Cities in Social Unrest (Discussion)
Z. Barbu, Nationalism as a Source of Aggression
Internal Conflict and Overt Aggression (Discussion)
Harold Lasswell, Conflict and Leadership: The Process of Decision and
the Nature of Authority
Objective Appraisal of Conflict (Discussion)
Kenneth Boulding, Conflict Management as a Learning Process
Regulation of Conflict (Discussion)
Anatol Rapoport, Models of Conflict: Cataclysmic and Strategic
Strategic Thinking and State Interests (Discussion)
Karl W. Deutsch, Power and Communication in International Society
Compliance in Modern Society (Discussion)
Bert V. Röling, The Role of Law in Conflict Resolution
Karol Lapter, External and Internal Sources of International Tension
John W. Burton, Conflict as a Function of Change
International Aspects of Conflict (Discussion)
A. Haddow, Chairman's Closing Remarks

Farrell, John C., and Asa P. Smith (eds.). *Image and Reality in World
Politics*, New York: Columbia University Press (1967).
Kenneth E. Boulding, The Learning and Reality-Testing Process in the
International System
Ole R. Holsti, Cognitive Dynamics and Images of the Enemy
Reinhold Niebuhr, The Social Myths in the "Cold War"
Stanley Hoffmann, Perceptions, Reality, and the Franco-American
Conflict
John G. Stoessinger, China and America: The Burden of Past Misper-
ceptions
Benjamin I. Schwartz, The Maoist Image of World Order
Robert C. North, Perception and Action in the 1914 Crisis
Ralph K. White, Misperception of Aggression in Vietnam

Farrell, John C., and Asa P. Smith (eds.). *Theory and Reality in Inter-
national Relations*, New York: Columbia University Press (1967).
Raymond Aron, What is a Theory of International Relations?
Hans Morgenthau, Common Sense and Theories of International Rela-
tions
Kenneth N. Waltz, International Structure, National Force, and the
Balance of World Power
Karl W. Deutsch, On the Concepts of Politics and Power
Francis H. Hinsley, The Concept of Sovereignty and the Relations
between States
Roger D. Masters, The Lockean Tradition in American Foreign Policy
Kenneth W. Thompson, Normative Theory in International Relations

Farrell, R. Barry (ed.). *Approaches to Comparative and International
Politics*, Evanston, Ill.: Northwestern University Press (1966).

Karl W. Deutsch, External Influences in the Internal Behavior of States

James N. Rosenau, Pre-theories and Theories of Foreign Policy

Carl J. Friedrich, International Politics and Foreign Policy in Developed (Western) Systems

Pablo Gonzalez Casanova, Internal and External Politics of Developing Countries

Norton E. Long, Open and Closed Systems

R. Barry Farrell, Foreign Policies of Open and Closed Political Societies

Vernon V. Aspaturian, Internal Politics and Foreign Policy in the Soviet System

Roland Young, Political and Legal Systems of Order

Chadwick F. Alger, Comparison of Intranational and International Politics

Raoul Naroll, Scientific Comparative Politics and International Relations

Oliver Benson, Challenges for Research in International Relations and Comparative Politics

Fisher, Roger (ed.). *International Conflict and Behavioral Science: The Craigville Papers*, New York: Basic Books (1964).

Anatol Rapoport, Perceiving the Cold War

William A. Gamson, Evaluating Beliefs about International Conflict

Kathleen Gough, The Crisis of the Nation-State

Kenneth E. Boulding, Toward a Theory of Peace

Roger Fisher, Fractionating Conflict

E. James Lieberman, Threat and Assurance in the Conduct of Conflict

Arthur Waskow, Nonlethal Equivalents of War

Morton Deutsch, Producing Change in an Adversary

Urie Bronfenbrenner, Allowing for Soviet Perceptions

Amitai Etzioni, Atlantic Union, the Southern Continents, and the United Nations

Anatol Rapoport, Critique of Strategic Thinking

Lester Grinspoon, Interpersonal Constraints and the Decision-Maker

Roger Fisher, Defects in the Governmental Decision Process

Elliot G. Mishler, The Peace Movement and the Foreign Policy Process

James A. Robinson, The Social Scientist and Congress

Lester Grinspoon, The Truth Is Not Enough

Fox, William T. R. (ed.). *Theoretical Aspects of International Relations*, Notre Dame, Ind.: University of Notre Dame Press (1959).

Paul H. Nitze, Necessary and Sufficient Elements of a General Theory of International Relations

Hans J. Morgenthau, The Nature and Limits of a Theory of International Relations

William T. R. Fox, The Uses of International Relations Theory

Kenneth N. Waltz, Political Philosophy and the Study of International Relations

Charles P. Kindleberger, International Political Theory from Outside

Arnold Wolfers, The Actors in International Politics

Reinhold Niebuhr, Power and Ideology in National and International
Affairs

Goodwin, Geoffrey L. (ed.). *The University Teaching of International
Relations*, London: Blackwell (1951).
**Documents of a Meeting Convened by the International
Studies Conference at St. Catharine's, Windsor Great Park,
England, 16–20 March 1950**
C. A. W. Manning, International Relations: An Academic Discipline;
Report of the General Rapporteur
J. Lambert, International Relations: A Special Kind of Specialism?
**Notes on the Provision Made for the Teaching
of International Relations**
Paul Mantoux, Geneva
G. Arangio Ruiz, Italy
Jacques Chapsal, France
Edgar S. Furniss, Jr., United States of America
Geoffrey L. Goodwin, United Kingdom

Haas, Michael (ed.). *International Systems: A Behavioral Approach*,
New York: Chandler (1974).
Michael Haas, The Scope and Method of International Relations
Michael Haas, International Socialization
Lloyd Jensen, Foreign Policy Calculation
John D. Sullivan, International Alliances
Nazli Choucri, International Nonalignment
Werner Levi, International Statecraft
Warren R. Phillips, International Communications
Michael Haas, International Integration
Louis Kriesberg, International Decisionmaking
Irvin L. White, International Law
Michael Haas, International Administration
John R. Raser, International Deterrence
Michael Haas, International Conflict Resolution
Michael Haas, The Future of International Relations Theory

Harrison, Horace V. (ed.). *Role of Theory in International Relations*,
Princeton, N.J.: Van Nostrand (1964).
Quincy Wright, Development of a General Theory of International
Relations
Kenneth W. Thompson, The Origins, Uses, and Problems of Theory in
International Relations
William T. R. Fox, Theories as Forces in Modern World Politics
Hans J. Morgenthau, The Intellectual and Political Functions of a
Theory of International Relations

Hoffmann, Stanley (ed.). *Contemporary Theory in International Rela-
tions*, Englewood Cliffs, N.J.: Prentice-Hall (1960).
Frederick S. Dunn, The Scope of International Relations
Kenneth W. Thompson, Toward a Theory of International Politics

Hans Morgenthau, Politics among Nations
Hans Morgenthau, Another Great Debate: The National Interest of the
United States
Raymond Aron, The Quest for a Philosophy of Foreign Affairs
Kenneth W. Thompson, Toynbee and the Theory of International Poli-
tics
Morton Kaplan, System and Process in International Politics
Jessie Bernard, The Sociological Study of Conflict
George Liska, International Equilibrium
Richard C. Snyder et al., Decision-Making as an Approach
Raymond Aron, Conflict and War from the Viewpoint of Historical
Sociology
Herbert C. Kelman, Societal, Attitudinal and Structural Factors in In-
ternational Relations
Ernst B. Haas, The Challenge of Regionalism
Arnold Wolfers, The Anglo-American Tradition in Foreign Affairs
Edward H. Carr, The Twenty Years' Crisis
Arnold Wolfers, Statesmanship and Moral Choice

Kaplan, Morton A. (ed.). *New Approaches to International Relations*,
New York: St. Martin's Press (1968).
Morton A. Kaplan, The New Great Debate: Traditionalism vs. Science
in International Relations
Albert Wohlstetter, Theory and Opposed-Systems Design
John Golden, System, Process, and Decision Making: A Developing
Method
Herman Kahn, The Alternative World Futures Approach
Karl Deutsch, New Approaches to International Relations
Hayward R. Alker, Jr., The Long Road to International Relations
Theory: Problems of Statistical Nonadditivity
Arthur Lee Burns, Quantitative Approaches to International Politics
Harold Guetzkow, Some Correspondences between Simulations and
Realities in International Relations
Johan Galtung, Small Group Theory and the Theory of International
Relations
Robert C. North, The Behavior of Nation-States: Problems of Conflict
and Integration
Richard A. Falk, New Approaches to the Study of International Law
Morton A. Kaplan, The Systems Approach to International Politics
Hsi-shen Chi, The Chinese Warlord System as an International System
Donald L. Reinken, Computer Explorations of the Balance of Power

Knorr, Klaus, and James Rosenau (eds.). *Contending Approaches to
International Politics*, Princeton, N.J.: Princeton University Press
(1969).
Klaus Knorr and James N. Rosenau, Tradition and Science in the Study
of International Politics
Hedley Bull, International Theory: The Case for a Classical Approach
Morton A. Kaplan, The New Great Debate: Traditionalism vs. Science
in International Relations

J. David Singer, The Incompleat Theorist: Insight Without Evidence
Marion J. Levy, Jr., Does it Matter if He's Naked? Bawled the Child
Richard A. Brody, The Study of International Politics qua Science: The
Emphasis on Methods and Techniques
Oran R. Young, Aron and the Whale: A Jonah in Theory
David Vital, Back to Machiavelli
Michael Haas, A Plan for Bridge Building in International Relations
Robert Jervis, The Costs of the Quantitative Study of International
Relations
Robert C. North, Research Pluralism and the International Elephant
Johan Galtung, The Social Sciences: An Essay on Polarization and
Integration

Knorr, Klaus, and Sidney Verba (eds.). *The International System:
Theoretical Essays*, Princeton, N.J.: Princeton University Press
(1961).
Morton A. Kaplan, Problems of Theory Building and Theory Confirma-
tion in International Politics
Arthur Lee Burns, Prospects for a General Theory of International
Relations
Thomas C. Schelling, Experimental Games and Bargaining Theory
Richard E. Quandt, On the Use of Game Models in Theories of Inter-
national Relations
J. David Singer, The Level-of-Analysis Problem in International Rela-
tions
Sidney Verba, Assumptions of Rationality and NonRationality in Mod-
els of the International System
George Modelski, Agraria and Industria: Two Models of the Interna-
tional System
Fred W. Riggs, International Relations as a Prismatic System
Charles A. McClelland, The Acute International Crisis
Stanley Hoffmann, International Systems and International Law

McNeil, Elton B. (ed.). *The Nature of Human Conflict*, Englewood
Cliffs, N.J.: Prentice-Hall (1965).
Ross Stagner, The Psychology of Human Conflict
Stephen Withey and Daniel Katz, The Social Psychology of Human
Conflict
Robert C. Angell, The Sociology of Human Conflict
Margaret Mead and Rhoda Metraux, The Anthropology of Human
Conflict
J. David Singer, The Political Matrix of Human Conflict
Ole R. Holsti and Robert C. North, The History of Human Conflict
Kenneth E. Boulding, The Economics of Human Conflict
Anatol Rapoport, Game Theory and Human Conflict
Richard A. Falk, World Law and Human Conflict
Charles A. McClelland, Systems Theory and Human Conflict
Chadwick F. Alger, Decision-making Theory and Human Conflict
Donald F. Keys, The American Peace Movement
Elton B. McNeil, The Future of Human Conflict

Palmer, Norman D. (ed.). A *Design for International Relations Research: Scope, Theory, Methods, and Relevance*, Philadelphia: American Academy of Political and Social Science, Monograph 10 (Oct. 1970).

Norman D. Palmer, The Study of International Relations: An Agendum

Chadwick F. Alger, Trends in International Relations Research

William T. R. Fox, After International Relations, What?

Kenneth W. Thompson, The Social-Psychological Approach: Overview or Single View?

Raymond Aron, Theory and Theories in International Relations: A Conceptual Analysis

Hans J. Morgenthau, International Relations: Quantitative and Qualitative Approaches

Charles A. McClelland, Conceptualization, Not Theory

Bruce M. Russett, Methodological and Theoretical Schools in International Relations

Richard C. Snyder, Communication and Influence Patterns in the International Relations Community

Robert C. North, Cohesion and Divisiveness in the Field of International Relations: The Problem of Free Will and Determinism

J. David Singer, Knowledge, Practice, and the Social Sciences in International Politics

Ralph K. White, Quantification and the Crucial Intangibles

Elton B. McNeil, 2001: A Social Science Odyssey

James M. Roherty, Policy Implications and Applications of International Relations Research for Defense and Security

Amos A. Jordan, International Relations Research and Defense Policy

Ernest W. Lefever, The Limits of Hard and Soft Research in Foreign Policy

Joseph E. Johnson, Policy Implications and Applications of International Relations Research for Foreign Policy and Diplomacy

E. Raymond Platig, Research and Foreign Policy/Diplomacy

Roger Hilsman, Research, Policy, and the Political Process

Norman D. Palmer, International Relations Research: An Assessment of Progress and Relevance

Problems of War and Peace: A Critical Analysis of Bourgeois Theories [ed(s). unknown; tr. Bryan Bean], Moscow: Progress Publishers (1972).

The Quest for Peace in the Social Thought of the Past

Utopian Socialism and Problems of Peace

The Idea of Universal Peace in the Theories of the Bourgeois Humanists (16th–18th Centuries)

The Origins and Essence of War

The Dialectics of War and Peace

Politics and War in Our Time

The Monopolies and War

Bourgeois Philosophy and Problems of War and Peace

National Sovereignty and War
Against Justification of War by Malthusianism and Geopolitics
Western Social Psychology on the Causes of Wars and the Means of
 Averting Them
Against the Ideology of Militarism and Reaction.
For Peace and Social Progress
American Doctrines of Power Politics
The Theory of Games in International Affairs
Who Is Opposed to Peaceful Coexistence
Criticism of the Interpretation of Peaceful Coexistence As Preserving
 the Social *Status Quo*
Against the Theory of Ideological Disarmament
Modern Catholicism and Problems of War and Peace
Pacifist Ideology Today. The American Quaker Movement
Western Scientists and Intellectuals and the Quest for Peace
The Pugwash Movement
The Soviet Disarmament Programme and Its Critics
The Peace Movement and Socialist Humanism

Riggs, Fred W. (ed.). *International Studies: Present Status and Future
 Prospects*, Philadelphia: American Academy of Political and Social
 Science, Monograph 12 (Oct. 1971).
    Cyril E. Black, Foreign Area Studies: Emergent Changes and Trends
    David Apter, Comparative Studies: A Commentary
    Michael Haas, International Relations: A Commentary
    Kalman H. Silvert, Area Studies Look Outward
    Wendell Bell, Comparative Studies: A Commentary
    E. Raymond Platig, International Relations: A Commentary
    Lucian W. Pye, Advances and Frustrations in Comparative Politics
    Vincent Davis, International Relations: A Commentary
    Robert T. Holt, Comparative Studies Look Outward
    Raymond Tanter, International Relations: A Commentary
    Glenn D. Paige, Area Studies: A Commentary
    Richard A. Brody, Convergences and Challenges in International Rela-
 tions
    Eliezer B. Ayal, Comparative Studies: A Commentary
    Leonard Binder, Area Studies: A Commentary
    James N. Rosenau, Adaptive Strategies for Research and Practice in
 Foreign Policy
    Davis B. Bobrow, Comparative Studies: A Commentary
    Frederick W. Frey, Area Studies: A Commentary

Rosenau, James N., Vincent Davis, and Maurice East (eds.). *The
 Analysis of International Politics: Essays in Honor of Harold and
 Margaret Sprout*, New York: Free Press (1972).
    Charles A. McClelland, On the Fourth Wave: Past and Future in the
 Study of International Systems
    Raymond Tanter, Explanation, Prediction, and Forecasting in Interna-
 tional Politics

Charles F. Hermann, Policy Classification: A Key to the Comparative Study of Foreign Policy

J. David Singer, Theorists and Empiricists: The Two-Culture Problem in International Politics

Morton A. Kaplan, Freedom in History and International Politics

Bruce M. Russett, A Macroscopic View of International Politics

Oran R. Young, The Actors in World Politics

James N. Rosenau, The External Environment as a Variable in Foreign Policy Analysis

Robert Gilpin, Has Modern Technology Changed International Politics?

Klaus Knorr, Notes on the Analysis of National Capabilities

Richard A. Falk, Zone II as a World Order Construct

Dina A. Zinnes, Some Evidence Relevant to the Man-Milieu Hypothesis

Michael Haas, Sources of International Conflict

Chadwick F. Alger, Negotiation, Regional Groups, Interaction and Public Debate in the Development of Consensus in the United Nations General Assembly

Maurice A. East, Status Discrepancy and Violence in the International System: An Empirical Analysis

Burton M. Sapin, The Politico-Military Approach to American Foreign Policy

Vincent Davis, The Office of the Secretary of Defense and the U.S. Department of Defense

Cyril E. Black, Russian Interpretations of World History

Russett, Bruce M. (ed.). *Economic Theories of International Politics*, Chicago: Markham (1968).

Alliances and the Collective Pursuit of Benefits

Malcolm W. Hoag, What Interdependence for NATO?

Mancur Olson and Richard Zeckhauser, An Economic Theory of Alliances

James M. Buchanan, An Economic Theory of Clubs

Stanislaw Wellisz, On External Diseconomies and the Government-Assisted Invisible Hand

James S. Coleman, The Possibility of a Social Welfare Function

Duncan Black, The Elasticity of Committee Decisions with Alterations in the Members' Preference Schedules

John G. Cross, Some Theoretic Characteristics of Economic and Political Coalitions

Markets and International Systems

Mancur Olson, Jr., A Theory of Groups and Organizations

Martin Shubik, Strategy and Market Structure

George J. Stigler, A Theory of Oligopoly

Michael Gort, Analysis of Stability and Change in Market Shares

Oliver E. Williamson, A Dynamic Theory of Interfirm Behavior

John Kenneth Galbraith, The Economics of Technical Development

Martin McGuire, The Arms Race: An Interaction Process

Irvin M. Grossack, Duopoly, Defensive Strategies, and the Kinked Demand Curve

Charles Wolf, Some Aspects of the Value of Less-Developed Countries
to the United States

Albert O. Hirschman, The Stability of Neutralism: A Geometric Note

Bruce M. Russett, Is There a Long-Run Trend Toward Concentration
in the International System?

Kenneth E. Boulding, The Theory of Viability

Internal Determinants of National Behavior

R. Joseph Monsen and Anthony Downs, A Theory of Large Managerial
Firms

Oliver E. Williamson, Managerial Discretion and Business Behavior

Harry G. Johnson, A Theoretical Model of Nationalism in New and
Developing States

Anne O. Kreuger, The Economics of Discrimination

E. R. Livernash, The Relation of Power to the Structure and Process of
Collective Bargaining

Clark Kerr and Abraham Siegel, The Interindustry Propensity to
Strike—An International Comparison

**Alternative Organizations for
International Decision Making**

James M. Buchanan and Gordon Tullock, The Costs of Decision Making

Albert O. Hirschman and Charles E. Lindblom, Economic Development, Research and Development, Policy Making: Some Converging
Views

Daniel E. Suits, Forecasting and Analysis with an Econometric Model

Alfred E. Kahn, The Tyranny of Small Decisions: Market Failures,
Imperfections, and the Limits of Econometrics

Singer, J. David (ed.). *Human Behavior and International Politics:
Contributions from the Social Psychological Sciences*, Chicago:
Rand McNally (1965).

The International System as Environment

Amos H. Hawley, Ecology and Human Ecology

Otis Dudley Duncan and Leo F. Schnore, Cultural, Behavioral, and
Ecological Perspectives in the Study of Social Organization

Lauriston Sharp, Steel Axes for Stone-Age Australians

Julian H. Steward et al., Irrigation Civilizations: A Comparative Study

Eleanor E. Maccoby et al., Community Integration and the Social
Control of Juvenile Delinquency

Theodore Caplow, Organizational Size

The Nation as Primary Actor

Donald T. Campbell, Common Fate, Similarity, and Other Indices of
the Status of Aggregates of Persons as Social Entities

Raymond B. Cattell, Concepts and Methods in the Measurement of
Group Syntality

Emily M. Nett, An Evaluation of the National Character Concept in
Sociological Theory

Politics as Interaction

Ralph Cassady, Taxicab Rate War: Counterpart of International Conflict
Paul Diesing, Bargaining Strategy and Union-Management Relationships
Igor Kopytoff, Extension of Conflict as a Method of Conflict Resolution among the Suku of the Congo
Muzafer Sherif et al., Intergroup Conflict and Cooperation: The Robber's Cave Experiment
Morton Deutsch, Trust and Suspicion
Leonard Solomon, The Influence of Some Types of Power Relationships and Game Strategies upon the Development of Interpersonal Trust

System Transformation

Smith, Clagett G. (ed.). *Conflict Resolution: Contributions of the Behavioral Sciences*, Notre Dame, Ind.: University of Notre Dame Press (1971).

Raymond W. Mack and Richard C. Snyder, The Analysis of Social Conflict—Toward an Overview and Synthesis
Morton Deutsch, Conflict and Its Resolution
Lewis A. Coser, Social Conflict and the Theory of Social Change
Irving Louis Horowitz, Consensus, Conflict and Cooperation: A Sociological Inventory
Daniel Katz, Current and Needed Psychological Research in International Relations
Judson S. Brown, Principles of Intrapersonal Conflict
Ross Stagner, Personality Dynamics and Social Conflict
Irving L. Janis, Problems of Theory in the Analysis of Stress Behavior
Martin Patchen, Decision Theory in the Study of National Action: Problems and a Proposal
Martin Shubik, On the Study of Disarmament and Escalation
William A. Gamson, A Theory of Coalition Formation
Roger Fisher, Fractionating Conflict
Joseph S. Himes, The Functions of Racial Conflict
Thomas F. Pettigrew, Social Psychology and Desegregation Research
Richard T. Morris and Vincent Jeffries, Class Conflict: Forget It!
Russell R. Dynes and E. L. Quarantelli, The Absence of Community Conflict in the Early Phases of Natural Disasters
Daniel Katz, Group Process and Social Integration: A System Analysis of Two Movements of Social Protest
Irving L. Janis and Daniel Katz, The Reduction of Intergroup Hostility: Research Problems and Hypotheses
Raymond Tanter, Dimensions of Conflict Behavior Within and Between Nations, 1958–60
Rudolph J. Rummel, Dimensions of Conflict Behavior within Nations, 1946–59
Franz Schurmann, On Revolutionary Conflict
Johan Galtung, A Structural Theory of Aggression
Marc Pilisuk and Thomas Hayden, Is There a Military-Industrial Com-

plex Which Prevents Peace?: Consensus and Countervailing Power in Pluralistic Systems
Werner Levi, On the Causes of War and the Conditions of Peace
Frank H. Denton and Warren Phillips, Some Patterns in the History of Violence
Philip M. Hauser, Demographic Dimensions of World Politics
Quincy Wright, The Escalation of International Conflicts
Dina A. Zinnes, An Analytical Study of the Balance of Power Theories
Paul Smoker, Nation State Escalation and International Integration
Janusz K. Zawodny, Unconventional Warfare
Harold Guetzkow, Isolation and Collaboration: A Partial Theory of Inter-nation Relations
Daniel Katz, Nationalism and Strategies of International Conflict Resolution
Herbert C. Kelman, Societal, Attitudinal and Structural Factors in International Relations
Frank L. Klingberg, Predicting the Termination of War: Battle Casualties and Population Losses
Lewis A. Coser, The Termination of Conflict
Kenneth E. Boulding, The Prevention of World War III
I. Glagolev and M. Goryainov, Some Problems of Disarmament Research
Inis L. Claude, Jr., United Nations Use of Military Force
Charles E. Osgood, Graduated Unilateral Initiatives for Peace
Erich Fromm, The Case for Unilateral Disarmament
Gordon W. Allport, Guide Lines for Research in International Cooperation
Amitai Etzioni, Strategic Models for a De-Polarizing World

Tanter, Raymond, and Richard H. Ullman (eds.). *Theory and Policy in International Relations*, Princeton, N.J.: Princeton University Press (1972).
Raymond Tanter, International System and Foreign Policy Approaches: Implications for Conflict Modelling and Management
Graham T. Allison and Morton H. Halperin, Bureaucratic Politics: A Paradigm and Some Policy Implications
Nazli Choucri and Robert C. North, Dynamics of International Conflict: Some Policy Implications of Population, Resources, and Technology
Edward L. Morse, Crisis Diplomacy, Interdependence, and the Politics of International Economic Relations
Norman Frohlich and Joe A. Oppenheimer, Entrepreneurial Politics and Foreign Policy
Oran R. Young, The Perils of Odysseus: On Constructing Theories of International Relations
Davis B. Bobrow, The Relevance Potential of Different Products
Allen S. Whiting, The Scholar and the Policy-Maker
Stephen M. Shaffer, Conceptual Index

Wright, Quincy, et al. (eds.). *Research for Peace*, Amsterdam: North Holland Publishers (1954).
Quincy Wright, Criteria for Judging the Relevance of Researches on the Problems of Peace
W. Fred Cottrell, Men Cry Peace
Charles Boasson, The Relevance of Research to the Problems of Peace
Ingemund Gullvåg, A Review of the Contributions to the Prize Contest on the Relevance of Research to Problems of Peace

Zawodny, Janusz K. (ed.). *Man and International Relations: Contributions of the Social Sciences to the Study of Conflict and Integration*, 2 vols., San Francisco: Chandler (1966).
Due to vast number of articles, no table of contents reproduced here.

Zimmern, Sir Alfred (ed.). *University Teaching of International Relations: A Record of the Eleventh Session of the International Studies Conference*, Paris: International Institute of Intellectual Cooperation (1939).
Individual Statements of Opinion on the Problem of the University Teaching of International Relations
Alfred Verdross, Austria: International Relations
Norman Mackenzie, Canada: The University Teaching of International Relations
Julio Escudero, Chile: The Necessity of the Study of International Relations
Emanuel Chalupny, Czechoslovakia: The University Teaching of International Relations
F. J. Pavelka, The Study of International Relations
Manuel Moreno Sanchez, Mexico: The University Teaching of International Relations
Waclaw Komarnicki, Poland: The Study and Teaching of International Relations
Antoni Deryng, Methods of Scientific Research and Methods of University Teaching Used for the Subject of International Relations
Bohdan Winiarski, International Politics as a Science of International Relations
George Sofronie, Rumania: The Teaching of International Law in Connection with the Study of International Relations
Mihai A. Antonesco, The University Teaching of International Relations
University Teaching of International Relations in Various Countries
Erich Voegelin, Austria: The Teaching of International Relations
W. E. C. Harrison, Canada: The University Teaching of International Relations in Canada
J. H. W. Verzijl, Netherlands: The University Teaching of International Relations in the Netherlands
Frede Castberg, Norway: The Study of International Relations in Norway

Radu Meitani, Rumania: The University Teaching of International Relations
Paul Guggenheim, Switzerland: The Study of International Relations in the Swiss Universities
M. Andrassy, Yugoslavia: The University Teaching of International Relations
Andre Tibal, Carnegie Endowment: The Teaching of International Relations in the French Faculties of Letters; The Activity of the European Centre of the Carnegie Endowment in the Field of the University Teaching of International Relations
Records of the Meetings of the Eleventh Session of the Conference

C. Articles

Alger, Chadwick. "Comparison of Intranational and International Politics," *American Political Science Review* 57 (June 1963): 406–419.

Berki, R. N. "On Marxian Thought and the Problem of International Relations," *World Politics* 24 (Oct. 1971): 80–105.

Davis, Harry R., and Robert C. Good. "The Illusion of Scientific Politics: A Critique," in Davis and Good (eds.), *Reinhold Niebuhr on Politics*, New York: Scribner's (1960), pp. 43–63.

DeRivera, Joseph. "Teaching a Course in the Psychology of International Relations," *American Psychologist* 1710 (Oct. 1962): 695–699.

Deutsch, Karl W. "The Place of Behavioral Sciences in Graduate Training in International Relations," *Behavioral Science* 3/3 (July 1958): 278–284.

Dunn, Frederick S. "The Scope of International Relations," *World Politics* 1 (Jan. 1948): 142–146.

_____. "The Present Course of International Relations Research," *World Politics* 2 (Oct. 1949): 80–95.

Fagen, Richard. "The Behavioral Scientist and International Relations," *American Behavioral Scientist* 4/8 (Apr. 1961): 29–30.

Fernback, Alfred. "The Doctorate in International Affairs," *Journal of Politics* 17 (May 1955): 275–286.

Fifield, Russell H. "The Introductory Course in International Relations," *American Political Science Review* 42 (Dec. 1948): 1189–1196.

Finkelstein, Lawrence S. "New Trends in International Affairs," *World Politics* 18 (Oct. 1965): 117–126.

Fox, William T. R. "Interwar International Relations Research: The American Experience," *World Politics* 2 (Oct. 1949): 67–79.

————, and Annette Baker Fox. "The Teaching of International Relations in the United States," *World Politics* 13 (Apr. 1961): 339–359.

Friedlander, Saul, and Raymond Cohen. "Some Thoughts on Current Trends in International Relations Research," *International Social Science Journal* 26/1 (1974): 34–52.

Guetzkow, Harold. "Long Range Research in International Relations," *American Perspective* 4/4 (1950): 421–440.

Gurian, Waldemar. "On the Study of International Relations," *Review of Politics* 8/3 (July 1946): 275–282.

Haas, Michael. "International Relations Theory," in M. Haas and Kariel (eds.), *Approaches to the Study of Political Science*, New York: Chandler (1970), pp. 444–476.

Holsti, Kal J. "Retreat from Utopia: International Relations Theory, 1945–1970," *Canadian Journal of Political Science* 4 (June 1971): 165–177.

Hughes, Barry B. "Teaching International Studies: Involved Organizations and Available Teaching Aids," *Consortium for International Studies Education Occasional Papers* 4 (1974): 3–30.

Kaplan, Morton A. "Is International Relations a Discipline?" *Journal of Politics* 23 (Aug. 1961): 462–476.

Kirk, Grayson. "Materials for the Study of International Relations, *World Politics* 1 (Oct. 1948): 426–430.

Knorr, Klaus. "Economics and International Relations: A Problem in Teaching," *Political Science Quarterly* 62/4 (Dec. 1947): 552–568.

Landecker, Werner S. "The Scope of a Sociology of International Relations," *Social Forces* 17 (Dec. 1938): 175–183.

Lijphart, Arend. "The Structure of the Theoretical Revolution in International Relations," *International Studies Quarterly* 18/1 (Mar. 1974): 41–74.

Lyon, Peter H. "Texts and the Study of International Relations," *Political Studies* 13/1 (Feb. 1965): 79–84.

Marchant, P. D. "Theory and Practice in the Study of International Relations," *International Relations* 1/3 (Apr. 1955): 95–102.

Masters, Roger D. "A Multi-Bloc Model of the International System," *American Political Science Review* 55 (Dec. 1961): 780–798.

20 ARTICLES

_____. "World Politics as a Primitive Political System," *World Politics* 16 (July 1964): 595–614.

McClelland, Charles A. "Systems and History in International Relations: Some Perspectives for Empirical Research and Theory," *General Systems* 3 (1958): 221–247.

Moul, William B. "The Levels of Analysis Problem Revisited," *Canadian Journal of Political Science* 6 (Sept. 1973): 494–513.

Nicholson, Michael B., and Phillip A. Reynolds. "General Systems, the International System, and the Eastonian Analysis," *Political Studies* 15/1 (Feb. 1967): 12–31.

Ransom, Harry H. "International Relations," *Journal of Politics* 30 (May 1968): 345–371.

Russett, Bruce M. "Toward a Model of Competitive International Politics," *Journal of Politics* 25 (Feb. 1963): 226–247.

Singer, J. David. "The Relevance of the Behavioral Sciences to the Study of International Relations," *Behavioral Science* 6/4 (Oct. 1961): 324–335.

_____. "Cosmopolitan Attitudes and International Relations Courses: Some Tentative Correlations," *Journal of Politics* 27 (May 1965): 318–338.

_____. "The Graduate Curriculum in World Politics: A Pedagogical Note," *Consortium for International Studies Education Occasional Papers* 4 (1974): 31–54.

Snyder, Richard C. "Some Recent Trends in International Relations Theory and Research," in Ranney (ed.), *Essays on the Behavioral Study of Politics*, Urbana: University of Illinois Press (1962), pp. 103–172.

Speer, James P. "Hans Morgenthau and the World State," *World Politics* 20 (Jan. 1968): 207–227.

Spykman, Nicholas J. "Methods of Approach to the Study of International Relations," Proceedings of the Fifth Conference of Teachers of International Law and Related Subjects, Washington, D.C.: Carnegie Endowment for International Peace (1933), pp. 60–69.

Stephens, Jerone. "An Appraisal of Some System Approaches in the Study of International Systems," *International Studies Quarterly* 16/3 (Sept. 1972): 321–349.

Sullivan, Michael P. "The Question of Relevance in Foreign Policy Studies," *Western Political Quarterly* 26 (1973): 314–324.

Thompson, Kenneth W. "The Study of International Politics," *Review of Politics* 14/4 (Oct. 1952): 433–467.

Van Dyke, Vernon. "The Improvement of Teaching in International Relations: The Iowa Seminars," *American Political Science Review* 51 (June 1957): 579–581.

Young, Oran R. "Political Discontinuities in the International System," *World Politics* 20 (Apr. 1968): 369–392.

Zimmerman, William. "Elite Perspectives and the Explanation of Soviet Foreign Policy," *Journal of International Affairs* 24/1 (1970): 84–98.

D. Course Outlines

Davis, Vincent, and Arthur M. Gilbert (eds.). *Basic Courses in International Relations: An Anthology of Syllabi*, Beverly Hills, Ca.: Sage (1968).

Hermann, Charles F., and Kenneth N. Waltz (eds.). *Foreign Policy: An Anthology of Syllabi*, Beverly Hills, Ca.: Sage (1970).

Rohn, Peter H., et al. (eds.). *Basic Course in International Organization: An Anthology of Syllabi*, Beverly Hills, Ca.: Sage (1970).

―――. *Basic Courses in International Law: An Anthology of Syllabi*, Beverly Hills, Ca.: Sage (1970).

II. Texts and General Treatises on International Politics

A. Authored Volumes

Aron, Raymond. *Peace and War: A Theory of International Relations* [tr. Richard Howard and Annette Baker Fox], New York: Doubleday (1967).

Atwater, Elton, William Butz, Kent Forster, and Neal Riemer. *World Affairs: Problems and Prospects*, New York: Appleton-Century-Crofts (1958).

Atwater, Elton, Kent Forster, and Jan Prybyla. *World Tensions: Conflict and Accommodation*, New York: Appleton-Century-Crofts (1967).

Axline, W. Andrew, and James A. Stegenga. *The Global Community: A Brief Introduction to International Relations*, New York: Dodd, Mead (1972).

Ball, M. Margaret, and Hugh B. Killough. *International Relations*, New York: Ronald Press (1956).

Barnes, Harry E. *World Politics in Modern Civilization: The Contributions of Nationalism, Capitalism, Imperialism and Militarism to Human Culture and International Anarchy*, New York: Knopf (1930).

Beres, Louis R., and Harry R. Targ. *Reordering the Planet: Constructing Alternative World Futures*, Boston: Allyn & Bacon (1974).

Boulding, Kenneth. *Conflict and Defense: A General Theory*, New York: Harper (1962).

Brucan, Silviu. *Dissolution of Power: A Sociology of International Relations and Politics*, New York: Knopf (1971).

Bryce, James. *International Relations*, Port Washington, N.Y.: Kennikat (1922; 1966).

Buell, Raymond L. *International Relations*, New York: Holt (1925).

Burton, J. W. *International Relations: A General Theory*, Cambridge, Mass.: Harvard University Press (1965).

Cantor, Robert D. *Introduction to International Politics*, Itasca, Ill.: Peacock (1976).

Carr, Edward H. *Twenty Years' Crisis, 1919–1939: An Introduction to the Study of International Relations*, New York: St. Martin's Press (1946).

―――. *International Relations between the Two World Wars (1919–1939)*, New York: St. Martin's Press (1947).

Clark, Grenville, and Louis B. Sohn. *World Peace through World Law*, Cambridge, Mass.: Harvard University Press (1960).

Claude, Inis L. *Power and International Relations*, New York: Random House (1962).

Clemens, Walter C. *Toward a Strategy of Peace*, New York: Rand Mc-Nally (1965).

Coplin, William D. *Introduction to International Politics: A Theoretical Overview*, Chicago: Markham (1971; 1974).

Crabb, Cecil V. *Nations in a Multipolar World*, New York: Harper & Row (1968).

DeGrazia, Alfred, and Thomas H. Stevenson. *World Politics, A Study of International Relations*, College Outline Series, New York: Barnes & Noble (1962).

Deutsch, Karl W. *The Analysis of International Relations*, Englewood Cliffs, N.J.: Prentice-Hall (1968).

Edwards, David V. *International Political Analysis*, New York: Holt, Rinehart & Winston (1969).

―――. *Creating a New World Politics: From Conflict to Cooperation*, New York: David McKay (1973).

Eisenstadt, Shmuel. *The Political Systems of Empires*, New York: Free Press (1963).

Finlay, David J., and Thomas Hovet. *International Relations on the Planet Earth*, New York: Harper & Row (1975).

Fliess, Peter J. *International Relations in the Bipolar World*, New York: Knopf (1968).

Forward, Nigel. *The Field of Nations*, Boston: Little, Brown (1971).

Frankel, Joseph. *International Relations*, New York: Oxford University Press (1964; 1969).

―――. *Contemporary International Theory and the Behavior of States*, New York: Oxford University Press (1973).

Friedmann, Wolfgang. *An Introduction to World Politics*, New York: Macmillan (1951; 1952; 1956; 1960).

Gibbons, Herbert A. *An Introduction to World Politics*, New York: Century (1922).

Goodwin, Geoffrey. *International Society*, The Hague: Nijhoff (1972).

Greene, Fred. *Dynamics of International Relations: Power, Security and Order*, New York: Holt, Rinehart & Winston (1964).

Haas, Ernst. *Beyond the Nation State*, Stanford, Ca.: Stanford University Press (1964).

_____, and Allen Whiting. *Dynamics of International Relations*, New York: McGraw-Hill (1956).

Hartmann, Frederick H. *The Relations of Nations*, New York: Macmillan (1957; 1962; 1967; 1973).

Herz, John H. *International Politics in the Atomic Age*, New York: Columbia University Press (1959).

Hill, Norman L. *International Politics*, New York: Harper & Row (1963).

Hinsley, Francis H. *Power and the Pursuit of Peace: Theory and Practice in the History of Relations between States*, Cambridge: At the University Press (1963).

Hodges, Charles. *The Background of International Relations*, New York: Wiley (1931).

Holsti, Kal J. *International Politics: A Framework for Analysis*, Englewood Cliffs, N.J.: Prentice-Hall (1967; 1972).

Hopkins, Raymond F., and Richard W. Mansbach. *Structure and Process in International Politics*, New York: Harper & Row (1973).

Jordan, David C. *World Politics in Our Time*, Lexington, Mass.: Heath (1970).

Kalijarvi, Thorsten. *Modern World Politics*, New York: Crowell (1953).

Kaplan, Morton. *System and Process in International Politics*, New York: Wiley (1957).

Kulski, W. W. *International Politics in a Revolutionary Age*, New York: Lippincott (1964).

Legg, Keith R., and James F. Morrison. *Politics and the International System: An Introduction*, New York: Harper & Row (1971).

Lerche, Charles O., Jr. *Principles of International Relations*, New York: Oxford University Press (1956).

_____, and Abdul A. Said. *Concepts of International Politics*, Englewood Cliffs, N.J.: Prentice-Hall (1963).

Levi, Werner. *International Politics: Foundations of the System*, Minneapolis: University of Minnesota Press (1974).

Liska, George. *International Equilibrium: A Theoretical Essay on the Politics and Organization of Security*, Cambridge, Mass.: Harvard University Press (1957).

Luard, Evan. *Conflict and Peace in the Modern International System*, Boston: Little, Brown (1968).

Mander, Linden A. *Foundations of Modern World Society*, Stanford, Ca.: Stanford University Press (1947).

Manning, C. A. W. *The Nature of International Society*, London: G. Bell & Sons (1962).

Maxwell, Bertram W. *International Relations*, New York: Crowell (1939).

Middlebush, Frederick A., and Chesney Hill. *Elements of International Relations*, New York: McGraw-Hill (1940).

Mills, Lennox A., and Charles H. McLaughlin. *World Politics in Transition*, New York: Holt (1956).

Modelski, George. *Principles of World Politics*, New York: Free Press (1972).

Moon, Parker T. *Imperialism and World Politics*, New York: Macmillan (1926).

Morgenthau, Hans J. *Politics among Nations: The Struggle for Power and Peace*, New York: Knopf (1948; 1954; 1960; 1967; 1974).

Mowat, Robert B. *International Relations*, New York: Macmillan (1931).

Niebuhr, Reinhold. *Nations and Empires: Recurring Patterns in the Political Order*, London: Faber & Faber (1959).

Northedge, Fred S., and M. J. Grieve. *A Hundred Years of International Relations*, New York: Praeger (1971).

Olson, William C., and Fred Sondermann. *The Theory and Practice of International Relations*, Englewood Cliffs, N.J.: Prentice-Hall (1960; 1966).

Organski, A. F. K. *World Politics*, New York: Knopf (1958; 1968).

Padelford, Norman J. *International Politics*, New York: Macmillan (1954).

————, and George Lincoln. *Dynamics of International Politics*, New York: Macmillan (1962; 1967; 1976).

Palmer, Norman, and Howard Perkins. *International Relations: The World Community in Transition*, New York: Houghton Mifflin (1953; 1957).

Pettman, Ralph. *Human Behavior and World Politics: An Introduction to International Relations*, New York: St. Martin's Press (1975).

Potter, Pitman B. *This World of Nations: Foundations, Institutions, Practices*, New York: Macmillan (1929).

Puchala, Donald. *International Politics Today*, New York: Dodd, Mead (1971).

Quester, George H. *The Continuing Problem of International Politics*, New York: Harper & Row (1974).

Rahman, Hafiz H. *International Law, Politics and Organisation*, Dacca, India: Ideal (1962).

Read, Elizabeth. *International Law and International Relations*, American Foundation (1925).

Renouvin, Pierre, and J. B. Duroselle. *Introduction to the History of International Relations*, New York: Praeger (1967).

Reuter, Paul. *International Institutions* [tr. J. M. Chapman], London: Allen & Unwin (1958).

Reynolds, R. A. *An Introduction to International Relations*, Cambridge, Mass.: Schenkman (1971).

Robertson, Charles L. *International Politics since World War II: A Short History*, New York: Wiley (1966).

Rosecrance, Richard. *Action and Reaction in World Politics: International Systems in Perspective*, Boston: Little, Brown (1963).

_____. *International Relations: Peace or War?* New York: McGraw-Hill (1973).

Rosen, Steven, and Walter S. Jones. *The Logic of International Relations*, Cambridge, Mass.: Winthrop (1974).

Russett, Bruce M. *Trends in World Politics*, New York: Macmillan (1965).

_____. *Power and Community in World Politics*, San Francisco: Freeman (1974).

Schleicher, Charles. *Introduction to International Relations*, Englewood Cliffs, N.J.: Prentice-Hall (1953).

_____. *International Relations: Cooperation and Conflict*, Englewood Cliffs, N.J.: Prentice-Hall (1962).

Schuman, Frederick L. *International Politics: The Western State System i Mid-Century*, New York: McGraw-Hill (1933; 1937; 1941; 1948; 1953; 1969).

Schwarzenberger, George. *Power Politics: A Study of International Society*, New York: Praeger (1951).

Sharp, Walter R., and Grayson Kirk. *Contemporary International Politics*, New York: Farrar & Rinehart (1940).

Simonds, Frank H., and Brooks Emeny. *The Great Powers in World Politics: International Relations and Economic Nationalism*, New York: American (1935; 1937; 1939).

Singer, Marshall R. *Weak States in a World of Powers: The Dynamics of International Relationships*, New York: Free Press (1972).

Spanier, John W. *World Politics in an Age of Revolution*, New York: Praeger (1967).

————. *Games Nations Play: Analyzing International Politics*, New York: Praeger (1972; 1975).

Spiegel, Steven L. *Dominance and Diversity: The International Hierarchy*, Boston: Little, Brown (1972).

Spiro, Herbert J. *World Politics: The Global System*, Homewood, Ill.: Dorsey (1966).

Sprout, Harold, and Margaret Sprout. *Foundations of International Politics*, New York: Van Nostrand (1962).

————. *Toward a Politics of the Planet Earth*, New York: Van Nostrand-Reinhold (1971).

Steiner, H. Arthur. *Principles and Problems of International Relations*, New York: Harper (1940).

Sterling, Richard W. *Macropolitics: International Relations in a Global Society*, New York: Knopf (1974).

Stoessinger, John G. *The Might of Nations: World Politics in Our Time*, New York: Random House (1962; 1969).

Strausz-Hupé, Robert, and Stefan Possony. *International Relations in the Age of the Conflict between Democracy and Dictatorship*, New York: McGraw-Hill (1950; 1954).

Sullivan, Michael. *International Relations: Theory and Practice*, Englewood Cliffs, N.J.: Prentice-Hall (1976).

Surindar, S. *International Relations*, New Delhi, India: Sudha Publications (1962).

Van Dyke, Vernon. *International Politics*, New York: Appleton-Century-Crofts (1957; 1966; 1972).

Vital, David. *The Inequality of States: A Study of the Smaller Powers in International Relations*, New York: Oxford University Press (1967).

Walsh, Edmund A. *History and Nature of International Relations*, New York: Macmillan (1922).

Wolfers, Arnold. *Discord and Collaboration: Essays on International Politics*, Baltimore: Johns Hopkins Press (1962).

Wright, Quincy. *Causes of War and the Conditions of Peace*, London: Longmans, Green (1935).

B. Edited Volumes

Art, Robert, and Robert Jervis (eds.). *International Politics: Anarchy, Force, Imperialism*, Boston: Little, Brown (1973).
Kenneth Waltz, International Conflict and International Anarchy
Hedley Bull, Society and Anarchy in International Relations
Arnold Wolfers, National Security as an Ambiguous Symbol
Edward H. Carr, The Harmony of Interests
Jean-Jacques Rousseau, A Lasting Peace through the Federation of Europe
Stanley Hoffmann, The Uses and Limits of International Law
Hans Morgenthau, The Future of Diplomacy
Inis Claude, The Balance of Power
Marina Finkelstein and Lawrence Finkelstein, The Future and Collective Security
Joseph Nye, Regional Organizations and Peace
Robert E. Osgood, The Expansion of Force
Thomas Schelling, The Diplomacy of Violence
Herman Kahn, Two Types of Deterrence
Glenn Snyder, The Balance of Power and the Balance of Terror
Karl Deutsch, A Critique of Deterrence Theory
Kenneth Waltz, The Function of Force
A. F. K. Organski, Nuclear Weapons as Deterrents
Henry Kissinger, The Problems of Limited War
Mao Tse-tung, What is Guerrilla Warfare?
John A. Hobson, The Economic Taproot of Imperialism
Lionel Robbins, Defensive Economic Imperialism
Harry Magdoff, The American Empire and the U.S. Economy
S. M. Miller et al., Does the U.S. Economy Require Imperialism?
Joseph Schumpeter, The Sociology of Imperialisms
Richard Barnet, The National-Security Manager
John Galbraith, The Turbulent Frontier as a Factor in British Expansion
Robert W. Tucker, America's Commitments and World Order
Stanley Hoffmann, The Future International System
Michel Tatu, The Great Power Triangle: Washington-Moscow-Peking
Anthony Hartley, Western Europe in the 1970s
Kei Wakaizumi, Japan Beyond 1970
Joseph Nye and Robert Keohane, Transnational Relations and World Politics
Raymond Vernon, Multinational Enterprise and National Security

Mancur Olson, Rapid Growth as a Destabilizing Force
Ivan Illich, Outwitting the Developed Countries

Brook, David (ed.). *Search for Peace: Readings in International Relations*, New York: Dodd, Mead (1972).
Does Human Nature Make War Inevitable?
Thomas Hobbes, On the Natural Condition of Mankind
Hans J. Morgenthau, Politics among Nations
Margaret Mead, Warfare Is Only an Invention—Not a Biological Necessity
Sigmund Freud, Why War?
Past International Systems
Thucydides, The History of the Peloponnesian War
Crane Brinton, From Many One
Adda Bozeman, Politics and Culture in International History
Nationalism
Hans Kohn, What Is Nationalism?
Carlton J. H. Hayes, Historical Development
William J. Foltz, Building the Newest Nations
Giuseppe Mazzini, The Duties of Man
Benito Mussolini, The Political and Social Doctrine of Fascism
Gamal Abdel Nasser Closes the Gulf of Aqaba and Blockades the Port of Elat
Sovereignty
Jean Bodin, Six Books of the Commonwealth
Lassa Oppenheim, The Problem of Sovereignty in the Twentieth Century
Power in International Relations
Nicholas Spykman, America's Strategy in World Politics
George Modelski, A Theory of Foreign Policy
Technology and Power
Bertie Kennedy Blount, Science Will Change the Balance of Power
Harold Sprout, Geopolitical Hypotheses in Technological Perspective
Bernard Brodie, Strategy in the Missile Age
Thomas C. Schelling, Arms and Influence
Glenn H. Snyder, Deterrence and Defense
Robert Endicott Osgood, Limited War
Che Guevara, Guerrilla Warfare
Henry A. Kissinger, Nuclear Weapons and Foreign Policy
James E. King, Nuclear Plenty and Limited War
Basil H. Liddell Hart, Deterrent or Defense?
Pierre M. Gallois, Nuclear Strategy: A French View
John H. Herz, The Rise and Demise of the Territorial State
Herman Kahn, Thinking About the Unthinkable
Balance of Power
Edward Vose Gulick, The Balance of Power
Morton A. Kaplan, Systems and Process in International Politics
Jessie Bernard, The Theory of Games of Strategy as a Modern Sociology of Conflict

Quincy Wright, Why Balances of Power Have Collapsed
Ernst B. Haas, The Balance of Power as a Guide to Policy-Making
A. F. K. Organski, World Politics
Pierre M. Gallois, The Balance of Terror
Bertrand Russell, Common Sense and Nuclear Warfare
Herman Kahn, How War Might Come
The Role of International Law in the Struggle to Maintain International Peace
James L. Brierly, The Law of Nations
David Brook, The U.N. and the China Dilemma
Percy E. Corbett, Morals, Laws, and Power in International Relations
Philip C. Jessup, A Modern Law of Nations
Lassa Oppenheim, International Law
Grenville Clark and Louis B. Sohn, World Peace Through World Law
Filmer S. C. Northrop, The Taming of the Nations
International Organization
Paul S. Reinsch, Public International Unions
Woodrow Wilson, Address Delivered at the First Annual Assemblage of the League to Enforce Peace
Leland M. Goodrich, Efforts to Establish an International Police Force Down to 1950
Inis L. Claude, Power and International Relations
John G. Stoessinger, The Might of Nations
Inis L. Claude, The O.A.S., the U.N., and the United States
Paul H. Nitze, Where and Under What Circumstances Might a United Nations Police Force Be Useful in the Future?
David Brook, Preface to Peace
Werner Levi, Fundamentals of World Organization
Building a World Community
Emery Reves, The Anatomy of Peace
David Mitrany, A Working Peace System
Karl W. Deutsch et al., Political Community and the North Atlantic Area
David B. Truman, The Governmental Process
Ernst B. Haas, The Uniting of Europe
Postscript: Toward the Future—The 1970's and Beyond
William and Paul Paddock, Famine—1975
Arvid Pardo, A Statement Before the First Committee of the General Assembly of the U.N.
Morton A. Kaplan, NATO and the International Systems of the 1970's

Clemens, Walter C. (ed.). *World Perspectives on International Politics*, Boston: Little, Brown (1965).
    J. William Fulbright, A Concert of Free Nations
    Jacques Vernant, Foundations and Objectives of French Foreign Policy
    John F. Kennedy, Toward a Strategy of Peace
    Robert Strausz-Hupé and William R. Kintner, A Forward Strategy Beyond Survival

Max F. Millikan and Donald L. M. Blackmer, The Third Choice
Edward C. Banfield, Foreign Aid Doctrines
Mikhail A. Suslov, On the Struggle of the C.P.S.U. for the Unity of the
  International Communist Movement
The Editors of "People's Daily" and "Red Flag," The Leaders of the
  C.P.S.U. Are the Greatest Splitters of Our Times
A. A. Arzumanyan, Peaceful Coexistence and the World Revolutionary
  Process
Shao Tieh-chen, Revolutionary Dialectics and How to Appraise Im-
  perialism
G. Mirsky, Whither the Newly Independent Countries
The Editors of "People's Daily" and "Red Flag," Apologists of Neo-
  Colonialism
Achmed Sukarno, Let a New Asia and a New Africa Be Born!
Gamal Abdel Nasser, Ours Is the Side of Peace and Freedom
E. M. Debrah, The Commitment of the Uncommitted Nations
N. Parameswaran Nayar, The Growth of Nonalignment in World Af-
  fairs
Robert S. McNamara, Spectrum of Defense
Walt W. Rostow, Guerrilla Warfare in the Underdeveloped Areas
Pierre M. Gallois, The Raison d'Etre of French Defense Policy
N. I Krylov, Strategic Rockets
V. I. Chuikov, Soviet Land Forces in Nuclear War
Mao Tse-tung, On the Protracted War
Ernesto Che Guevara, Guerrilla Warfare: A Means
Lucius D. Clay, Berlin
Nikita S. Khrushchev, On German Revanchism
L. Erven, About the Berlin Crisis
Conference of Nonaligned Nations, Declaration at Belgrade, Sep-
  tember 6, 1961
John F. Kennedy, Statement at Conclusion of Visit of President
  Sukarno and President Keita, September 13, 1961
Soviet Foreign Ministry, Statement, September 14, 1961
Nikita S. Khrushchev, Letter to Prime Minister Nehru, September 16,
  1961
Osvaldo Dorticós Torrado, On Yankee Aggression
John F. Kennedy, The Soviet Threat to the Americas
Nikita S. Khrushchev, Speech to the Supreme Soviet, December 12,
  1962
The Editors of "People's Daily," Editorial, December 31, 1962
K. S. Shelvankar, China's Himalayan Frontiers: India's Attitude
The Editors of "People's Daily," More on Nehru's Philosophy in the
  Light of the Sino-Indian Boundary Question
"Pravda," Serious Hotbed of Tension in Asia
George E. Pugh, Restraints, Strategy, and Arms Control
Seymour Melman, Too Much U.S. War Power? A Scientist's View
I. Glagolev and V. Larionov, Soviet Defense Might and Peaceful
  Coexistence

Chinese Government Statement, Against the Test Ban
Kwame Nkrumah, Africa, Disengagement and Peace
Simha Flapan, For an Atom-Bomb Free Middle East
Aftab Ahmad Khan, Economic and Social Consequences of Disarmament
Charles de Gaulle, Press Conference, April 11, 1961
Mohammad Nawaz, Afro-Asians and the United Nations
M. Volodin, United Nations in a Changed World
The Editors of "People's Daily," Editorial, December 18, 1963
Dean Rusk, The First Twenty-Five Years of the United Nations—From San Francisco to the 1970's

Coplin, William D., and Charles W. Kegley, Jr. (eds.). A *Multi-Method Introduction to International Politics: Observation, Explanation, and Prescription*, Chicago: Markham (1971).
The Actors
Hans J. Morgenthau, The Intellectual, Political, and Moral Roots of U.S. Failure in Vietnam
Ole R. Holsti, The Belief System and National Images: A Case Study
Graham T. Allison, Conceptual Models and the Cuban Missile Crisis
Gabriel A. Almond, The Elites and Foreign Policy
R. Barry Farrell, Foreign Policies of Open and Closed Political Societies
Samuel P. Huntington, The Changing Locus of Violence in World Politics
Walter Millis, The Uselessness of Military Power
Peter Wallensteen, Characteristics of Economic Sanctions
Glenn D. Paige, A Prescriptive Evaluation of the Korean Decision
Eugene Wittkopf, Containment Versus Underdevelopment in the Distribution of United States Foreign Aid
Jonathan Wilkenfeld, Domestic and Foreign Conflict Behavior of Nations
International Interactions
Chadwick F. Alger, Non-resolution Consequences of the United Nations and Their Effect on International Conflict
Robert C. Angell, The Growth of Transnational Participation
Bruce M. Russett, The Calculus of Deterrence
Amitai Etzioni, Strategic Models for a De-Polarizing World
George Kent, An Experimental Approach to the Study of the Determinants of Bargaining Outcomes
The International Political System
Ernst B. Haas, The Balance of Power: Prescription, Concept, or Propaganda?
Kenneth N. Waltz, The Stability of the Bipolar World
Karl W. Deutsch and J. David Singer, Multipolar Power Systems and International Stability
Kenneth E. Boulding, National Images and International Systems
Donald J. Puchala, The International Political Future of Europe

Charles W. Kegley, Jr., and J. Martin Rochester, Assessing the Impact of Trends on the International System: The Growth of Intergovernmental Organizations

Duchacek, Ivo D. (ed.). *Discord and Harmony: Readings in International Politics*, New York: Holt, Rinehart & Winston (1972).
States and Nations
Kenneth E. Boulding, The Map-Shape of Nations
Robert Ardrey, The Territorial Imperative
John H. Herz, The Territorial State Revisited
J. David Singer, Trends away from the Nation-State
Edward Hallett Carr, Nationalism Socialized: Socialism Nationalized
Mao Tse-tung, Can a Communist be a Patriot?
Karl W. Deutsch, Nationalism and World Unity
Rupert Emerson, National Self-Determination
Ernest Renan, Nation: A Soul
Chiang Kai-shek et al., Fear of Losing National Soul
J. David Singer, Territorial States and Their System
John G. Stoessinger, The Superpowers and the United Nations
Lassa F. L. Oppenheim et al., The Myth and Reality of World Community: A Controversy
John H. E. Fried and Hans J. Morgenthau, Observance and Enforcement of International Law
Richard A. Falk, International Law: A New Approach
Decisions in Foreign Policy
Hans J. Morgenthau, The Key Concept of Political Realism: Interest in Terms of Power
Stanley Hoffmann, A Critique of Political Realism
Arthur M. Schlesinger, Bay of Pigs: A Case Study
Theodore C. Sorensen, The First Nuclear Confrontation in History— The Cuban Missile Crisis of 1962: A Case Study
Nikita S. Khrushchev et al., Missiles in the Caribbean: A Postscript
Ole R. Holsti, Enemies are those Whom We Define as Such: A Case Study
Vladimir I. Lenin, Capitalism = Imperialism = War
Jen-min Pao, Leninism or Social Imperialism
Richard J. Barnet, The Third World: Why Do We Interfere?
Max Weber, Ethical Paradoxes of Politics
Kautilya et al., Ends and Means for a State, a Prince, and a Revolutionary
American Friends Service Committee, The Politics of Nonviolence
Thomas F. Farrell, The Birth of the Atomic Age
Louis Morton, The Decision to Use the Atomic Bomb
War, Deterrence, and Diplomacy
Karl von Clausewitz, War as an Instrument of National Policy
Archives of the German Foreign Office, How World War II Came: Nazi-Soviet Cooperation, 1939–1941

Herman Kahn, How Nuclear War Might Come
Robert S. McNamara, The U.S. Nuclear Strategy: Assumptions and
Dangers
Arkady S. Sobolev, Are They Geese or Missiles?
Amitai Etzioni, Never Has a Non-War Cost so Much
Philip Green, Nuclear Deterrence and Moral Considerations
Kenneth N. Waltz, The Modern Balance of Power: Duopoly at the Top
John H. Herz, Nuclear Stalemate: Cause of Stability or Instability?
Graham T. Allison, Ernest May, and Adam Yarmolinsky, Limits to
Intervention
Kenneth W. Thompson, The Concept of Collective Security
Fred Charles Iklé, What is Negotiation?
Harold Nicolson, Open Covenants Secretly Arrived At
Justice Potter Stewart et al., The Pentagon Papers
Thomas C. Schelling, Tacit Coordination of Expectations and Behavior
Charles Burton Marshall, The Impenetrable Blank of the Future: A
Postscript

Duchacek, Ivo, and Kenneth Thompson (eds.). *Conflict and Coopera-
tion Among Nations*, New York: Holt, Rinehart & Winston
(1960).
The Nature of International Society
Ernest Renan, Is Nationalism Constructive or Destructive? What is a
Nation?
Hans Kohn, Hebrew and Greek Roots of Modern Nationalism
Carlton J. H. Hayes, Five Types of Nationalism
Edward Hallett Carr, Socialization of Nationalism
Woodrow Wilson, Self-Determination as the Basis for Peace
Alfred Cobban, National Self-Determination
The United Nations General Secretariat, Definition and Classification
of Minorities
Charter of the United Nations, Non-Self-Governing Territories
Reports on the Progress Towards Self-Government or Independence in
Trust Territories
Gaganvihari L. Mehta, Asian Nationalism vis-à-vis other Asian Nations
Edict Closing Japan, 1936, Asian Isolationism: Japan
Chiang Kai-shek, Asian Isolationism: China
Ho Chi Minh, Viet-Nam to be Free From the French
Achmed Sukarno, The Shot at Lexington Heard in Indonesia
P. Kodanda Rao, Different Languages—A Threat to Indian Unity?
Joseph Stalin, Marxism and the National and Colonial Question
Mao Tse-tung, Can a Communist be a Patriot?
Milovan Djilas, National Communism is Communism in Decline
John H. Herz, The Demise of the Territorial State
Reinhold Niebuhr, The Illusion of World Government
The Struggle for Power and Order
Nicholas John Spykman, Civilized Life Rests on Power
Herbert Butterfield, Force and the Ethical Order

Louis J. Halle, What Constitutes Power?
Louis J. Halle, Checks and Balances
Thucydides, The Growth of Athenian Power Has to be Checked
David Hume, The Balancing Process: An Ancient Wisdom
Arnold Wolfers, The Balancing Process: Is It Outdated?
Kenneth W. Thompson, The Idea of World Police and Its Fallacies
Albert Einstein, Nations Should be Deprived of Their Sovereignty
Sigmund Freud, Might is Not the Opposite of Right
Gabriel Almond, Anthropology and International Politics
Kenneth W. Thompson, Theories on the Nature of War
Nicholas John Spykman, Elements of Power Do Not Stay Put
Allen W. Dulles, How Strong is the U.S.S.R.?
Evaluation of Intentions
Hans J. Morgenthau, What is National Interest?
William T. R. Fox, The Desirable and the Possible
Stanley H. Hoffmann, Critique of Realism
Charles Burton Marshall, Foresight and Blindness in Foreign Policy
Vladimir I. Lenin, Capitalism Equals Imperialism
Nikita S. Khrushchev, Yes, Capitalism Imperialism will Wither and Die
George F. Kennan, Soviet Advances can be Contained
Historicus, Communist Doctrine on War and Coexistence
Nikita S. Khrushchev, Peaceful Coexistence—The Soviet View
Walter Lippmann, Rivals Should Negotiate
George F. Kennan, Peaceful Coexistence—A Western View
Paul Schmidt, Munich, 1938
Raymond J. Sontag, The Yalta Conference
Protocol of Proceedings, The Yalta Agreements
Raymond J. Sontag, The Last Months of Peace
Nazi Archives, Nazi-Soviet Coexistence, 1939–1941
Choice of Responses
Charles Burton Marshall, Errors in the Calculation of Means
Paul H. Nitze, A Shaky Balance of Brinkmanship
Henry L. Roberts, Minimum Requirements
Hans J. Morgenthau, American and Soviet Alliance Policies
Arnold Wolfers, Stresses and Strains in Going It with Others
Karl von Clausewitz, What is War?
Quincy Wright, The Main Characteristics of War
Kenneth W. Thompson, Nuclear Weapons: Four Crucial Questions
Niccolò Machiavelli, In What Way Princes Must Keep Faith
Arnold Wolfers, Statesmanship and Moral Choice
Dwight D. Eisenhower, Crusade in Europe
Winston Churchill, Passion Ran High in England about the Darlan Deal
Louis Morton, The Decision to Use the Atomic Bomb
Negotiations
Harold Nicolson, The Evolution of Diplomatic Method
Charles Burton Marshall, The Problem of Incompatible Purposes
John C. Campbell, Negotiations with the Soviets: Lessons of the Past

International Law and Organization
Lassa F. L. Oppenheim, Community and Law
Kenneth W. Thompson, The Absence of Common Standards
Hans Kelsen, Centralized Enforcement and Self-Help
Leland M. Goodrich, The United Nations Security Council
Dag Hammarskjöld, The United Nations: An Added Instrument to Diplomacy
Vernon V. Aspaturian, World Organization's Three Phases
Inis L. Claude, The Theory of Functionalism

Edwards, David V. (ed.). *International Political Analysis: Readings*, New York: Holt, Rinehart & Winston (1970).
Elements of Explanation in International Politics
Dean G. Pruitt, Definition of the Situation as a Determinant of International Action
Henry A. Kissinger, Domestic Structure and Foreign Policy
Paul Y. Hammond, The Political Order and the Burden of External Relations
Kenneth E. Boulding, Towards a Pure Theory of Threat Systems
J. David Singer, Inter-Nation Influence: A Formal Model
Jan F. Triska and David D. Finley, Soviet-American Relations: A Multiple Symmetry Model
From Explanation to Theorizing: Crisis
and War as Examples
Charles A. McClelland, The Acute International Crisis
Allen R. Ferguson, Tactics in a Local Crisis
Nicholas S. Timasheff, The Movement from Peace to War
Theorizing about International Politics
Alan James, Power Politics
Charles A. McClelland, Applications of General Systems Theory in International Relations
Arthur Lee Burns, From Balance to Deterrence: A Theoretical Analysis
Morton A. Kaplan, Some Problems of International Systems Research
George Liska, Continuity and Change in International Systems
Kenneth N. Waltz, The Stability of a Bipolar World
Karl W. Deutsch and J. David Singer, Multipolar Power Systems and International Stability
Richard N. Rosecrance, Bipolarity, Multipolarity, and the Future
Applications of International Political Theory
Daniel Bell, Twelve Modes of Prediction—A Preliminary Sorting of Approaches in the Social Sciences
Robert A. LeVine, The Logical Structure of a Policy Position
Kenneth E. Boulding, Dare We Take the Social Sciences Seriously?

Falk, Richard A., and Saul H. Mendlovitz (eds.). *The Strategy of World Order: Toward a Theory of War Prevention*, vol. 1, New York: World Law Fund (1966).
The Problem, the Plan, and Some
Preliminary Considerations
Kenneth E. Boulding, The Prevention of World War III

Herman Kahn, The Arms Race and Some of Its Hazards
Richard J. Barnet, Preparations for Progress
Walter Millis, Order and Change in a Warless World
Robert M. Hutchins, Constitutional Foundations for World Order
Quincy Wright, Toward a Universal Law for Mankind
Albert Wohlstetter, Technology, Prediction, and Disorder
Pope John XXIII, Pacem in Terris, Part IV
Hugh Gaitskell, An Eight Point Programme for World Government

The Causes of War and Peace
Quincy Wright, Analysis of the Causes of War
Kenneth N. Waltz, Political Philosophy and the Study of International Relations
Werner Levi, On the Causes of War and the Conditions of Peace
Harold L. Nieburg, Uses of Violence

The Nature of International Society
Roberto Ducci, The World Order in the Sixties
Kenneth N. Waltz, The Stability of a Bipolar World
Ronald J. Yalem, Regionalism and World Order
J. David Singer, The Level-of-Analysis Problem in International Relations
Anatol Rapoport, Systemic and Strategic Conflict
Harold D. Lasswell, The Political Science of Science: An Inquiry into the Possible Reconciliation of Mastery and Freedom

The Shimoda Case: Challenge and Response
Richard A. Falk, The Claimants of Hiroshima
Shimoda and Others versus Japan. Decision of the Tokyo District Court, December 7, 1963
Karl Jaspers, The New Fact (and) Initial Political Thinking about the New Fact
Saul H. Mendlovitz, The Study of War Prevention: Toward a Disciplined View

International Legal Order in the Contemporary World
Richard A. Falk and Saul H. Mendlovitz, Towards a Warless World: One Legal Formula to Achieve Transition
Morton A. Kaplan and Nicholas deB. Katzenbach, Law in the International Community
Myres S. McDougal and Harold D. Lasswell, The Identification and Appraisal of Diverse Systems of Public Order
Roger Fisher, Bringing Law to Bear on Governments
Kenneth S. Carlston, The Individual Interest and the Growth of International Law and Organization
Max F. Millikan, Inquiry and Policy: The Relation of Knowledge to Action
Myres S. McDougal, Some Basic Theoretical Concepts about International Law: A Policy-Oriented Framework of Inquiry
Stanley Hoffmann, International Systems and International Law

Diverse Challenges to International Legal Order
Richard A. Falk, Historical Tendencies, Modernizing and Revolutionary Nations, and the International Legal Order

Edward McWhinney, Soviet and Western International Law and the Cold War in the Era of Bipolarity

J. J. G. Syatauw, Peaceful Coexistence: The Asian Attitude

Oliver J. Lissitzyn, The Less Developed Nations

International Legal Order and the Management of World Power

Morton A. Kaplan and Nicholas deB. Katzenbach, Resort to Force: War and Neutrality

Richard A. Falk, The Legal Control of Force in the International Community

Wolfgang Friedmann, The International Organization of Security and the Use of Force: "Indirect" Aggression, National Sovereignty, and Collective Security

Louis Henkin, Force, Intervention, and Neutrality in Contemporary International Law

Inis L. Claude, Jr., The Management of Power in the Changing United Nations

Ruth B. Russell, The Management of Power and Political Organization: Some Observations on Inis L. Claude's Conceptual Approach

The League of Nations and the United Nations: Continuities and Discontinuities

Clyde Eagleton, Covenant of the League of Nations and the Charter of the United Nations: Points of Difference

Leland M. Goodrich, From League of Nations to United Nations

Coordinated Reading in WPTWL: The United Nations Charter

The Relevance of Law to the Operations of the United Nations

Rosalyn Higgins, Law, Politics and the United Nations

A. J. P. Tammes, The Introduction of a New Legislative Technique

Report of Committee on Study of Legal Problems of the United Nations. Should the Laws of War Apply to United Nations Enforcement Action?

Extract from Oral Argument before the International Court of Justice in the *South West Africa Cases*

Excerpts from the Separate Opinion of Judge Sir Percy Spender in the Case of the *Certain Expenses of the United Nations*

Oscar Schachter, The Relation of Law, Politics and Action in the United Nations

Membership in the United Nations

The Advisory Opinion of the International Court of Justice in *Conditions of Admission of a State to Membership in the United Nations*

Sixteenth Session General Assembly Debate on Question of Representation of China in the United Nations and Restoration of the Lawful Rights of the People's Republic of China in the United Nations

Coordinated Reading in WPTWL: pp. 12–17

The Security Council

Leland M. Goodrich, The UN Security Council

D. W. Bowett, The Security Council: Functions and Powers
Excerpts from 18th Session of the General Assembly Special Political
Committee Debates
Coordinated Reading in WPTWL: pp. 66-131
The General Assembly
Gabriella R. Lande, The Changing Effectiveness of General Assembly
Resolutions
Krzysziof Skubiszewski, The General Assembly of the United Nations
and its Power to Influence National Action
Coordinated reading in WPTWL: pp. 34-65
The Uniting for Peace Resolution
Keith S. Petersen, The Uses of the Uniting for Peace Resolution Since
1950
Francis O. Wilcox, Representation and Voting in the United Nations
General Assembly
Thomas Hovet, Jr., How the African Bloc Uses Its Votes
United States Department of State, Would Weighted Voting Help the
U.S.?
Coordinated Reading in WPTWL: pp. 20-33
The Secretariat and the Secretary-General
Charles Henry Alexandrowicz, The Secretary-General of the United
Nations
Sydney D. Bailey, The Troika and the Future of the United Nations:
The Secretary-General
Coordinated Reading in WPTWL: pp. 183-186
**The Limitations on the Authority of the United Nations.
Article 2(7) and Apartheid in the Republic of South Africa**
United Nations Materials on Apartheid in the Republic of South Africa
Coordinated Reading in WPTWL: pp. 6-11
Procedures for Pacific Settlement
Morton A. Kaplan and Nicholas deB. Katzenbach, The Institutions of
International Decision-Making
Louis B. Sohn, Step-by-Step Acceptance of the Jurisdiction of the In-
ternational Court of Justice
Lon L. Fuller, Adjudication and the Rule of Law
Coordinated Reading in WPTWL: pp. 89-110; 335-344
**Procedures of Coercive Settlement:
Sanctions, Peace-Keeping and Police**
James L. Brierly, The Prohibition of War by International Law
Hans Kelsen, Sanctions in International Law under the Charter of the
United Nations
Wolfgang Friedmann, National Sovereignty, International Cooperation
and the Reality of International Law
U Thant, United Nations Peace Force
Herbert Nicholas, An Appraisal
Dag Hammarskjöld, United Nations Emergency Force
Marion H. McVitty, Wanted: Rules to Guide United Nations Peace-
Keeping Operations of the Future

Louis B. Sohn, The Role of the United Nations in Civil Wars
Coordinated reading in WPTWL: pp. 111–131
D. W. Bowett, Structure and Control of United Nations Forces (and) Conclusions
Arthur I. Waskow, Quis Custodiet? Controlling the Police in a Disarmed World
Hans Morgenthau, Political Conditions for a Force
Thomas C. Schelling, Strategy: A World Force in Operation
Coordinated Reading in WPTWL: pp. 314–334

The Financing and the So-Called Financing Problem
International Court of Justice. Certain Expenses of the United Nations
Norman J. Padelford, Financial Crisis and the Future of the United Nations
Special Committee on Peace-Keeping Operations: Report of the Secretary-General and the President of the General Assembly
Coordinated Reading in WPTWL: pp. 52–65; 349–358

Evaluating the United Nations
Stanley Hoffmann, An Evaluation of the United Nations
Dag Hammarskjöld, Two Differing Views of the United Nations Assayed
Alvin Z. Rubinstein, More Responsibility for Russia?

The Military Environment: Arms Competition and the Idea of Stable Deterrence
P. M. S. Blackett, Steps Toward Disarmament
Jerome Wiesner and Herbert F. York, National Security and the Nuclear-Test Ban
Freeman J. Dyson, Defence Against Ballistic Missiles
General Nikolai Talensky, Antimissile Systems and Disarmament
Robert Gomer, The ABM Debate: A Soviet View
Adrian S. Fisher, Arms Control and Disarmament in International Law

Theories of Arms Control and Disarmament
Hedley Bull, The Objectives of Arms Control
Thomas C. Schelling, Reciprocal Measures for Arms Stabilization
Charles Osgood, Reciprocal Initiative
Walter Goldstein, Keeping the Genie in the Bottle: The Feasibility of a Nuclear Non-Proliferation Agreement
Coordinated Reading in WPTWL: pp. 206–213

Transitional Steps Toward a Disarmable World
Robert C. Tucker, No First Use of Nuclear Weapons: A Proposal
No First Use of Nuclear Weapons: FAS Resolution
Betty Goetz Lall, Questions and Answers on the U.S. Production Freeze Proposal
Paul Doty, A Freeze on Strategic Delivery Systems
Louis B. Sohn, European Security—Interrelation of Political, Military, and Economic Factors

The Idea of General and Complete Disarmament
Hedley Bull, General and Comprehensive Disarmament
The McCloy-Zorin Agreement—Joint Statement of Agreed Principles for Disarmament Negotiations

Marion H. McVitty, A Comparison and Evaluation of Current Disarmament Proposals
Klaus Knorr, Supranational versus International Models for General and Complete Disarmament
Richard A. Falk, Respect for International Law and Confidence in Disarmament
Maintaining Security During Disarmament: Verified Compliance and Response
Richard J. Barnet, Inspection: Shadow and Substance
Louis B. Sohn, Phasing of Arms Reduction: The Territorial Method
Coordinated reading in WPTWL: pp. 263–280
Fred Charles Iklé, After Detection—What?
Verification and Response in Disarmament Agreements, Summary Report on the Woods Hole Summer Study of 1962
Roger Fisher, International Police: A Sequential Approach to Effectiveness and Control, Part I
Roger Fisher, International Police: A Sequential Approach to Effectiveness and Control, Part II
Coordinated Reading in WPTWL: pp. 306–313
World Economic Development: Some Trends and Models
Kenneth E. Boulding, The Concept of World Interest
P. N. Rosenstein-Rodan, International Aid for Underdeveloped Countries
Gustavo Lagos, International Stratification and Atimia
U Thant, The United Nations Development Decade
Emile Benoit, The Economic Impact of Disarmament in the United States

Forsyth, M. G., et al. (eds.). *The Theory of International Relations: Selected Texts*, Chicago: Aldine-Atherton (1972).
Alberico Gentili, Extracts from On the Law of War
Hugo Grotius, Extracts from On the Law of War and Peace
Emmerich De Vattel, Extracts from The Law of Nations on the Principles of Natural Law
Jean-Jacques Rousseau, Extracts from Abstract of the Abbe Saint-Pierre's Project for Perpetual Peace
Immanuel Kant, Extracts from Idea for a Universal History from a Cosmopolitical Point of View
Lord Brougham, Extracts from Balance of Power
Friedrich Von Gentz, Extracts from Fragments upon the Present State of the Political Balance of Europe
Richard Cobden, Extracts from Russia
Heinrich Von Treitschke, Extracts from Politics

Garnett, John (ed.). *Theories of Peace and Security*, New York: Macmillan (1970).
The Role of Force in International Politics
Michael Howard, Military Power and International Order
Klaus Knorr, The International Purposes of Military Power
Thomas C. Schelling, The Diplomacy of Violence

42   EDITED VOLUMES

Peace and Security Through Deterrence
Bernard Brodie, The Anatomy of Deterrence
Glenn Snyder, Deterrence: A Theoretical Introduction
Laurence W. Martin, Ballistic Missile Defence and the Strategic Balance
Peace and Security Through Disarmament
Inis L. Claude, Disarmament as an Approach to Peace
Hedley Bull, Disarmament and the International System
J. David Singer, Tensions, Political Settlement and Disarmament
Robert R. Bowie, Basic Requirements of Arms Control
Thomas C. Schelling, Surprise Attack and Disarmament
Wayland Young, The Problem of Verification
Peace and Security Through Limited War
Bernard Brodie, Limited War
Morton H. Halperin, The Limitation of Central War
Herman Kahn, The Concept of Escalation

Gray, Richard B. (ed.). *International Security Systems: Concepts and Models of World Order*, Itasca, Ill.: Peacock (1969).
Charles A. McClelland, General Systems Theory in International Relations
Morton A. Kaplan, Balance of Power, Bipolarity and Other Models of International Systems
Herbert S. Dinerstein, The Transformation of Alliance Systems
Richard J. Barnet, Regional Security Systems
Richard N. Rosecrance, Diplomacy in Security Systems
Inis L. Claude, The United Nations and Collective Security
Stanley H. Hoffmann, International Systems and International Law
Richard A. Falk, Law in Future International Systems
Saul H. Mendlovitz, Models of World Order
Kenneth E. Boulding, Stability in International Systems: The Role of Disarmament and Development

Gyorgy, Andrew, et al. (eds.). *Problems in International Relations*, Englewood Cliffs, N.J.: Prentice-Hall (1955; 1962; 1970).
John R. Thomas, Wars of National Liberation: Internal and External Factors
Ishwer Ojha, The Chinese Revolutionary Model: Mao's Ideal Type
Harold Hinton, The Chinese Road to Communism: Twenty Years of Maoism
Ferengc Vali, The Hungarian Revolution
Andrew Gyorgy, Cohesive and Disruptive Forces in Soviet-East European Relations
Andrew Gyorgy, A Note on the Significance and Impact of the Sino-Soviet Dispute
Anita M. Dasbach, The Political Attitudes of East European Youth
Hubert Gibbs, Containment: Europe and the United States
Hubert Gibbs, The American Alliance System
Edward Drachman, The United States Decision to Bomb North Vietnam

Harold Jacobson and Robert Jordan, Economic and Political Integration: From the Schuman Plan to the European Communities
Robert Jordan, The French Decision to Withdraw from the NATO Military Structure
James McBrayer, The Political Role of the Latin-American Elite
Carl Schneider, The Arab-Israeli Conflict: The Impact of the Six-day War
Carl Leiden and Karl Schmitt, The Cuban Revolution
Andrew Gyorgy, The Ideology of the Newly Emerging Nations
Henry Bretton, The Overthrow of Kwame Nkrumah
Carl Schneider, The Suez Crisis of 1956 and Its Aftermath
Peter Toma, Competitive Coexistence and World Food Supply Problems
Daniel Cheever, The Role of International Organization in Ocean Development

Hartmann, Frederick H. (ed.). *World in Crisis: Readings in International Relations*, New York: Macmillan (1952; 1962; 1967).
Niccolò Machiavelli, Concerning the Way in Which Princes Should Keep Faith
Edward H. Carr, International Politics: Idealism vs. Realism
Martin Wight, Power Politics
Royal Institute of International Affairs, Nationalism: What It Is and What It Means
C. J. H. Hayes, Liberal vs. Integral Nationalism
Salvador de Madariaga, The Fundamentals of National Power
Harold Nicolson, National Character and National Policy
Frank W. Notestein and Others, The Future Population of Europe and the Soviet Union
H. E. Wimperis, Atomic Energy and National Defence
Dean Acheson, Economic Policy and National Security
Nicholas J. Spykman, Geography and Geopolitics
Parker T. Moon, Imperialism and World Politics
Vladimir I. Lenin, Imperialism, the Highest Stage of Capitalism
E. M. Winslow, The Non-economic Roots of Imperialism
Willard Waller, The Causes of War
Thucydides, The Old Diplomacy
Harold Nicolson, The New Diplomacy
Lord Vansittart, The Decline of Diplomacy
Nicholas J. Spykman, The Balance of Power as Policy
Sir Eyre Crowe, The Balance of Power in Action
Grayson Kirk, The Atlantic Pact and International Security
William G. Carleton, Ideology or Balance of Power?
Alexandre Parodi, Peaceful Settlement of Disputes
Dean Rusk, Mutual Understanding—Key to Peace
Erich Hula, Four Years of the United Nations
Woodrow Wilson, Collective Security versus Balance of Power
Edwin Borchard, The Impracticability of "Enforcing" Peace
Edward H. Buehrig, Collective Security in a Bi-Polar World

James L. Brierly, The Outlook for International Law
Grant Gilmore, The Feasibility of Compulsory Legal Settlement
Emery Reves, The Need for World Government
Reinhold Niebuhr, The Illusion of World Government
"X," The Sources of Soviet Conduct
Walter Lippmann, A Critique of Containment
Hans J. Morgenthau, Strategy of Error
George F. Kennan, Is War with Russia Inevitable? Five Solid Arguments for Peace
Winston Churchill, Will There Be War?
Frederick H. Hartmann, Settlement for Germany
John K. Fairbank, The Problem of Revolutionary Asia
Dean Acheson, Crisis in Asia
Frederick H. Hartmann, A Crossroads in Foreign Policy

Hekhuis, Dale J., Charles McClintock, and Arthur Burns (eds.). *International Stability: Military, Economic and Political Dimensions*, New York: Wiley (1964).
International Stability and the Underdeveloped Areas
Dale J. Hekhuis and John F. Youngblood, The Nature of the Underdeveloped Areas
Lucian W. Pye, The Underdeveloped Areas as a Source of International Tension Through 1975
Paul N. Rosenstein-Rodan and Dale J. Hekhuis, Programs for Alleviating Instability
International Stability and Mutual Deterrence
Robert E. Osgood, Stabilizing the Military Environment
Arthur L. Burns, The Nth Country Problem, Mutual Deterrence and International Stability
Charles G. McClintock and Dale J. Hekhuis, European Community Deterrence: Its Organization, Utility, and Political and Economic Feasibility
Thomas W. Milburn, What Constitutes Effective U.S. Deterrence
Disarmament, Arms Control, and International Stability
Arthur L. Burns, Problems of Disarmament
Thomas C. Schelling, Arms Control: Proposal for a Special Surveillance Force
International Instrumentalities and Stability
Ernst B. Haas, International Integration: The European and the Universal Process
Arthur L. Burns and Nina Heathcote, The United Nations as a Peace-Preserving Force

Hill, Norman (ed.). *International Relations: Documents and Readings*, New York: Oxford University Press (1950).
International Relations and Organization
The State in International Relations
The Earlier Search for Security
The United Nations—A New System of Security

Regionalism and the United Nations
International Law and Courts
The Conduct of International Relations
Power Politics and War
Power Politics
The Geographic Setting
Nationalism
The Economic Basis
Imperialism
The Problem of War
World Economics and Social Problems
Technology in the Atomic Era
Trade and the World Economy
Social Problems
Labor and Agriculture
The Individual and the World of Ideas
Human Rights and Minority Rights
Ethics and Religion
Opinion, Education, and World Affairs

Kaplan, Morton A. (ed.). *The Revolution in World Politics*, New York: Wiley (1962).
Robert Waelder, Protest and Revolution against Western Societies
Norman Birnbaum, Great Britain: The Reactive Revolt
Stanley Hoffmann, Protest in Modern France
Herbert Passin, The Stratigraphy of Protest in Japan
George I. Blanksten, Fidel Castro and Latin America
Immanuel Wallerstein, Pan-Africanism as Protest
Leonard Binder, Nasserism: The Protest Movement in the Middle East
Leonard Binder, Egypt's Positive Neutrality
Joseph J. Zasloff, Peasant Protest in South Viet Nam
Vernon Aspaturian, The Challenge of Soviet Foreign Policy
A. M. Halpern, Communist China's Demands on the World
Morton A. Kaplan, Bipolarity in a Revolutionary Age
Ernst B. Haas, Dynamic Environment and Static System: Revolutionary Regimes in the United Nations
Richard A. Falk, Revolutionary Nations and the Quality of International Legal Order
Herman Kahn, The Arms Race and World Order
Bert F. Hoselitz and Ann R. Willner, Economic Development, Political Strategies, and American Aid
Charles Wolf, Defense and Development in Less-Developed Countries
Malcolm W. Hoag, On Stability in Deterrent Races
R. C. Nairn, Counterguerrilla Warfare in Southeast Asia
Morton A. Kaplan, United States Foreign Policy in a Revolutionary Age

Kaplan, Morton A. (ed.). *Great Issues of International Politics*, Chicago: Aldine (1970; 1974).
Robert Hutchins, Constitutional Foundations for World Order

Walter Millis, Order and Change in a Warless World
Morton A. Kaplan, International Law and the International System
Richard A. Falk and Quincy Wright, On Legal Tests of Aggressive War
Richard A. Falk, The Beirut Raid and the International Law of Retaliation
W. E. Butler, Socialist International Law or Social Principles of International Relations?
Stanley Hoffmann, Sisyphus and the Avalanche: The United Nations, Egypt, and Hungary
Stanley Hoffmann, Obstinate or Obsolete? The Fate of the Nation-State and the Case of Western Europe
Seymour C. Yuter, Preventing Nuclear Proliferation through the Legal Control of China's Bomb
Morton A. Kaplan, The Nuclear Non-Proliferation Treaty: Its Rationale, Prospects, and Possible Impact on International Law
Morton A. Kaplan, Changes in United States Perspectives on the Soviet Union and Detente
R. Judson Mitchell, The Revised Two Camps Doctrine in Soviet Foreign Policy
J. William Fulbright, The Foundations of National Security
Morton A. Kaplan, Old Realities and New Myths
Morton A. Kaplan, United States Foreign Policy in a Revolutionary Age
Frank Church, The Global Crunch
Eqbal Ahmad and Edwin Reischauer, The Lessons of Vietnam
Earl C. Ravenal, The Nixon Doctrine and Our Asian Commitments
Simon Serfaty, America and Europe in the Seventies: Integration or Disintegration?
François Duchene, A New European Defense Community
Paul Taylor, Britain, the Common Market, and the Forces of History
Dennis L. Bark, Changing East-West Relations in Europe: The Bonn-Moscow Treaty of August 1970
Edward A. Kolodziej, France Ensnared: French Strategic Policy and Bloc Politics after 1968
Albert Wohlstetter, Japan's Security: Balancing after the Shocks
Ian Clark, Sino-American Relations in Soviet Perspective
Robert E. Hunter, The Diplomacy of Unpredictability
Robert E. Hunter, In the Middle in the Middle East
R. M. Burrell, Opportunity Knocks for the Kremlin's Drive East
McGeorge Bundy, To Cap the Volcano
Uri Ra'anan, The Changing American-Soviet Strategic Balance: Some Political Implications
Jonathan D. Pollack, Chinese Attitudes Towards Nuclear Weapons: 1964–69
Herbert Scoville, Beyond SALT One
Donald G. Brennan, When the SALT Hit the Fan
George McGovern, An Alternative National Defense Posture
Secretary of Defense Melvin R. Laird, Excerpts from the Annual Defense Department Report for the Fiscal Year 1973
William R. Kintner, Unwrapping the McGovern Defense Package

Kelman, Herbert C. (ed.). *International Behavior: A Social-Psychological Analysis*, New York: Holt, Rinehart & Winston (1965).

> Herbert C. Kelman, Social-Psychological Approaches to the Study of International Relations: Definition of Scope
>
> Robert A. LeVine, Socialization, Social Structure, and Intersocietal Images
>
> William A. Scott, Psychological and Social Correlates of International Images
>
> Ithiel de Sola Pool, Effects of Cross-National Contact on National and International Images
>
> Karl W. Deutsch and Richard L. Merritt, Effects of Events on National and International Images
>
> Irving L. Janis and M. Brewster Smith, Effects of Education and Persuasion on National and International Images
>
> Ralph K. White, Images in the Context of International Conflict: Soviet Perceptions of the U.S. and the U.S.S.R.
>
> Milton J. Rosenberg, Images in Relation to the Policy Process: American Public Opinion on Cold-War Issues
>
> Harold D. Lasswell, The Climate of International Action
>
> Daniel Katz, Nationalism and Strategies of International Conflict Resolution
>
> Dean G. Pruitt, Definition of the Situation as a Determinant of International Action
>
> James A. Robinson and Richard C. Snyder, Decision-Making in International Politics
>
> Jack Sawyer and Harold Guetzkow, Bargaining and Negotiation in International Relations
>
> Chadwick F. Alger, Personal Contact in Intergovernmental Organizations
>
> Anita L. Mishler, Personal Contact in International Exchanges
>
> Herbert C. Kelman, Social-Psychological Approaches to the Study of International Relations: The Question of Relevance

Kriesberg, Louis (ed.). *Social Processes in International Relations: A Reader*, New York: Wiley (1968).

> **Processes and Conditions**
>
> Louis Wirth, World Community, World Society, and World Government: An Attempt at a Clarification of Terms
>
> Marshall G. S. Hodgson, The Interrelations of Societies in History
>
> Lewis Coser, The Termination of Conflict
>
> **Societies and International Relations**
>
> William A. Gamson and Andre Modigliani, Knowledge and Foreign Policy Opinions: Some Models for Consideration
>
> Erich Reigrotski and Nels Anderson, National Stereotypes and Foreign Contact
>
> Bruce M. Russett, International Communications and Legislative Behavior
>
> Morris Janowitz, The Professional Soldier, Political Behavior, and Coalition Warfare

Suzanne Keller, Diplomacy and Communication
Lewis Anthony Dexter, Where the Elephant Fears to Dance Among the
Chickens: Business in Politics? The Case of du Pont
Joan W. Moore and Burton M. Moore, The Role of the Scientific Elite
in the Decision to Use the Atomic Bomb
Edward Shils, The Intellectuals in the Political Development of the
New States
Raymond Tanter, Dimensions of Conflict Behavior within and between
Nations, 1958–1960

Relatively Noninstitutionalized International Relations
Robert C. Angell, The Growth of Transnational Participation
Karl W. Deutsch, The Propensity to International Transactions
Edward T. Hall and William Foote Whyte, Intercultural Communica-
tion: A Guide to Men of Action
Johan Galtung, East-West Interaction Patterns
Feliks Gross, Seizure of Tension Areas
John W. Riley and Leonard S. Cattreil, Jr., Research for Psychological
Warfare
Elmo C. Wilson and Frank Bonilla, Evaluating Exchange of Persons
Programs
Bernhardt Lieberman, i-Trust: A Notion of Trust in Three-Person
Games and in International Affairs
John R. Raser and Wayman J. Crow, A Simulation Study of Deterrence
Theories
Ole R. Holsti, Richard A. Brody, and Robert C. North, Measuring
Affect and Action in International Reaction Models: Empirical Mate-
rials from the 1962 Cuban Crisis
Amitai Etzioni, The Kennedy Experiment

Relatively Institutionalized International Relations
Amitai Etzioni, The Epigenesis of Political Communities at the Interna-
tional Level
Louis Kriesberg, U.S. and U.S.S.R. Participation in International
Non-Governmental Organizations
Paul Smoker, Nation State Escalation and International Integration
Chadwick F. Alger, United Nations Participation as a Learning Experi-
ence
Hayward Alker, Supranationalism in the United Nations
Kal J. Holsti, Resolving International Conflicts: A Taxonomy of Be-
havior and Some Figures on Procedures

Lanyi, George A., and Wilson C. McWilliams (eds.). *Crisis and Con-
tinuity in World Politics: Readings in International Relations,*
New York: Random House (1966; 1972).
Niccolò Machiavelli, The Real Truth of the Matter and One's Country
Must Be Defended
Immanuel Kant, Perpetual Peace
Edward H. Carr, Utopia and Reality
Kenneth W. Thompson, American Approaches to International Politics

J. David Singer, The Relevance of the Behavioral Sciences to the Study of International Relations

Stanley Hoffmann, The Long Road to Theory

Joseph Mazzini, The Question of Nationalities: The Alliance of the Peoples

Alfred Cobban, National Self-Determination

Louis Wirth, Types of Nationalism

Rupert Emerson, Nationalism and Political Development

Marc J. Swartz, Negative Ethnocentrism

Douglas E. Ashford, The Irredentist Appeal in Morocco and Mauritania

Karl Marx, The British Rule in India

Friedrich Engels, The Conquest of Algeria

E. M. Winslow, Marxian Liberal and Sociological Theories of Imperialism

William L. Langer, Farewell to Empire

Richard Pipes, Russifying the Nationalities

Michael Rywkin, Central Asia and the Price of Sovietization

Hugh Seton-Watson, Moscow's Imperialism

Hans Speier, Risk, Security, and Modern Hero Worship

Guglielmo Ferrero, Napoleon: The Aggressive Fear of Illegitimate Power

Alan Bullock, Hitler's Empire

R. N. Carew Hunt, The Importance of Doctrine

Samuel L. Sharp, National Interest: Key to Soviet Politics

Richard Lowenthal, The Logic of One-Party Rule

Sigmund Freud, Why War?

Talcott Parsons, The Structure of Group Hostility

Sir Thomas More, On Just War

Karl von Clausewitz, On War

Thornton Read, Nuclear Strategy

Aaron B. Wildavsky, Nuclear Clubs or Nuclear Wars

Robert LeVine, Facts and Morals in the Arms Debate

Harold Lasswell, The Garrison State

David Hume, Of the Balance of Power

Sir Eyre Crowe, England, the Holder of the Balance

Morton A. Kaplan, Balance of Power: A Model of an International System

Ernst B. Haas, The Balance of Power as a Guide to Policy-Making

A. F. K. Organski, Collective Security

Gerhart Niemeyer, The Balance Sheet of the League Experiment

Niccolò Machiavelli, The End Justifies the Means

Immanuel Kant, The Conflict Between Morals and Politics

David Hume, Are Nations Less Moral Than Men?

Hans J. Morgenthau, The Twilight of International Morality

Brand Blanshard, Theology of Power

Oliver J. Lissitzyn, International Law in a Divided World

Adam Smith, Free Trade Without Constraint is Always Advantageous

Friedrich List, Industrial Development Needs Protective Tariffs
Committee of Experts Convened by UNESCO, Final Statement:
Humanism of Tomorrow and the Diversity of Cultures
Francisco Ayala, The Place of Spanish Culture
Sir Harold Nicolson, The Old Diplomacy
A. P. Herbert, From the Chinese: The Ambassador
Sir Ivone Kirkpatrick, As a Diplomat Sees the Art of Diplomacy
Charles B. Marshall, Afterthoughts on the Cuban Blockade
C. Wright Mills, We Can't Trust the Power Elites
Dag Hammarskjöld, Preventive Diplomacy in the United Nations
Hans Speier, International Political Communications: Elite vs. Mass
Inis L. Claude, The Management of Power in the Changing United
Nations
Ernst B. Haas, Regional Integration and National Policy
Amitai Etzioni, The Dialectics of Supranational Unification
James L. Busey, Central American Union: The Latest Attempt
Wilson C. McWilliams and Jonathon W. Polier, Pan-Africanism and
the Dilemmas of National Development
Inis L. Claude, The Functional Approach
Kathleen Freeman, The Lesson of the Greek City-State
Dean Acheson, The First Line of Action
George F. Kennan, Disengagement Revisited
Henry A. Kissinger, A Neutral Germany?
Richard Lowenthal, The Illusion of Stability
Arthur P. Whitaker, Protracted Conflict in Latin America
Barbara Ward, A New Direction for the West
P. T. Bauer, International Economic Development
Bandung Conference, Final Communique
Julius K. Nyerere, The Belgrade Declaration of Nonaligned Nations
George Liska, The Third Party: The Rationale of Nonalignment
A. Nove, The Soviet Model and Underdeveloped Countries
Morton A. Kaplan, Loose Bipolarity: A Model of an International System
Nikita S. Khrushchev, On Peaceful Coexistence
Tang Tsou, Mao Tse-tung and Peaceful Coexistence
Bernard Morris, Soviet Policy Toward National Communism: The Limits of Diversity
John F. Kennedy, Toward a Strategy of Peace
Zbigniew Brzezinski, Threat and Opportunity in the Communist
Schism
Countess Marion Donhoff, The End of the Postwar Era
Herbert Luthy, Culture and the Cold War: The Prospects of East-West
Exchanges
George Orwell, Triangular Perpetual War
Kenneth N. Waltz, The Stability of a Bipolar World

Larus, Joel (ed.). *Comparative World Politics: Readings in Western and
Premodern Non-Western International Relations*, Belmont, Ca.:
Wadsworth (1966).

John H. Herz, Rise and Demise of the Territorial State
M. Frederick Nelson, The World Outlook of the Chinese Empire
A. L. Basham, Some Fundamentals of Hindu Statecraft
Costi K. Zurayk, Muslim Universalism
Robert Montagne, The Nation-State System in Modern Africa and Asia
Stephen B. Jones, Gauging Power in the Western State System
U. N. Ghoshal, Gauging Power of the Hindu State
Edward V. Gulick, The Western Concept of Balance of Power in Historical Perspective
Martin Wight, The Mechanics of Balance of Power among Western States
U. N. Ghoshal, The Hindu Concept of Balance of Power: Constituents of the Mandala
Benoy Kumar Sarkar, The Hindu Concept of Balance of Power: Theory of the Mandala
Glenn H. Snyder, Balance of Power in the Missile Age
Quincy Wright, The Nature of Conflict
Kung-chuan Hsiao, The Chinese Philosophy of War: The Traditionalists
Shu-ching Lee, Comment
Morton H. Fried, Rejoinder
Majid Khadduri, The Islamic Philosophy of War
Nikolai Talensky, The Soviet Philosophy of War
François de Callieres, The Methods and Objectives of Diplomacy
John K. Fairbank and S. Y. Teng, The Chinese Tradition of Diplomacy
Muhammad Hamidullah, The Islamic Tradition of Diplomacy
Lord Vansittart, Diplomacy in the Missile Age
Baron S. A. Korff, An Introduction to the History of International Law
Majid Khadduri, An Introduction to the Islamic Law of Nations
Oliver J. Lissitzyn, International Law in the Missile Age
Arnold Wolfers, The Pole of Power and the Pole of Indifference
The Mahabharata, Hindu and Western Realism: Kanika's Advice
D. Mackenzie Brown, Hindu and Western Realism: A Study of Contrasts

Lepawsky, Albert, et al. (eds.). *The Search for World Order*, New York: Appleton-Century-Crofts (1971).
Arnold J. Toynbee, War in Our Time
Karl W. Deutsch and Dieter Senghaas, A Framework for a Theory of War and Peace
J. David Singer, Modern International War: From Conjecture to Explanation
Bernard Brodie, Military Technology and International Strategy
Morton A. Kaplan, The Sociology of Strategic Thinking
William L. Tung, Settlement of Disputes Through Nonamicable Means
Johan Galtung, Peace Thinking
R. P. Anand, The Development of a Universal International Law
Percy E. Corbett, The International Definition and Protection of Human Rights

Vernon Van Dyke, Violations of Human Rights as Threats to Peace
Philip C. Jessup, Untried Potentials of the International Court of Justice
Bert V. A. Röling, The Limited Significance of the Prohibition of War
Gabriel A. Almond, National Politics and International Politics
Rouhollah K. Ramazani, Treaty Relations: An Iranian-Soviet Case
Study
Frederick L. Schuman, The Neuroses of the Nations
Arthur N. Holcombe, The American Presidency in the Nuclear Age
Walter H. C. Laves, United Nations Assistance for Political Develop-
ment: A Rationale
Richard A. Falk, The Trend Toward World Community: An Inventory
of Issues
Charles A. McClelland, Field Theory and System Theory in Interna-
tional Relations
William T. R. Fox, The Study of Relations in International Relations
Klaus Knorr, Transnational Phenomena and the Future of the Nation-
State
Harold D. Lasswell, The Cross-Disciplinary Manifold: The Chicago
Prototype
Kenneth W. Thompson, International Policy in War and Peace:
Wright's Contribution
A Select Bibliography of the Writings of Quincy Wright

Lerche, Charles O., and Margaret E. Lerche (eds.). *Readings in Inter-
national Politics: Concepts and Issues*, New York: Oxford Univer-
sity Press (1958).
E. Bassert, Power Politics vs. Political Ecology
Harry Rudin, Diplomacy, Democracy, Security: Two Centuries in Con-
trast
John Foster Dulles, Challenge and Response in United States Policy
Hans J. Morgenthau, The Paradoxes of Nationalism
Carlos P. Romulo, Whither, Submerged Millions?
Hans Kohn, Some Reflections on Colonialism
B. K. Blount, Science as a Factor in International Relations
Howard Trivers, Morality and Foreign Affairs
Harold Callender, Footnotes on Modern Diplomacy
Ben C. Limb, Speech: The Life of a Diplomat
Charles O. Lerche, The United States, Great Britain, and SEATO: A
Case Study in the Fait Accompli
Oleg Anisimov, A New Policy for American Psychological Warfare
Robert R. Bowie, United States Foreign Economic Policy
Andreas and Lois Grotewold, Some Geographic Aspects of Interna-
tional Trade
Sir Anthony W. Buzzard, Massive Retaliation and Graduated Deter-
rence
Basil H. Liddell Hart, Military Strategy vs. Common Sense
Stephen B. Jones, Global Strategic Views
Norton Ginsburg, Natural Resources and Economic Development
Richard P. Longaker, The President as International Leader

Robert H. Cory, The Role of Public Opinion in US Policies Toward the UN

Andrew M. Scott, Challenge and Response: A Tool for the Analysis of International Affairs

Ernst B. Haas, Types of Collective Security: An Examination of Operational Concepts

Edgar S. Furniss, A Re-examination of Regional Arrangements

John Foster Dulles, The Institutionalizing of Peace

Stanley Hoffmann, The Role of International Organization

Hans Kohn, The UN in a Revolutionary Age

Robert Strausz-Hupé, The Balance of Tomorrow

Chester Bowles, The Challenge of the Next Decade

David J. Dallin, Soviet Postwar Foreign Policy

James E. McSherry, Soviet Diplomacy from Stalin to Suez

Vernon V. Aspaturian, The Metamorphosis of the United Nations

Ahmed S. Bokhari, Parliaments, Priests and Prophets

Gunnar Myrdal, Trade and Aid

Paul G. Hoffman, Blueprint for Foreign Aid

Gerhart Niemeyer, The Probability of War in Our Time

Drew Middleton, War or Peace: What Are the Chances?

Raymond L. Garthoff, The Only Wars We Can Afford

Ephriam M. Hampton, Unlimited Confusion over Limited War

Lijphart, Arend (ed.). *World Politics: The Writings of Theorists and Practitioners, Classical and Modern*, Boston: Allyn & Bacon (1966; 1971).

Morton A. Kaplan, Is International Relations a Discipline?

William T. R. Fox and Annette Baker Fox, The Teaching of International Relations in the United States

Niccolò Machiavelli, The Prince

Dean Acheson, Ethics in International Relations Today

Stanley H. Hoffmann, International Relations: The Long Road to Theory

Jean Bodin, On Sovereignty

Thomas Hobbes, The State of Nature

Jean-Jacques Rousseau, The State of War

Clement Attlee, The Perils of Absolute Sovereignty

Dante Alighieri, On World-Government

Alexander Hamilton, Concerning Dangers from War Between the States

Reinhold Niebuhr, The Illusion of World Government

Ernest Renan, What Is a Nation?

Giuseppe Mazzini, Duties Toward Your Country

Karl W. Deutsch, The Growth of Nations

Niccolò Machiavelli, How to Measure the Power of States

Alexis de Tocqueville, Democracy and Foreign Policy

Stephen B. Jones, Global Strategic Views

Lin Piao, Long Live the Victory of People's War!

Thucydides, The Melian Conference

Quincy Wright, The Decline of Classic Diplomacy
Michael H. Cardozo, Diplomatic Immunities, Protocol, and the Public
Kenneth N. Waltz, Man, the State, and War
Plato, The Origin of War
Desiderius Erasmus, On Going to War
Frederick S. Dunn, Politics, Culture, and Peace
Theodore Roosevelt, The Strenuous Life
Vladimir I. Lenin, Imperialism: The Highest Stage of Capitalism
William L. Langer, Farewell to Empire
Karl von Clausewitz, What Is War?
Mao Tse-tung, Problems of Strategy in Guerrilla War
Herman Kahn, Some Possible Sizes and Shapes of Thermonuclear War
Douglas MacArthur, The Abolition of War
David Hume, Of the Balance of Power
Ernst B. Haas, The Balance of Power: Prescription, Concept, or Prop-
    aganda?
Glenn H. Snyder, The Balance of Power and the Balance of Terror
Immanuel Kant, Second Definitive Article of Perpetual Peace
Woodrow Wilson, A League to Enforce Peace
Kenneth W. Thompson, Collective Security Reexamined
Inis L. Claude, Preventive Diplomacy as an Approach to Peace
Jean-Jacques Rousseau, Sketch of a Project for Permanent Peace
U Thant, The League of Nations and the United Nations
Dag Hammarskjöld, Two Differing Concepts of United Nations
Charles de Gaulle, The Disunited Nations
David Mitrany, The Functional Approach to World Organization
Paul G. Hoffman, Success, Failure . . . and the Future
Napoleon Bonaparte, The Unification of Europe
Walter Hallstein, Economic Integration and Political Unity in Europe
Hugo Grotius, Prolegomena to the Law of War and Peace
John Stuart Mill, The Custom of Nations
Philip C. Jessup, On the World Community
Richard M. Nixon, World Peace Through World Law
Jeremy Bentham, Treaties Limiting the Number of Troops
Pope John XXIII, Disarmament
John F. Kennedy, Toward a Strategy of Peace
Jerome D. Frank, Emotional and Motivational Aspects of the Disar-
    mament Problem
Alexis de Tocqueville, Two Great Nations Marked Out to Sway the
    Destinies of Half the Globe
Friedrich Engels, The Division of Europe
Nikita S. Khrushchev, Communism Will Ultimately Be Victorious
Karl W. Deutsch, The Future of World Politics

Martin, Laurence W. (ed.). *Neutralism and Nonalignment: The New
    States in World Affairs*, New York: Praeger (1962).
    Laurence W. Martin, Introduction: The Emergence of the New States
    Robert C. Good, State-Building as a Determinant of Foreign Policy in
    the New States

Charles Burton Marshall, On Understanding the Unaligned
Robert C. Good, The Congo Crisis: A Study of Postcolonial Politics
Laurence W. Martin, A Conservative View of the New States
George Liska, The "Third Party": The Rationale of Nonalignment
Ernest W. Lefever, Nehru, Nasser, and Nkrumah on Neutralism
Francis O. Wilcox, The Nonaligned States and the United Nations
Arnold Wolfers, Allies, Neutrals, and Neutralists in the Context of U.S. Defense Policy
Vernon V. Aspaturian, Revolutionary Change and the Strategy of the Status Quo
Reinhold Niebuhr, The Relation of Strength to Weakness in the World Community
George Liska, Tripartism: Dilemmas and Strategies

McLellan, David S., et al. (eds.). *The Theory and Practice of International Relations*, Englewood Cliffs, N.J.: Prentice-Hall (1960; 1974).
Arnold Wolfers, The Actors in International Politics
Walker Connor, Nation-Building or Nation-Destroying?
Herbert C. Kelman, The Role of the Individual in International Relations: Some Conceptual and Methodological Considerations
Mostafa Rejai and Cynthia H. Enloe, Nation-States and State-Nations
Kenneth W. Terhune, Nationalistic Aspiration, Loyalty, and Internationalism
Werner Feld, Nongovernmental Entities and the International System
Peter P. Gabriel, MNCs in the Third World: Is Conflict Unavoidable?
Leon Gordenker, The "New Nationalism" and International Organization
Leon N. Lindberg, Decision Making and Integration in the European Community
Henry A. Kissinger, The End of Bipolarity
Zbigniew Brzezinski, The Balance of Power Delusion
Walter Laqueur, The World of the 70s
Harold Sprout, Political Potential
David O. Wilkenson, Capability
Stephen B. Jones, The Power Inventory and National Strategy
David W. Paul, Sources of Soviet Foreign Policy
Morton Schwartz, Sources of Soviet Policy: A Second View
Franklin B. Weinstein, The Uses of Foreign Policy in Indonesia: An Approach to the Analysis of Foreign Policy in the Less Developed Countries
Herbert C. Kelman, The Role of the Individual in Decision-Making
Michael P. Sullivan, Vietnam: Calculation or Quicksand? An Analysis of Competing Decision-Making Models
Leon B. Poullada, Diplomacy: The Missing Link in the Study of International Politics
Fred Charles Iklé, Negotiating Effectively
W. Phillips Davison, Political Communication as an Instrument of Foreign Policy

Bryant Wedge, International Propaganda and Statecraft
Richard Pipes, Soviet Propaganda Techniques
Michael J. Flack, International, Educational, and Cultural Relations
and the Transforming World
Charles Frankel, Cultural Affairs in Action
Council of Economic Advisers, Freedom and Stability in the World
Economy
Theodore Geiger, A World of Trading Blocs?
Hans Morgenthau, A Political Theory of Foreign Aid
Thomas Franck and Edward Weisband, Three Case Studies of Intervention
Edward H. Carr, Military Power
Harold L. Nieburg, Uses of Violence
Kenneth N. Waltz, International Structure, National Force, and the
Balance of Power
Andrew J. Pierre, America Down, Russia Up: The Changing Political
Role of Military Power
Fred Charles Iklé, The Purpose of Fighting [and of Ceasing to Fight]
Coral Bell, Instruments and Techniques of Crisis Management
John W. Burton, Resolution of Conflict
Jean-Pierre Cot, Critical Remarks on John Burton's Paper on Resolution of Conflict with Special Reference to the Cyprus Conflict
Laura Nader, Some Notes on John Burton's Papers on "Resolution of Conflict"
William D. Coplin, International Law and Assumptions about the State
System
Ralph Littauer and Norman Uphoff, The Air War in Indochina and
International Law
Edwin H. Fedder, The Concept of Alliance
Amitai Etzioni, European Unification: A Strategy of Change
Herbert Goldhamer, The Soviet Union in a Period of Strategic Parity
Alton H. Quanbeck and Barry M. Blechman, After Salt
Hedley Bull, The New Balance of Power in Asia and the Pacific
Bruce M. Russett, Trends in World Inequality
Theodore H. Moran, The Politics of Economic Nationalism
Robert L. Heilbroner, Counterrevolutionary America
Louis J. Cantori and Steven L. Spiegel, International Regions: A Comparative Approach to Five Subordinate Systems
Larry W. Bowman, The Subordinate State System of Southern Africa
Seyom Brown, The Changing Essence of Power
Kenneth W. Thompson, Paths Toward Peace
William Jackson, Durable Peace

Morgenthau, Hans J., and Kenneth W. Thompson (eds.). *Principles
and Problems of International Relations: Selected Readings*, New
York: Knopf (1951; 1956).
The Science of International Politics
Herbert A. L. Fisher, Political Prophecies

Sir Alfred Zimmern, Introductory Report to the Discussion in 1935 on University Teaching of International Relations

Nicholas J. Spykman, Methods of Approach to the Study of International Relations

What Foreign Policy is all About

Alexander Hamilton, The Federalist No. VI; The Pacificus Papers; The Americanus Papers

Woodrow Wilson, The Fourth Liberty Loan; Essential Terms of Peace in Europe; For Declaration of War against Germany

William E. Gladstone, Bulgarian Horrors and Russia in Turkestan

Benjamin Disraeli, Speech in the House of Lords on the Berlin Treaty

Lord Salisbury, Speech to the Middlesex Conservative Association; Speech in Manchester

National Power

Report of the Nye Committee to the United States Senate on Munitions Industry

Vladimir Lenin, Imperialism: The Highest Stage of Capitalism

William Scott Ferguson, Greek Imperialism

Guchi Tanaka, Japan's Dream of World Empire: The Tanaka Memorial

Nicholas J. Spykman, Geography and Foreign Policy

Sir Arthur Salter, The Economic Causes of War

Dudley Kirk, Population Changes and the Postwar

Salvador de Madariaga, Englishmen, Frenchmen, Spaniards

International Order and Peace

David Hume, Of the Balance of Power

H. W. V. Temperley, The Domestic and Foreign Policy of William of Orange

Arnold D. McNair, International Law in Practice

Erich Hula, Four Years of the United Nations

Reinhold Niebuhr, The Myth of World Government

Robert Maynard Hutchins, The Constitutional Foundations for World Order

Hugh Gibson, The Road to Foreign Policy

The Foreign Policies of the Great Powers

Hans J. Morgenthau, Conduct of American Foreign Policy

James Reston, Debate Over China Shows Seven Misconceptions

Alfred Vagts, The United States and the Balance of Power

Harry S. Truman, Recommendations of Greece and Turkey

George C. Marshall, The European Recovery Program

Text of the Atlantic Defense Treaty

George F. Kennan, Foreign Aid in the Framework of National Policy

Dean Acheson, Crisis in Asia—An Examination of United States Policy

John Price, Foreign Affairs and the Public

Sir Eyre Crowe, Memorandum on British Relations with France and Germany

Winston S. Churchill, The Second World War

W. Gurian, Permanent Features of Soviet Foreign Policy

The Earl of Malmesbury, Diaries and Correspondence

Present Problems of Foreign Policy
Jacob Viner, The Implications of the Atomic Bomb for International
Relations
Hans J. Morgenthau, The Conquest of the United States by Germany
Winston Churchill, How to Stop War; Speeches in House of Commons
William Pitt, Speech in House of Commons
Edmund Burke, Correspondence (Letter of August 1793)
Charles James Fox, Speeches in House of Commons
Earl Russell, The Life and Times of Charles James Fox
Edmund Burke, Speech in House of Commons
William Pitt, Speech in House of Commons
Lord Salisbury, Biographical Essays
C. K. Webster, The Foreign Policy of Castlereagh, 1815–1822
Lord Salisbury, Biographical Essays
Oliver Goldsmith, The Citizen of the World
Prince de Talleyrand, Memoirs
Lord Salisbury, Circular of April 1, 1878, to the British Embassies
Earl Russell, Communication to Lord Napier
Report of the Crimea Conference
Philips Price, Speech in House of Commons

Mueller, John E. (ed.). *Approaches to Measurement in International
Relations*, New York: Appleton-Century-Crofts (1969).
Samuel P. Huntington, Arms Races: Prerequisites and Results
Bruce M. Russett, The Calculus of Deterrence
William A. Gamson and Andre Modigliani, Knowledge and Foreign
Policy Opinions: Some Models for Consideration
James N. Rosenau, Consensus-Building in the American National
Community: Some Hypotheses and Some Supporting Data
Gerald H. Shure, Robert J. Meeker, and Earle A. Hansford, The Effec-
tiveness of Pacifist Strategies in Bargaining Games
Richard A. Brody, Some Systematic Effects of the Spread of Nuclear
Weapons Technology: A Study Through Simulation of a Multi-
Nuclear Future
Hayward R. Alker, Jr., Dimensions of Conflict in the General Assembly
Raymond Tanter, Dimensions of Conflict Within and Between Nations
Masakatsu Kato, A Model of U.S. Foreign Aid Allocation: An Applica-
tion of a Decision-Making Scheme
Ole R. Holsti, The 1914 Case
Russell H. Fitzgibbon, Measuring Democratic Change in Latin
America
Daniel Ellsberg, The Crude Analysis of Strategic Choices
Michael D. Intriligator, Some Simple Models of Arms Races

Olson, William C., and Fred Sondermann (eds.). *The Theory and Practice of International Relations*, Englewood Cliffs, N.J.: Prentice-
Hall (1960; 1966; 1974).
William T. R. Fox and Annette Baker Fox, The Teaching of International Relations in the United States

Kenneth W. Thompson, The Study of International Politics: A Survey of Trends and Developments

Fred A. Sondermann, The Linkage Between Foreign Policy and International Politics

George Liska, Continuity and Change in International Systems

Philip C. Jessup, The Equality of States as Dogma and Reality

John H. Herz, Rise and Demise of the Territorial State

Kenneth E. Boulding, National Images and International Systems

Morton Grodzins, The Basis of National Loyalty

William C. Olson, Forms and Variations of Nationalism

Martin Wight, Power Politics

Ernst Haas, The Balance of Power: Concept, Prescription or Propaganda

Harold Sprout, Geopolitical Hypotheses in Technological Perspective

Stephen B. Jones, The Power Inventory and National Strategy

Jean Gottmann, Geography and International Relations

Stephen B. Jones, Global Strategic Views

Fred A. Sondermann, Political Implications of Population Growth in Underdeveloped Countries

Kingsley Davis, The Demographic Transition

Klaus Knorr, The Concept of Economic Potential for War

James R. Schlesinger, Economic Growth and National Security

Edward H. Carr, Military Power

Charles M. Fergusson, Jr., Military Forces and National Objectives

Robert E. Marshak, Reexamining the Soviet Scientific Challenge

Warner R. Schilling, Science, Technology, and Foreign Policy

James D. Thompson and William J. McEwen, Organizational Goals and Environment: Goal-Setting as an Interaction Process

Hans J. Morgenthau, Another "Great Debate": The National Interest of the United States

Arnold Wolfers, National Security as an Ambiguous Symbol

Harold Nicolson, Diplomacy Then and Now

Gordon A. Craig, Totalitarian Approaches to Diplomatic Negotiation

William C. Olson, Democratic Approaches to Diplomacy

Dean G. Pruitt, National Power and International Responsiveness

W. Phillips Davison, Political Communication as an Instrument of Foreign Policy

Walt Whitman Rostow, A Non-Communist Manifesto

John Kenneth Galbraith, Economic Development: Rival Systems and Comparative Advantage

Gordon A. Craig, The Diplomacy of New Nations

Henry A. Kissinger, The New Cult of Neutralism

Harold L. Nieburg, Uses of Violence

Herman Kahn, The Arms Race and Some of Its Hazards

Glenn H. Snyder, Deterrence and Power

J. David Singer, Threat-Perception and the Armament-Tension Dilemma

David Frisch, Disarmament: Theory or Experiment

Wesley W. Posvar, The New Meaning of Arms Control
René Maheu, The Triple Role of International Organizations Today
Leland M. Goodrich, The Maintenance of International Peace and
Security
Inis L. Claude, United Nations Use of Military Force
Harry W. Jones, Law and the Idea of Mankind
John N. Hazard, A Pragmatic View of the New International Law
Lincoln P. Bloomfield, Law, Politics and International Disputes
Arnold Wolfers, Statesmanship and Moral Choice
Charles Burton Marshall, The Problem of Incompatible Purposes
Reinhold Niebuhr, History's Limitations in the Nuclear Age

Pfaltzgraff, Robert L., Jr. (ed.). *Politics and the International System*,
Philadelphia: Lippincott (1969; 1972).
Quincy Wright, The Meaning of International Relations
E. Raymond Platig, International Relations as a Field of Inquiry
Edward H. Carr, The Utopian Background
Hans J. Morgenthau, Six Principles of Political Realism
Morton A. Kaplan, The New Great Debate: Traditionalism versus Sci-
ence in International Relations
Robert L. Pfaltzgraff, Jr., International Studies in the 1970's
J. David Singer, The Level-of-Analysis Problem in International Rela-
tions
Charles A. McClelland, Theory and the International System
Oran R. Young, Political Discontinuities in the International System
Hans Kohn, Nationalism
John H. Kautsky, Nationalism in Underdeveloped Countries
Walker Connor, National Self-Determination and National Disintegra-
tion
Kal J. Holsti, The Concept of Power in the Study of International
Relations
Vladimir I. Lenin, Imperialism
General Karl von Clausewitz, What is War?
Glenn H. Snyder, The Balance of Terror
William R. Kintner, The Nuclear Thrust: From Alamogordo to Cuba
Morton H. Halperin, Limited War
Mao Tse-tung, What is Guerrilla Warfare?
Victor Basiuk, The Impact of Technology in the Next Decades
Zbigniew Brzezinski, The Emerging Technetronic Age
Robert Strausz-Hupé and Stefan T. Possony, Economics and Statecraft
Norman D. Palmer, Foreign Aid and Foreign Policy: The New State-
craft Reassessed
Johan Galtung, Economic Sanctions and Statecraft
Raymond Vernon, The Internationalization of Production and the
Multinational Corporation
Nicholas J. Spykman, Geography and Foreign Policy
Harold and Margaret Sprout, The Ecological Perspective
Henry A. Kissinger, Domestic Sources of Foreign Policy
Gabriel A. Almond, American Character and Foreign Policy

Henry A. Kissinger, On Negotiations
Thomas C. Schelling, Negotiation in Warfare
Sir Eyre Crowe, England's Foreign Policy
Ernst B. Haas, The Balance of Power: Prescription, Concept, or Prop-
aganda?
Robert E. Osgood, The Nature of Alliances
Leo Mates, Nonalignment
Hedley Bull, The Objectives of Arms Control
James E. Dougherty, Arms Control in the 1970's
Karl W. Deutsch et al., Some Essential Requirements for the Estab-
lishment of Amalgamated Security Communities
William D. Coplin, Law and International Politics
Philip E. Jacob, Organizing Nations in the 1970's
Inis L. Claude, Appraisal of the Case for World Government

Pruitt, Dean G., and Richard C. Snyder (eds.). *Theory and Research on
the Causes of War*, Englewood Cliffs, N.J.: Prentice-Hall (1969).
The Study of War: Theory and Method
Motives and Perceptions Underlying
Entry into War
Werner Levi, War and the Quest for National Power
J. David Singer, Threat Perception and National Decision Makers
Thomas Schelling and Morton Halperin, Pre-emptive, Premeditated,
and Accidental War
Movement toward War: From Motives and
Perceptions to Actions
Karl W. Deutsch, The Point of No Return in the Progression toward
War
Ole R. Holsti et al., The Management of International Crisis: Affect and
Action in American-Soviet Relations
James A. Robinson et al., Search under Crisis in Political Gaming and
Simulation
Charles A. McClelland, The Acute International Crisis
Restraints against the Use of Violence:
Military Preparations
Glenn Snyder, The Balance of Power and the Balance of Terror
Bruce Russett, Refining Deterrence Theory: The Japanese Attack on
Pearl Harbor
John Raser and Wayman Crow, A Simulation Study of Deterrence
Theories
Raoul Naroll, Deterrence in History
Richard Brody and Alexandra Benham, Nuclear Weapons and Alliance
Cohesion
Nonmilitary Restraints and the Peaceful
Resolution of Controversy
Ithiel de Sola Pool, Deterrence as an Influence Process
Chadwick Alger, Non-resolution Consequences of the United Nations
and their Effect on International Conflict
Charles E. Osgood, Calculated De-escalation as a Strategy

The Incidence of War: Statistical Evidence
Rudolph J. Rummel, Dimensions of Foreign and Domestic Conflict
Behavior: A Review of Empirical Findings
James Paul Wesley, Frequency of Wars and Geographical Opportunity
Toward an Integrated Theory and Cumulative Research
Clark C. Abt and Morton Gorden, Report on Project Temper
Thomas W. Milburn, Intellectual History of a Research Program
Harold Guetzkow, Simulations in the Consolidation and Utilization of
Knowledge about International Relations

Quester, George H. (ed.). *Power, Action and Interaction: Readings on
International Politics*, Boston: Little, Brown (1971).
National Action in International Politics
Henry A. Kissinger, Domestic Structure and Foreign Policy
Dean Rusk, The President
Hans J. Morgenthau, Another Great Debate: The National Interest of
the United States
Thomas C. Schelling, Bargaining, Communication, and Limited War
Robert Jervis, Hypotheses on Misperception
National Interaction in International Politics
Arnold Wolfers, The Pole of Power and the Pole of Indifference
John H. Herz, Rise and Demise of the Territorial State
Arthur Lee Burns, From Balance to Deterrence: A Theoretical Analysis
Kenneth N. Waltz, The Stability of a Bipolar World
The Relevance of History
Ernst B. Haas, The Balance of Power: Prescription, Concept, or Prop-
aganda?
Francis H. Hinsley, The Development of the European States System
since the Eighteenth Century
William L. Langer, Farewell to Empire
Evan Luard, Conciliation and Deterrence: A Comparison of Political
Strategies in the Interwar and Postwar Periods
International Law and Structure
Stanley Hoffmann, International Systems and International Law
Robert L. Friedheim, The Satisfied and Dissatisfied States Negotiate
International Law: A Case Study
Leland M. Goodrich, From League of Nations to United Nations
Bruce M. Russett, Toward a Model of Competitive International Poli-
tics
Inis L. Claude, United Nations Use of Military Force
Military Power
Glenn H. Snyder, Balance of Power in the Missile Age
Albert Wohlstetter, The Delicate Balance of Terror
Samuel P. Huntington, Arms Races: Prerequisites and Results
Carl Kaysen, Keeping the Strategic Balance
Robert A. LeVine, Facts and Morals in the Arms Debate

Romani, Romano (ed.). *The International Political System: Introduction and Readings*, New York: Wiley (1972).
Arnold Wolfers, The Actors in International Politics

Carol Ann Cosgrove and Kenneth J. Twitchett, International Organizations as Actors
John H. Herz, Rise and Demise of the Territorial State
Karl W. Deutsch, The Growth of Nations: Some Recurrent Patterns of Political and Social Integration
Morton Grodzins, The Basis of National Loyalty
Kal J. Holsti, The Concept of Power in the Study of International Relations
Karl W. Deutsch, On The Concepts of Politics and Power
Klaus Knorr, The Concept of Military Potential
Morton Kaplan, Balance of Power, Bipolarity and Other Models of International Systems
Wolfram F. Hanrieder, The International System: Bipolar or Multibloc?
Kenneth N. Waltz, International Structure, National Force, and the Balance of World Power
Richard Rosecrance, Bipolarity, Multipolarity, and the Future
George Liska, The World Today: Multistate and Imperial Orders
Louis J. Cantori and Steven L. Spiegel, The International Relations of Regions
Fred Charles Iklé, What is Negotiation?
Jack Sawyer and Harold Guetzkow, Bargaining and Negotiation in International Relations
Robert E. Osgood and Robert W. Tucker, The Persistence of Force
Samuel P. Huntington, Arms Races: Prerequisites and Results
Morton H. Halperin, Warfare in the Nuclear Age
Samuel P. Huntington, Guerrilla Warfare in Theory and Policy
David A. Baldwin, Foreign Aid, Intervention, and Influence
Terence Qualter, Psychological Warfare
James N. Rosenau, The Domestic Sources of Foreign Policy: Introduction
Carl J. Friedrich, Intranational Politics and Foreign Policy in Developed (Western) Systems
Stanley Hoffmann, The Functions of International Law
William Coplin, International Law and Assumptions About the State System
Werner Levi, The Relative Irrelevance of Moral Norms in International Politics
Harold and Margaret Sprout, Geography and International Politics in an Era of Revolutionary Change
Bruce M. Russett, The Ecology of Future International Politics
Ernst B. Haas, Toward Controlling International Change: A Personal Plea

Rosenau, James N. (ed.). *International Politics and Foreign Policy*, New York: Free Press (1961).
Fred A. Sondermann, The Linkage between Foreign Policy and International Politics
P. D. Marchant, International Relations as an Autonomous Discipline
Charles A. McClelland, The Social Sciences, History, and International Relations

Richard C. Snyder, Toward Greater Order in the Study of International Politics

Anatol Rapoport, Various Meanings of "Theory"

Harold Guetzkow, Long Range Research in International Relations

Harold and Margaret Sprout, Explanation and Prediction in International Politics

Henry L. Roberts, Problems of Choice and Decision

John H. Herz, The Rise and Demise of the Territorial State

Stewart E. Perry, Notes on the Role of the National: A Social-Psychological Concept for the Study of International Relations

Karl W. Deutsch, Security Communities

Harold and Margaret Sprout, Environmental Factors in the Study of International Politics

Talcott Parsons, Order and Community in the International Social System

Kingsley W. Davis, Social Changes Affecting International Relations

Arnold Wolfers, The Pole of Power and the Pole of Indifference

Harold Guetzkow, Isolation and Collaboration: A Partial Theory of Inter-Nation Relations

Morton A. Kaplan, The National Interest and Other Interests

Hans J. Morgenthau, Power and Ideology in International Politics

Thomas C. Schelling, The Retarded Science of International Strategy

Richard C. Snyder, H. W. Bruck, and Burton Sapin, The Decision-Making Approach to the Study of International Politics

Richard C. Snyder and Glenn D. Paige, The United States Decision to Resist Aggression in Korea: The Application of an Analytical Scheme

Roger Hilsman, Jr., Intelligence and Policy-Making in Foreign Affairs

Bernard C. Cohen, Foreign Policy Makers and the Press

Charlton Ogburn, Jr., The Flow of Policy-Making in The Department of State

Samuel P. Huntington, Strategic Planning and the Political Process

Felix M. Keesing and Marie M. Keesing, Opinion Formation and Decision-Making in Samoa

Richard C. Snyder, H. W. Bruck, and Burton Sapin, Motivational Analysis of Foreign Policy Decision-Making

Stephen B. Jones, The Power Inventory and National Strategy

Gabriel A. Almond, The Elites and Foreign Policy

Henry A. Kissinger, The Policymaker and the Intellectual

Bernard C. Cohen, Political Communication on the Japanese Peace Settlement

Lucian W. Pye, The Non-Western Political Process

Klaus Knorr, Motivation for War

Arvid Brodersen, National Character: An Old Problem Re-Examined

Boyd C. Shafer, Toward a Definition of Nationalism

Filmer S. C. Northrop, The Normative Inner Order of Societies

Ernst B. Haas, The Balance of Power: Prescription, Concept, or Propaganda?

George Liska, Toward an Equilibrium Theory of International Relations and Institutions

Maurice A. Ash, An Analysis of Power, with Special Reference to International Politics

Morton A. Kaplan, Balance of Power, Bipolarity and Other Models of International Systems

Arthur Lee Burns, From Balance to Deterrence: A Theoretical Analysis

A. F. K. Organski, The Power Transition

Andrew M. Scott, Challenge and Response: A Tool for the Analysis of International Affairs

Richard C. Snyder, Game Theory and the Analysis of Political Behavior

Kenneth E. Boulding, National Images and International Systems

Quincy Wright, The Form of a Discipline of International Relations

Charles A. McClelland, Applications of General Systems Theory in International Relations

Stanley H. Hoffmann, International Relations: The Long Road to Theory

Urban G. Whitaker, Jr., Actors, Ends, and Means: A Coarse-Screen Macro-Theory of International Relations

Karl W. Deutsch, Toward an Inventory of Basic Trends and Patterns in Comparative and International Politics

Dina A. Zinnes, Robert C. North, and Howard E. Koch, Jr., Capability, Threat, and the Outbreak of War

Frank L. Klingberg, Studies in Measurement of the Relations among Sovereign States

Anatol Rapoport, The Mathematics of Arms Races

Herbert Goldhamer and Hans Speier, Some Observations on Political Gaming

Oliver Benson, A Simple Diplomatic Game

Rosenau, James N. (ed.). *International Politics and Foreign Policy*, New York: Free Press (1969).

Charles A. McClelland, International Relations: Wisdom or Science?

E. Raymond Platig, International Relations as a Field of Inquiry

J. David Singer, The Level-of-Analysis Problem in International Relations

Stanley Hoffmann, Theory and International Relations

Harold and Margaret Sprout, Environmental Factors in the Study of International Politics

T. B. Millar, On Writing About Foreign Policy

J. David Singer, The Behaviorial Science Approach to International Relations: Payoff and Prospects

John H. Herz, The Territorial State Revisited: Reflections on the Future of the Nation-State

Fred W. Riggs, The Nation-State and Other Actors

Bruce M. Russett, The Ecology of Future International Politics

Roger D. Masters, World Politics as a Primitive Political System

Bruce M. Russett, Toward a Model of Competitive International Politics

Michael Haas, A Functional Approach to International Organization

William D. Coplin, International Law and Assumptions About the State System

Michael Brecher, The Subordinate State System of Southern Asia
Arnold Wolfers, The Pole of Power and the Pole of Indifference
Thomas W. Robinson, National Interests
Werner Levi, The Relative Irrelevance of Moral Norms in International
Politics
Richard C. Snyder, H. W. Bruck, and Burton Sapin, The Decision-
Making Approach to the Study of International Politics
David Braybrooke and Charles E. Lindblom, Types of Decision-Making
Sidney Verba, Assumptions of Rationality and Non-Rationality in
Models of the International System
Roger Hilsman, Policy-Making Is Politics
Robert Jervis, Hypotheses on Misperception
Karl W. Deutsch, On the Concepts of Politics and Power
Henry A. Kissinger, Domestic Structure and Foreign Policy
Herbert C. Kelman, Patterns of Personal Involvement in the National
System: A Social-Psychological Analysis of Political Legitimacy
Morton A. Kaplan, Variants on Six Models of the International System
Kenneth N. Waltz, International Structure, National Force, and the
Balance of World Power
Karl W. Deutsch and J. David Singer, Multipolar Power Systems and
International Stability
Richard N. Rosecrance, Bipolarity, Multipolarity, and the Future
Oran R. Young, Political Discontinuities in the International System
Amitai Etzioni, The Epigenesis of Political Communities at the Interna-
tional Level
Bruce M. Russett, The Calculus of Deterrence
John C. Harsanyi, Game Theory and the Analysis of International Con-
flict
J. David Singer, Inter-Nation Influence: A Formal Model
Dean G. Pruitt, Stability and Sudden Change in Interpersonal and
International Affairs
Charles F. Hermann, International Crisis as a Situational Variable
Kenneth E. Boulding, National Images and International Systems
John R. Raser, Learning and Affect in International Politics
Quincy Wright, The Form of a Discipline of International Relations
Glenn D. Paige, The Korean Decision
Charles A. McClelland, Action Structures and Communication in Two
International Crises: Quemoy and Berlin
Chadwick F. Alger, Interaction and Negotiation in a Committee of the
United Nations General Assembly
Karl W. Deutsch, Toward an Inventory of Basic Trends and Patterns in
Comparative and International Politics
J. David Singer and Melvin Small, National Alliance Commitments and
War Involvement, 1818–1945
Ole R. Holsti, The Belief System and National Images: A Case Study
Johan Galtung, Foreign Policy Opinion as a Function of Social Position
Paul Smoker, Fear in the Arms Race: A Mathematical Study
Steven J. Brams, The Structure of Influence Relationships in the Inter-
national System

Rudolph J. Rummel, Some Dimensions in the Foreign Behavior of
Nations
Charles F. Hermann and Margaret G. Hermann, An Attempt to Simu-
late the Outbreak of World War I
Philip M. Burgess and James A. Robinson, Alliances and the Theory of
Collective Action: A Simulation of Coalition Processes
Lincoln P. Bloomfield and Barton Whaley, The Political-Military Exer-
cise: A Progress Report
Ithiel de Sola Pool and Allen Kessler, The Kaiser, The Tsar, and the
Computer: Information Processing in a Crisis
Ole R. Holsti, Richard A. Brody, and Robert C. North, Measuring
Affect and Action in International Reaction Models: Empirical Mate-
rials from the 1962 Cuban Crisis
Hayward R. Alker, Jr., Supranationalism in the United Nations
Charles A. McClelland and Gary D. Hoggard, Conflict Patterns in the
Interactions Among Nations

Rosenau, James N. (ed.). *Linkage Politics: Essays on the Convergence
of National and International Systems*, New York: Free Press
(1969).
James N. Rosenau, Introduction: Political Science in a Shrinking World
J. David Singer, The Global System and Its Subsystems: A Develop-
mental View
James N. Rosenau, Toward the Study of National-International Link-
ages
Douglas A. Chalmers, Developing on the Periphery: External Factors in
Latin American Politics
William G. Fleming, Sub-Saharan Africa: Case Studies of International
Attitudes and Transactions of Ghana and Uganda
Bernard C. Cohen, National-International Linkages: Superpolities
Ole R. Holsti and John D. Sullivan, National-International Linkages:
France and China as Nonconforming Alliance Members
Robert T. Holt and John E. Turner, Insular Polities
Richard L. Merritt, Noncontiguity and Political Integration
R. V. Burks, The Communist Polities of Eastern Europe
Lloyd Jensen, Postwar Democratic Polities: National-International
Linkages in the Defense Policy of the Defeated States
Michael O'Leary, Linkages Between Domestic and International Poli-
tics in Underdeveloped Nations

Rosenbaum, Naomi (ed.). *Readings on the International Political Sys-
tem*, Englewood Cliffs, N.J.: Prentice-Hall (1970).
The People: Personality, Attitude, and Opinion
J. David Singer, Man and World Politics: The Psycho-Cultural Inter-
face
Richard L. Merritt, Nation-Building in America: The Colonial Years
William A. Gamson and Andre Modigliani, Knowledge and Foreign
Policy Opinions: Some Models for Consideration
Seymour Martin Lipset, The President, the Polls, and Vietnam

The Governments: The Making of Foreign Policy
James A. Robinson, The Concept of Crisis in Decision-Making
Ithiel de Sola Pool and Allen Kessler, The Kaiser, The Tsar, and the Computer: Information Processing in a Crisis
Ole R. Holsti and Robert C. North, Perceptions of Hostility and Financial Indices during the 1914 Crisis: An Experiment in Validating Content Analysis Data
Arnold Wolfers, The Goals of Foreign Policy
David S. McLellan, The Role of Political Style: A Study of Dean Acheson
International Conflict: War, Weapons, and Strategy
Lewis Coser, Peace Settlements and the Dysfunctions of Secrecy
Clinton F. Fink, More Calculations about Deterrence
Anatol Rapoport, Critique of Strategic Thinking
Herman Kahn, The Arms Race and World Order
International Cooperation: International Organization
Inis L. Claude, Collective Legitimization as a Political Function of the United Nations
Chadwick F. Alger, Non-resolution Consequences of the United Nations and their Effect on International Conflict
Bruce M. Russett, Discovering Voting Groups in the United Nations
Ernst B. Haas, System and Process in the International Labor Organization: A Statistical Afterthought
The World Community: The Integrated International System
Roger D. Masters, World Politics as a Primitive Political System
Karl W. Deutsch, Integration and Arms Control in the European Political Environment: A Summary Report
Ronald Inglehart, An End to European Integration?
Morton A. Kaplan, Some Problems of International Systems Research

Russett, Bruce M. (ed.). *Peace, War, and Numbers*, Beverly Hills, Ca.: Sage (1972).
J. David Singer et al., Capability Distribution, Uncertainty, and Major Power War, 1820–1965
Michael D. Wallace, Status, Formal Organization, and Arms Levels as Factors Leading to the Onset of War, 1820–1964
Rudolph J. Rummel, U.S. Foreign Relations: Conflict, Cooperation, and Attribute Distances
John D. Sullivan, Cooperating to Conflict: Sources of Informal Alignments
Jeffrey S. Milstein, American and Soviet Influence, Balance of Power, and Arab-Israeli Violence
Steven Rosen, War Power and the Willingness to Suffer
Michael P. Sullivan and William Thomas, Symbolic Involvement as a Correlate of Escalation: The Vietnam Case
P. Terrence Hopmann, Internal and External Influences on Bargaining in Arms Control Negotiations: The Partial Test Ban
Nazli Choucri and Robert C. North, In Search of Peace Systems: Scandinavia and the Netherlands, 1870–1970

Jonathan Wilkenfeld, Models for the Analysis of Foreign Conflict Behavior of States

Bruce M. Russett, The Revolt of the Masses: Public Opinion on Military Expenditures

Said, Abdul A. (ed.). *Theory of International Relations: The Crisis of Relevance*, Englewood Cliffs, N.J.: Prentice-Hall (1968).

Abdul A. Said, Recent Theories of International Relations: An Overview

Kenneth W. Thompson, Theory and International Studies in the Cold War

Roger Fisher, International Relations Theory and the Policy Maker

William D. Coplin, The Impact of Simulation on Theory of International Relations

Karl W. Deutsch, The Impact of Communications upon Theory of International Relations

Abdul A. Said, The Impact of the Emergence of the Non-West Upon Theories of International Relations

John H. Herz, The Impact of the Technological-Scientific Process on the International System

Marian D. Irish, The Impact of Science and Technology Upon American Foreign Policy

Theodore A. Couloumbis, Traditional Concepts and the Greek Reality

Hans J. Morgenthau, The Impact of the Cold War on the Theories of International Law and Organization

Schou, August, and Arne Olav Brundtland (eds.). *Small States in International Relations*, New York: Wiley (1971).

A. Schou, Opening Address

H. Eek, The Conception of Small States

D. Vital, The Analysis of Small Power Politics

E. Bjøl, The Small State in International Politics

R. P. Barston, The External Relations of Small States

L. G. M. Jaquet, The Role of a Small State within Alliance Systems

L. Réczei, The Political Aims and Experiences of the Small Socialist States

I. Nicolae, The Role and Responsibility of the Small and Medium-Sized Countries in Maintaining International Peace

G. Stourzh, Some Reflections on Permanent Neutrality

R. Vukadinović, Small States and the Policy of Non-Alignment

S. F. Lemass, Small States in International Organizations

G. G. Schram, The Role of the Nordic States in the U.N.

A. O. Brundtland, The Nordic Countries as an Area of Peace

J. J. Okumu, The Place of African States in International Relations

A. Baker Fox, The Twenty and the One: Latin American Relations and the United States

P. M. Ledo, Developing Nations—A Mexican Point of View

J. Freymond, How the Small Countries Can Contribute to Peace

J. J. Holst, Small Powers in a Nuclear World

A. O. Brundtland, Summary of Discussion

Singer, J. David (ed.). *Quantitative International Politics: Insights and Evidence*, New York: Free Press (1968).
The Decision Maker's Level
James N. Rosenau, Private Preferences and Political Responsibilities: The Relative Potency of Individual and Role Variables in the Behavior of U.S. Senators
Chadwick F. Alger, Interaction in a Committee of the United Nations General Assembly
Dina A. Zinnes, The Expression and Perception of Hostility in Prewar Crisis: 1914
The National Level
Ole R. Holsti et al., Perception and Action in the 1914 Crisis
Charles A. McClelland, Access to Berlin: The Quantity and Variety of Events, 1948–1963
Rudolph J. Rummel, The Relationship between National Attributes and Foreign Conflict Behavior
Michael Haas, Social Change and National Aggressiveness, 1900–1960
The Systemic Level
J. David Singer and Melvin Small, Alliance Aggregation and the Onset of War, 1815–1945
Hayward Alker and Donald Puchala, Trends in Economic Partnership: The North Atlantic Area, 1928–1963
Bruce M. Russett, Delineating International Regions

Spiegel, Steven L. (ed.). *At Issue: Politics in the World Arena*, New York: St. Martin's Press (1973).
The Conflict of Peoples
Harold R. Isaacs, Color in World Affairs
Tom Engelhardt, Ambush at Kamikaze Pass
Theodore Caplow, Are the Poor Countries Getting Poorer?
Hans J. Morgenthau, To Intervene or Not to Intervene
Ronald Steel, Is America Imperialistic?
Francis G. Hutchins, On Winning and Losing by Revolution
Robert F. Lamberg, Che in Bolivia: The Revolution that Failed
John McAlister and Paul Mus, The Meaning of Revolution in Viet Nam
Shlomo Avineri, The Palestinians and Israel
Conor Cruise O'Brien, Violence in Ireland: Another Algeria?
The Burden of the Strong
Hans J. Morgenthau, Changes and Chances in American-Soviet Relations
Richard Lowenthal, Russia and China: Controlled Conflict
Allen S. Whiting, Turning Point in Asia
George W. Ball, We Are Playing a Dangerous Game with Japan
Richard J. Barnet, Nixon's Plan to Save the World
Benjamin S. Lambeth, The Soviet Strategic Challenge under SALT I
George H. Quester, Paris, Pretoria, Peking . . . Proliferation?
The Crises of Institutions
Miriam Camps, European Unification in the Seventies
Harlan Cleveland, Can We Revive the U.N.?

Robert L. Heilbroner, The Multinational Corporation and the Nation-State

Leslie H. Gelb and Morton H. Halperin, The Ten Commandments of the Foreign Affairs Bureaucracy

Richard Holbrooke, The Machine that Fails

James C. Thomson, How Could Vietnam Happen? An Autopsy

Stuart R. Schram, What Makes Mao a Maoist

Daniel Singer, Charles de Gaulle: Death of a Legendary Hero

The Problems of the Future

Paul R. Ehrlich, Population, Food, and Environment: Is the Battle Lost?

Zbigniew Brzezinski, America in the Technetronic Age

Spiegel, Steven L., and Kenneth N. Waltz (eds.). *Conflict in World Politics*, Cambridge, Mass.: Winthrop (1971).

Robert W. Tucker, The United States

William Zimmerman, The Soviet Union

Edward Friedman, The United States and China

Herbert S. Dinerstein, The Soviet Union and China

Abraham F. Lowenthal, The United States and the Dominican Republic

Joseph Rothschild, The Soviet Union and Czechoslovakia

Roy C. Macridis, France and Germany

Robert N. Burr, Argentina and Chile

Elke Frank, East and West Germany

Gregory Henderson, North and South Korea

David Vital, Israel and the Arab Countries

Wayne A. Wilcox, India and Pakistan

Samuel L. Popkin, South Vietnam

Charles R. Nixon, Nigeria and Biafra

Peter Lyon, Malaysia, the Philippines, and Indonesia

Saadia Touval, Somalia, Ethiopia, and Kenya

Larry W. Bowman, Portugal and South Africa

Donald C. Hellmann, The United States and Japan

Kal J. Holsti, The United States and Canada

Lawrence Scheinman, Great Britain and France

Samuel L. Popkin and George McT. Kahin, American Policy: Southeast Asia

George H. Quester, American Policy: Nuclear Proliferation

Kenneth N. Waltz, Conflict in World Politics

Sprout, Harold, and Margaret Sprout (eds.). *Foundations of National Power*, Princeton, N.J.: Princeton University Press (1945; 1951).

The Ways of International Politics

The Editors, Introduction

Brooks Emeny, The Multi-State System

Nicholas J. Spykman, Politics: Domestic and International

Edward H. Carr, Power and Morality in International Politics

Walter Lippmann, Ends and Means in International Politics

Crane Brinton, The Pattern of Aggression

The Anatomy of Power
The Editors, Introduction
Edward H. Carr, Forms of Power
Charles C. Abbott, Economic Aspects of Power
Bertrand Russell, The Power of Ideas
Harold D. Lasswell, Language and Power
Frederick S. Dunn, "Total Diplomacy"
Geography, Maps and World Politics
The Editors, Introduction
Brooks Emeny, Outlines of World Geography
Nicholas J. Spykman, Mapping the World
Robert E. Harrison and Robert Strausz-Hupé, Maps, Strategy, and
   World Politics
Samuel W. Boggs, Propaganda with Maps
Samuel W. Boggs, Political Geography Lesson for Americans
Why Some States Are Strong and Others Weak
The Editors, Introduction
Robert Strausz-Hupé, Population as an Element of National Power
The Editors, Supplementary Note on Population and Power
Karl Brandt, Foodstuffs and Raw Materials as Elements of National
   Power
The Editors, The Raw Materials That Count in War and in Peace
Ralph Turner, Technology and National Power
National Resources Committee, The Integration of Resources
The Editors, Morale as an Element of National Strength
Henry Brougham, Leadership as an Element of National Strength
The Editors, Form of Government as a Factor in National Strength
D. W. Brogan, Challenge to Democracy
J. K. Galbraith, The Weaknesses of Dictatorships: Post Mortem on the
   Third Reich
Power Patterns in World Politics: Some Theories and Their Critics
The Editors, Introduction
The Editors, From Mahan to Mackinder
Sir Halford J. Mackinder, Sea Power vs. Land Power
N. J. Spykman, The Eurasian Rimland in World Politics
H. W. Weigert, Critique of Mackinder
A. J. Toynbee, The Next Stage in World Politics?
The European Realm in World Politics
The Editors, Introduction
Dudley Kirk, The Expansion of Europe
R. H. Whitbeck and V. C. Finch, Europe: Terrain, Resources, and
   Regions
J. M. Keynes, Europe Before 1914
André Siegfried, Europe Between Wars
Committee on European Economic Cooperation, Europe After World
   War II
Hajo Holborn, The Collapse of the European Political System, 1914–45

The Afro-Asian Realm in World Politics
The Editors, Introduction
Vernon McKay, Africa: Land and People
The Editors, Africa in World Politics
C. H. Grattan, The Future of Empire in Africa
E. A. Mowrer and Marthe Rajchman, The Indian Ocean in World Politics
K. M. Panikkar, The Indian Ocean in World Politics (continued)
Guy Wint, What Follows Imperialism in the Indian Ocean Realm?
N. J. Spykman, Political Geography of the Far East
Eugene Staley, Problems of Economic Development in Asia
The American Realm in World Politics
The Editors, Introduction
N. J. Spykman, Political Geography of the Americas
S. F. Bemis, North and South America Consequences of Latitude and Altitude
E. P. Hanson, Revolt Against Economic Colonialism
The Soviet Union
The Editors, Introduction
G. B. Cressey, Land of the Soviets
G. B. Cressey, The Peoples of the Soviet Union
W. H. Chamberlin, The Russian Revolution
The Editors, The Rise of Soviet Power
Maurice Edelman, Machinery Before Butter
Nikolaus Basseches, Preparation for Total War
Edgar Snow, What the War Cost the Russians
John Fischer, An American Look at the Ukraine in 1946
The Editors, Soviet Population Trends
Harry Schwartz, The Soviet Economy: A Trial Balance
Editors of *The Economist*, Political Bases of Soviet Strength
The Editors, Postwar Geopolitical Position
The Editors, Soviet Land Frontiers
The Editors, Security Against Devastation
The Editors, Was Mackinder Right?
The Editors, Soviet Foreign Policy: The Problem of Interpretation
John Foster Dulles, Aims and Methods of Soviet Foreign Policy
C. D. Fuller, Soviet Behavior in the U.N.
Edward Crankshaw, Nationalism vs. Revolution in Soviet Statecraft
The Soviet Border Satellites
The Editors, Introduction
The Editors, The East-European Security Zone
C. E. Black, Soviet Objectives, Methods, and Results in Eastern Europe
Christopher Rand, Soviet Security Zone in Asia
Communist China
The Editors, Introduction
G. F. Winfield, The Land and the People
G. F. Winfield, China's Basic Problems

The Editors, The Transportation Bottleneck
The Secretary of State, China and the United States
H. H. Fisher, China and the Soviet Union
A. D. Barnett, Profile of Red China
The United States
The Editors, Introduction
The Editors, The American Land
J. S. Davis, How Many Americans?
J. F. Dewhurst, The United States Economy
C. C. Abbott, Are We Vulnerable to Economic Attack?
The Editors, Research and Learning in the United States
The Editors, Impact of War on Research and Higher Learning in the
   United States
Learning and Statecraft
Harold Sprout, Role of Military Persons and Military Ideas in American
   Statecraft
Herbert Hoover et al., Foreign Policy Machinery
Walter Lippmann, The American Approach to Foreign Policy
G. T. Robinson, Can We Win the Battle for Men's Minds?
R. B. Fosdick, The Requisites of World Leadership
Great Britain
The Editors, Introduction
H. and M. Sprout, Pax Britannica
H. and M. Sprout, British Sea Power in the Writings of Captain Alfred
   Thayer Mahan
Robert Strausz-Hupé, The Challenge of Land Power
The Editors, Economic Aspects of Britain's Changing World Position
Barbara Ward, The Core of the Problem
Eyre Crowe, Traditional Bases of British Foreign Policy
Sir Austen Chamberlain, British Foreign Policy Between Wars
The Editors of "Planning," Britain's Role in the Postwar World
Barbara Ward, Britain: Keystone of Western Union
France
The Editors, Introduction
S. K. Padover, France Today: Trial Balance
The British Empire and Commonwealth
The Editors, Introduction
C. B. Fawcett, The Historic Empire of Great Britain
The Editors, The British Empire in Transition
Francis Williams, The Postwar Commonwealth
The North Atlantic Community
The Editors, Introduction
Barbara Ward, The Case for Western Association
J. K. Galbraith, The Case for West-European Union: An American
   View
Klaus Knorr, Western Union: Problems and Difficulties
The Secretary of State, The North Atlantic Alliance

The Inter-American System
The Editors, Introduction
Frank Tannenbaum, A Commonwealth of Nations?
E. S. Furniss, Jr., The Organization of American States
Germany
The Editors, Introduction
The Editors, The German Reich
The Editors, Germany Since 1945
David Rodnik, Social Structure and Behavior in Postwar Germany
C. E. Schorske, German Politics and Foreign Relations
H. R. Trevor-Roper, The Soviet Dilemma in Germany
Dean Acheson, U.S. Aims in Germany
G. A. Craig, Germany: Satellite or Great Power?
Japan
The Editors, Introduction
The Editors, Post-Mortem on the Japanese Empire
Sir George Sansom, Historical Foundations of Modern Japan
G. B. Cressey, Nature's Gifts to the Japanese
U.N. Economic Commission for Asia and the Far East, Population
   Trends in Japan
The Editors, Japan's Economic Potential
J. B. Cohen, Japan's War Economy
D. G. Haring, Japanese Behavior
T. A. Bisson, The Japanese State
H. H. Fisher, Soviet Aims in Japan
W. M. Ball, Japan After the Occupation
India
The Editors, Introduction
G. B. Cressey, The Land and Its Resources
G. B. Cressey, The People and Their Way of Life
John Fischer, India on the Eve of Independence
India: Free and Hungry
An Indian Official, Aims of Indian Foreign Policy
L. K. Rosinger, India in World Politics
The Mediterranean and Middle East
The Editors, Introduction
The Editors, Political and Strategic Geography
J. S. Badeau, "Bridge to Asia"
The Editors, Demography and Manpower
The Editors, Economic Resources
The Editors, The Pattern of Economic Life
The Editors, Political Structure of the Region
The Editors, Russian Interests and Policies
The Editors, British Interests and Policies
The Editors, American Interests and Policies
William Reitzel, The Postwar Mediterranean in American Statecraft
William Reitzel, A Look Toward the Future

The Polar Regions
The Editors, Introduction
Elmer Plischke, Power Politics in the Polar Regions
S. B. Jones, Problems of Economic Development and Military Strategy
in the Arctic
What Price World War III?
The Editors, Introduction
C. H. Grattan, The Cost of World War II
E. M. Earle, The Consequences of Air Power
W. L. Laurence, What Happened at Bikini
Jerome Feiner, The Menace of Biological Warfare
R. B. Fosdick, What Follows the Cold War?
Security: How Can We Achieve It?
The Editors, Introduction
W. W. Kaufmann, Background of World Organization
P. C. Jessup, The United Nations: What It Is Becoming
Walter Lippmann, Two Worlds or Three?
R. B. Fosdick, The Road Ahead

Stoessinger, John G., and Alan F. Westin (eds.). *Power and Order: 6
Cases in World Politics*, New York: Harcourt, Brace & World
(1964).
Classical Diplomacy
Henry A. Kissinger, The Congress of Vienna
Modern Diplomacy
James J. Wadsworth, Atoms for Peace
Alliance Policy
Robert E. Osgood, NATO: The Entangling Alliance
Nationalism and Colonialism
L. Gray Cowan, Ghana's Fight for Independence
The United Nations
John G. Stoessinger, Financing Peace-Keeping Operations
International Law
Quincy Wright, The Cuban Quarantine of 1962

Toma, Peter A. (ed.). *Basic Issues in International Relations*, Boston:
Allyn & Bacon (1967; 1974).
The Scope of International Relations
Quincy Wright, Development of International Relations as a Discipline
Morton Kaplan, Is International Relations a Discipline?
Stanley Hoffmann, International Relations as a Discipline
George F. Kennan, Training for Statesmanship
Karl W. Deutsch, The Place of Behavioral Sciences in Graduate Train-
ing in International Relations
Methods of Inquiry in International Relations
Raymond Aron, Historical Determinism and Causal Thought
Neal D. Houghton, Historical Bases for Prediction in International Re-
lations
Charles A. McClelland, History in International Relations

Ladis K. D. Kristof, The Origins and Evolution of Political Geography
Harold and Margaret Sprout, Geography and International Politics in an Era of Revolutionary Change
Hans J. Morgenthau, International Politics as a Struggle for Power
Kal J. Holsti, The Concept of Power in the Study of International Relations
Benno Wasserman, The Cultural and Psychological Approach to the Study of International Relations
J. David Singer, The Relevance of the Behavioral Sciences to the Study of International Relations
Ole R. Holsti, The 1914 Case
Harold Guetzkow, A Use of Simulation in the Study of Inter-Nation Relations
Richard C. Snyder and Glenn D. Paige, The United States Decision to Resist Aggression in Korea: The Application of an Analytical Scheme
Charles A. McClelland, The Tools of System Analysis
John H. Herz, Balance Systems and Balance Policies in a Nuclear and Bipolar Age
Karl W. Deutsch, An Alternative to the "Equilibrium" Approach

International Politics

Statement of Hon. Dean Rusk, Secretary of State, before the Foreign Relations Committee of the U.S. Senate, on February 18, 1966
Hans J. Morgenthau, Johnson's Dilemma: The Alternatives Now in Vietnam
John H. Kautsky, Myth, Self-Fulfilling Prophecy, and Symbolic Reassurance in the East-West Conflict
Louis J. Halle, Strategy versus Ideology
Dean Acheson, The American Image Will Take Care of Itself
Dean Rusk, The Anatomy of Foreign Policy Decisions
Samuel P. Huntington, Strategic Planning and the Political Process
Franklin A. Lindsay, Program Planning: The Missing Elements
Klaus Knorr, Failures in National Intelligence Estimates: The Case of the Cuban Missiles
Charles Burton Marshall, Afterthoughts on the Cuban Blockade
J. David Singer, Negotiation by Proxy: A Proposal
Hollis B. Chenery, Objectives and Criteria for Foreign Assistance
Eugene R. Black, A Status for Development
Peter A. Toma, The Problem of Foreign Aid
Herbert Dinerstein, The Transformation of Alliance Systems
Charles Burton Marshall, Detente: Effects on the Alliance
George Liska, The Rationale of Non-Alignment
Thomas C. Schelling, Deterrence: Military Diplomacy in the Nuclear Age
Walter Goldstein, Disarmament, The U.N. and the Nuclear Club

International Organization

Stanley Hoffmann, The Role of International Organization: Limits and Possibilities
Ernst B. Haas, The Challenge of Regionalism

Inis L. Claude, Jr., The Management of Power in the Changing United Nations

Richard W. Van Wagenen, The Concept of Community and the Future of the United.Nations

Edward T. Rowe, The Emerging Anti-Colonial Consensus in the United Nations

Leland M. Goodrich, The Political Role of the Secretary General

W. Raymond Duncan, Red China's Admission to the United Nations: Obligation or Privilege?

Brian E. Urquhart, United Nations Peace Forces and the Changing United Nations: An Institutional Perspective

Wilkenfeld, Jonathan (ed.). *Conflict Behavior and Linkage Politics*, New York: David McKay (1973).

A Theoretical Perspective on Linkages

Lewis Coser, Conflict with Out-Groups and Group Structure

James Rosenau, Theorizing across Systems: Linkage Politics Revisited

Foreign Conflict Behavior Linkages

Rudolph Rummel, Dimensions of Conflict Behavior within and between Nations

Jonathan Wilkenfeld, Domestic and Foreign Conflict

Warren Phillips, The Conflict Environment of Nations: A Study of Conflict Inputs to Nations in 1963

Leo Hazlewood, Externalizing Systemic Stress: International Conflict as Adaptive Behavior

Michael Haas, Societal Development and International Conflict

Richard Van Atta, Field Theory and National-International Linkages

John Collins, Foreign Conflict Behavior and Domestic Disorder in Africa

Robert Burrowes and Bertram Spector, The Strength and Direction of Relationships between Domestic and External Conflict and Cooperation: Syria, 1961–1967

Domestic Conflict Behavior Linkages

Jonathan Wilkenfeld and Dina Zinnes, A Linkage Model of Domestic Conflict Behavior

C. Propositional Inventories

Alker, Hayward R., Jr., and P. G. Bock. "Propositions about International Relations: Contributions from the International Encyclopedia of the Social Sciences," *Political Science Annual: An International Review* 3 (1972): 385–495.

Berelson, Bernard, and Gary Steiner. *Human Behavior: An Inventory of Scientific Findings*, New York: Harcourt, Brace & World (1964).

Coplin, William D. *Introduction to International Politics: A Theoretical Overview*, Chicago: Markham (1971; 1974).

Munton, Don. "The Study of International Relations: Traditional Insight and Empirical Evidence," Behavioral Sciences Laboratory, Ohio State University, mimeographed (Jan. 1971).

Scott, Andrew M. *Functioning of the International Political System*, New York: Macmillan (1967).

Sullivan, Dennis G. "An Inventory of Major Propositions Contained in Contemporary Textbooks in International Relations," Ph.D. dissertation, Northwestern University (1962).

III. American and Comparative Foreign Policy

A. Authored Volumes

Adamec, Ludwig. *Afghanistan's Foreign Affairs to the Mid-Twentieth Century*, Tucson: University of Arizona Press (1974).

Agung, Ide Anak. *Twenty Years of Indonesian Foreign Policy, 1945–1965*, The Hague: Nijhoff (1973).

Allison, Graham T. *Essence of Decision: Explaining the Cuban Missile Crisis*, Boston: Little, Brown (1971).

Almond, Gabriel. *The American People and Foreign Policy*, New York: Harcourt, Brace (1950).

Appleton, Sheldon. *U.S. Foreign Policy: An Introduction with Cases*, Boston: Little, Brown (1968).

Aron, Raymond. *The Imperial Republic: American Foreign Policy, 1946–1973*, Englewood Cliffs, N.J.: Prentice-Hall (1974).

Aspaturian, Vernon. *The Soviet Union in the International Communist System*, Stanford, Ca.: Hoover Institution Press (1966).

_____. *Process and Power in Soviet Foreign Policy*, Boston: Little, Brown (1971).

Astiz, Carlos A. *Latin American International Politics: Ambitions, Capabilities, and the National Interest of Mexico, Brazil, and Argentina*, Notre Dame, Ind.: University of Notre Dame Press (1969).

Bailey, Thomas. *The Art of Diplomacy*, New York: Appleton (1968).

Barber, James. *South Africa's Foreign Policy 1945–1970*, New York: Oxford University Press (1973).

Beloff, Max. *The Foreign Policy of Soviet Russia: 1929–1941*, vol. 1, 1929–1936 (1947); vol. 2, 1936–1941 (1949), London: Oxford University Press.

_____. *Foreign Policy and the Democratic Process*, Baltimore: Johns Hopkins Press (1955).

Berkes, Ross N., and Mahinder S. Bedi. *The Diplomacy of India*, Stanford, Ca.: Stanford University Press (1958).

Bloomfield, Lincoln P. *In Search of American Foreign Policy: The Humane Use of Power*, New York: Oxford University Press (1974).

Borton, Hugh, et al. *Japan between East and West*, New York: Harper (1957).

Boyd, R. G. *Communist China's Foreign Policy*, London: Pall Mall (1962).

Brecher, Michael. *The Foreign Policy System of Israel: Setting, Images, Process*, New Haven, Conn.: Yale University Press (1972).

————. *Decisions in Israel's Foreign Policy*, New Haven, Conn.: Yale University Press (1974).

Brzezinski, Zbigniew K. *The Soviet Bloc*, Cambridge, Mass.: Harvard University Press (1960).

Buck, Philip W., and Martin Travis, Jr. *Control of Foreign Relations in Modern Nations*, New York: Norton (1957).

Burke, S. M. *Pakistan's Foreign Policy: An Historical Analysis*, New York: Oxford University Press (1973).

Campbell, John F. *The Foreign Affairs Fudge Factory*, New York: Basic Books (1971).

Chittick, William O. *The Analysis of Foreign Policy Output*, Columbus, Ohio: Merrill (1974).

Cho, Soon Sung. *Korea in World Politics, 1940–1950*, Berkeley: University of California Press (1967).

Chubin, Shahram, and Sepehr Zabih. *The Foreign Relations of Iran*, Berkeley: University of California Press (1975).

Conil Paz, Alberto. *Argentina's Foreign Policy, 1930–1962* [tr. John J. Kennedy], Notre Dame, Ind.: University of Notre Dame Press (1966).

Coplin, William D., et al. *American Foreign Policy: An Introduction to Analysis and Evaluation*, N. Scituate, Mass.: Duxbury (1973).

Crabb, Cecil V., Jr. *Bipartisan Foreign Policy: Myth or Reality?* Evanston, Ill.: Row, Peterson (1957).

————. *American Foreign Policy in the Nuclear Age: Principles, Problems, and Prospects*, Evanston, Ill.: Row, Peterson (1960).

Dahl, Robert. *Congress and Foreign Policy*, New York: Harcourt, Brace (1950).

Dallin, Alexander. *Soviet Conduct in World Affairs*, New York: Columbia University Press (1968).

Davis, Harold, et al. *Latin American Foreign Policies: An Analysis*, Baltimore: Johns Hopkins Press (1975).

deCarmoy, Guy. *The Foreign Policies of France 1944–1968* [tr. Elaine Halperin], Chicago: University of Chicago Press (1970).

Destler, Isidore M. *Presidents, Bureaucrats, and Foreign Policy: The Politics of Organizational Reform*, Princeton, N.J.: Princeton University Press (1972).

Deutsch, Karl W., et al. *France, Germany and the Western Alliance*, New York: Scribner's (1966).

Donovan, John C. *The Cold Warriors: A Policy-Making Elite*, Lexington, Mass.: Heath (1974).

Dutt, Vidya Prakash. *China and the World: An Analysis of Communist China's Foreign Policy*, New York: Praeger (1966).

Elder, Robert E. *The Policy Machine: The Department of State and American Foreign Policy*, Syracuse: Syracuse University Press (1960).

Emmerson, John K. *Arms, Yen and Power: The Japanese Dilemma*, New York: Dunellen (1971).

Farrell, Robert B. *The Making of Canadian Foreign Policy*, Scarborough, Ontario: Prentice-Hall of Canada (1969).

Fifield, Russell H. *The Diplomacy of Southeast Asia: 1945–1958*, New York: Harper (1958).

Fischer, Louis. *The Soviet in World Affairs*, Princeton, N.J.: Princeton University Press (1951).

Fitzsimons, Matthew A. *The Foreign Policy of the British Labour Government, 1945–1951*, Notre Dame, Ind.: University of Notre Dame Press (1953).

Frankel, Joseph. *Making of Foreign Policy*, New York: Oxford University Press (1963).

Freund, Gerald. *Germany between Two Worlds*, New York: Harcourt, Brace & World (1961).

Gerberding, William P. *United States Foreign Policy: Perspectives and Analysis*, New York: McGraw-Hill (1966).

Goldhamer, Herbert. *Foreign Powers in Latin America*, Princeton, N.J.: Princeton University Press (1972).

Goldman, Nahum. *Israel Foreign Policy*, Tel Aviv: New Outlook (1970).

Gorden, Morton, and Kenneth Vines. *Theory and Practice of American Foreign Policy*, New York: Crowell (1955).

Graham, Robert A. *Vatican Diplomacy: A Study of Church and State on the International Plane*, Princeton, N.J.: Princeton University Press (1959).

Gross, Feliks. *Foreign Policy Analysis*, New York: Philosophical Library (1954).

Grosser, Alfred. *French Foreign Policy under de Gaulle* [tr. Losi A. Pattison], Boston: Little, Brown (1967).

Gruber, Karl. *Between Liberation and Liberty: Austria in the Post-War World* [tr. Lionel Kochan], New York: Praeger (1955).

Halle, Louis J. *Civilization and Foreign Policy*, New York: Harper (1955).

————. *The Cold War as History*, New York: Harper & Row (1967).

Hammond, Paul Y. *Cold War Years: American Foreign Policy since 1945*, New York: Harcourt, Brace (1969).

Hanrieder, Wolfram F. *West German Foreign Policy, 1949–1963: International Pressure and Domestic Response*, Stanford, Ca.: Stanford University Press (1967).

————. *The Stable Crisis: Two Decades of German Foreign Policy*, New York: Harper & Row (1970).

Hartmann, Frederick H. *Germany between East and West: The Reunification Problem*, Englewood Cliffs, N.J.: Prentice-Hall (1965).

Hellmann, Donald C. *Japan and East Asia: The New International Order*, New York: Praeger (1972).

Hildebrand, Klaus. *The Foreign Policy of the Third Reich*, Berkeley: University of California Press (1973).

Hilsman, Roger. *The Politics of Policy Making in Defense and Foreign Affairs*, New York: Harper & Row (1971).

Hinton, Harold C. *China's Turbulent Quest: An Analysis of China's Foreign Relations since 1949*, Bloomington: Indiana University Press (1972).

Howard, John E. *Parliament and Foreign Policy in France*, London: Cresset (1948).

Hugo, Grant. *Britain in Tomorrow's World: Principles of Foreign Policy*, New York: Columbia University Press (1969).

Iman, Zafar. *World Powers in South and South-East Asia: The Politics of Super-Nationalism*, New Delhi, India: Sterling (1972).

International Studies Group. *Major Problems of U.S. Foreign Policy 1947*, Washington, D.C.: Brookings Institution (1947–).

Irish, Marian, and Elke Frank. *U.S. Foreign Policy: Context, Conduct, Content*, New York: Harcourt Brace Jovanovich (1975).

Johnstone, William C. *Burma's Foreign Policy: A Study in Neutralism*, Cambridge, Mass.: Harvard University Press (1963).

Kaiser, Karl. *German Foreign Policy in Transition: Bonn between East and West*, New York: Oxford University Press (1968).

Kajima, Morinosuke. *Modern Japan's Foreign Policy*, Rutland, Vt.: Tuttle (1969).

Kaplan, Lawrence S. *Recent American Foreign Policy: Conflicting Interpretations*, Homewood, Ill.: Dorsey (1973).

Kennan, George. *American Diplomacy 1900–1951*, Chicago: University of Chicago Press (1951).

_____. *Realities of American Foreign Policy*, Princeton, N.J.: Princeton University Press (1954).

Kennaway, Richard. *New Zealand Foreign Policy 1951–1971*, Wellington, New Zealand: Hicks Smith (1972).

Kieft, David O. *Belgium's Return to Neutrality: An Essay in the Frustration of Small Power Diplomacy*, Oxford: Clarendon Press (1972).

Knappen, Marshall. *An Introduction to American Foreign Policy*, New York: Harper (1956).

Koh, Byung C. *The Foreign Policy of North Korea*, New York: Praeger (1969).

Kolko, Gabriel. *The Roots of American Foreign Policy*, Boston: Beacon Press (1967).

Kolodziej, Edward A. *French International Policy under de Gaulle and Pompidou: The Politics of Grandeur*, Ithaca, N.Y.: Cornell University Press (1974).

Kulski, W. W. *The Soviet Union in World Affairs: A Documented Analysis, 1964–1972*, Syracuse: Syracuse University Press (1973).

Kundra, J. C. *Indian Foreign Policy: 1947–1954*, Bombay, India: Vora (1955).

Lall, Arthur. *How Communist China Negotiates*, New York: Columbia University Press (1968).

Langdon, Frank C. *Japan's Foreign Policy*, Vancouver: University of British Columbia Press (1973).

Leifer, Michael. *Cambodia: The Search for Security*, New York: Praeger (1967).

_____. *Foreign Relations of the New States*, New York: Longman (1974).

Lentner, Howard H. *Foreign Policy Analysis: A Comparative and Conceptual Approach*, Columbus, Ohio: Merrill (1974).

Lerche, Charles O. *Foreign Policy of the American People*, Englewood Cliffs, N.J.: Prentice-Hall (1958; 1961; 1967).

Levi, Werner. *Modern China's Foreign Policy*, Minneapolis: University of Minnesota Press (1953).

Levy, Reynold. *Nearing the Crossroads: Contending Approaches to Contemporary American Foreign Policy*, New York: Free Press (1975).

Lippmann, Walter. *U.S. Foreign Policy*, Boston: Little, Brown (1943).

London, Kurt. *The Making of Foreign Policy: East and West*, Philadelphia: Lippincott (1965).

Lyon, Peyton V. *The Policy Question: A Critical Appraisal of Canada's Role in World Affairs*, Toronto: McClelland & Stewart (1963).

Mackintosh, J. M. *Strategy and Tactics of Soviet Foreign Policy*, New York: Oxford University Press (1962).

Maclean, Donald D. *British Foreign Policy: The Years since Suez, 1956-1968*, New York: Stein & Day (1970).

Magdoff, Harry. *The Age of Imperialism: The Economics of U.S. Foreign Policy*, New York: Monthly Review Press (1969).

Marshall, Charles B. *The Limits of Foreign Policy*, New York: Holt, Rinehart & Winston (1955).

Marwick, Arthur C. *Britain in the Century of Total War: War, Peace and Social Change 1900-1967*, Boston: Little, Brown (1968).

Mathews, John M. *American Foreign Relations*, New York: Century (1968).

May, Ernest R. *Lessons of History: The Use and Misuse of History in American Foreign Policy*, New York: Oxford University Press (1973).

Mendel, Douglas U. *The Japanese People and Foreign Policy: A Study of Public Opinion in Post-Treaty Japan*, Westport, Conn.: Greenwood (1961; 1971).

Merkl, Peter H. *German Foreign Policies, West and East: On the Threshold of a New European Era*, Santa Barbara: ABC-Clio (1974).

Millar, Thomas B. *Australia's Foreign Policy*, Sydney, Australia: Angus & Robertson (1968).

Miller, J. D. B. *The Commonwealth in the World*, London: Gerald Duckworth (1959).

Minifie, James M. *Peacemaker or Powder-Monkey: Canada's Role in a Revolutionary World*, Toronto: McClelland & Stewart (1960).

Modelski, George. *A Theory of Foreign Policy*, New York: Praeger (1962).

Morgenthau, Hans. *In Defense of the National Interest*, New York: Knopf (1951).

Morse, Edward L. *Foreign Policy and Interdependence in Gaullist France*, Princeton, N.J.: Princeton University Press (1973).

Mosely, Phillip E. *The Kremlin and World Politics*, New York: Vintage (1960).

Muni, S. D. *Foreign Policy of Nepal*, Delhi, India: National (1973).

Nash, Henry T. *American Foreign Policy: Response to a Sense of Threat*, Homewood, Ill.: Dorsey (1973).

Nicolson, Harold. *The Evolution of Diplomatic Method*, New York: Harper (1955).

North, Robert C. *The Foreign Relations of China*, Encino, Ca.: Dickenson (1973).

Northedge, Fred S. *British Foreign Policy: The Process of Readjustment 1945–1961*, London: Allen & Unwin (1962).

Oglesby, Carl, and Richard Shaull. *Containment and Change*, New York: Macmillan (1969).

Ojha, Ishwer C. *Chinese Foreign Policy in an Age of Transition: The Diplomacy of Cultural Despair*, Boston: Beacon Press (1969).

Osgood, Robert E. *Ideals and Self-Interest in America's Foreign Relations*, Chicago: University of Chicago Press (1953).

Patel, Satayavrata R. *Foreign Policy of India: An Inquiry and Criticism*, Bombay, India: Tripathi (1960).

Perkins, Dexter. *The American Approach to Foreign Policy*, Cambridge, Mass.: Harvard University Press (1952).

Phillips, Claude S. *The Development of Nigerian Foreign Policy*, Evanston, Ill.: Northwestern University Press (1964).

Pratt, Julius W. *A History of United States Foreign Policy*, New York: Prentice-Hall (1955).

Radway, Laurence I. *Foreign Policy and National Defense*, Glenview, Ill.: Scott, Foresman (1969).

Rainey, Gene E. *Patterns of American Foreign Policy*, Boston: Allyn & Bacon (1975).

Reitzel, William, Morton Kaplan, and Constance Coblenz. *U. S. Foreign Policy 1945–1955*, Washington, D.C.: Brookings Institution (1956).

Richardson, James L. *Germany and the Atlantic Alliance*, Cambridge, Mass.: Harvard University Press (1966).

Robinson, James A. *Congress and Foreign Policy: A Study in Legislative Influence and Initiative*, Homewood, Ill.: Dorsey (1962; 1967).

Rubinstein, Alvin Z. *The Foreign Policy of the Soviet Union*, New York: Random House (1960).

Sapin, Burton M. *The Making of United States Foreign Policy*, New York: Praeger (1966).

Schlessinger, Thomas O. *Austrian Neutrality in Post-War Europe*, Vienna: Wilhelm Braunmuller (1972).

Schulman, Marshall. *Stalin's Foreign Policy Reappraised*, Cambridge, Mass.: Harvard University Press (1963).

Seabury, Paul. *The United States in World Affairs*, New York: McGraw-Hill (1973).

Sen, Chanakya. *The Fulcrum of Asia: Relations among China, India, Pakistan, and the USSR*, New York: Pegasus (1970).

Sharma, Phool K. *India, Pakistan, China, and the Contemporary World*, Delhi, India: National (1972).

Simmonds, John D. *China's World: The Foreign Policy of a Developing State*, New York: Columbia University Press (1970).

Simpson, Smith. *Anatomy of the State Department*, Boston: Beacon Press (1969).

Skurnik, W. A. E. *The Foreign Policy of Senegal*, Evanston, Ill.: Northwestern University Press (1972).

Smith, Roger M. *Cambodia's Foreign Policy*, Ithaca, N.Y.: Cornell University Press (1965).

Snyder, Richard C., and Edgar S. Furniss. *American Foreign Policy: Formulation, Principles, and Programs*, New York: Rinehart (1954).

Spanier, John W. *American Foreign Policy since World War II*, New York: Praeger (1971).

————, and Eric Uslaner. *How American Foreign Policy Is Made*, New York: Praeger (1974).

Spence, John E. *Republic under Pressure: A Study of South African Foreign Policy*, New York: Oxford University Press (1965).

Spykman, Nicholas J. *America's Strategy in World Politics: The U.S. and the Balance of Power*, New York: Harcourt, Brace (1942).

Steiner, H. Arthur. *Communist China in the World Community*, New York: Carnegie Endowment for International Peace (1961).

Stillman, Edmund, and William Pfaff. *The New Politics: America and the End of the Post-War World*, New York: Coward-McCann (1961).

Takeuchi, Sterling T. *War and Diplomacy in the Japanese Empire*, New York: Russell (1936).

Thiam, Doudou. *The Foreign Policy of African States: Ideological Bases, Present Realities, Future Prospects*, London: Phoenix (1965).

Thompson, Kenneth W. *American Diplomacy and Emergent Patterns*, New York: New York University Press (1962).

Thompson, W. Scott. *Ghana's Foreign Policy, 1957–1966: Diplomacy, Ideology, and the New State*, Princeton, N.J.: Princeton University Press (1969).

Tint, Herbert. *French Foreign Policy since the Second World War*, London: Weidenfeld & Nicolson (1972).

Triska, Jan. *The World Communist System*, Stanford, Ca.: Stanford Studies of the Communist System (1964).

————, and David D. Finley, *Soviet Foreign Policy*, New York: Mac-

Tucker, Robert W. *Nation or Empire?* Baltimore: Johns Hopkins Press (1968).

VanCampen, S. I. P. *The Quest for Security: Some Aspects of Netherlands Foreign Policy 1945–1950*, 2d ed., The Hague: Nijhoff (1968).

Vandenbosch, Amry. *Dutch Foreign Policy since 1815: A Study in Small Power Politics*, The Hague: Nijhoff (1959).

————. *South Africa and the World: The Foreign Policy of Apartheid*, Lexington: University of Kentucky Press (1970).

————, and Mary Vandenbosch. *Australia Faces Southeast Asia: The Emergence of a Foreign Policy*, Lexington: University of Kentucky Press (1967).

Van Ness, Peter. *Revolution and Chinese Foreign Policy*, Berkeley: University of California Press (1970).

Vital, David. *The Making of British Foreign Policy*, New York: Praeger (1968).

Waltz, Kenneth N. *Foreign Policy and Democratic Politics: The American and British Experience*, Boston: Little, Brown (1968).

Watt, D. C. *Personalities and Policies: Studies in the Formulation of British Foreign Policy in the Twentieth Century*, Notre Dame, Ind.: University of Notre Dame Press (1965).

Watt, Sir Alan S. *The Evolution of Australian Foreign Policy, 1938–1965*, London: Cambridge University Press (1967).

Weisband, Edward. *Turkish Foreign Policy: Great Power Politics and Small State Diplomacy*, Princeton, N.J.: Princeton University Press (1973).

Westerfield, H. Bradford. *Foreign Policy and Party Politics*, New Haven, Conn.: Yale University Press (1955).

Whetten, Lawrence L. *Contemporary American Foreign Policy*, Lexington, Mass.: Lexington Books (1974).

Williams, William A. *The Tragedy of American Diplomacy*, Cleveland, Ohio: World (1959).

Woodhouse, Christopher M. *British Foreign Policy since the Second World War*, London: Hutchinson (1961).

Worcester, Donald E. *Brazil, from Colony to World Power*, New York: Scribner's (1973).

Young, Kenneth T. *Negotiating with the Chinese Communists: The U.S. Experience 1953–1967*, New York: McGraw-Hill (1968).

Younger, Kenneth. *Changing Perspectives in British Foreign Policy*, London: Oxford University Press (1964).

Zabih, Sepehr, and Shahram Chubin. *Foreign Relations of Iran: A Small State in a Zone of Great-Power Conflict*, Berkeley: University of California Press (1975).

B. Edited Volumes

Armstrong, Hamilton F. (ed.). *Fifty Years of Foreign Affairs*, New York: Praeger (1972).

Barber, James, and Michael Smith (eds.). *The Nature of Foreign Policy: A Reader*, London: Open University Press (1974).

Barston, R. P. (ed.). *Other Powers: The Foreign Policies of Norway, the Netherlands, Switzerland, Zambia, Israel, Cyprus, Cuba, Singapore and New Zealand*, London: Allen & Unwin (1973).

Black, Joseph E., and Kenneth W. Thompson (eds.). *Foreign Policies in a World of Change*, New York: Harper & Row (1963).

Bliss, Howard, and M. Glen Johnson (eds.). *Consensus at the Crossroads: Dialogues in American Foreign Policy*, New York: Dodd, Mead (1972).

Chai, Winberg (ed.). *The Foreign Relations of the People's Republic of China*, New York: Capricorn (1972).

Clarkson, Stephen (ed.). *An Independent Foreign Policy for Canada*, Toronto: McClelland & Stewart (1968).

Dallin, Alexander (ed.). *Soviet Conduct in World Affairs*, New York: Columbia University Press (1960).

Dial, Roger L. (ed.). *Advancing and Contending Approaches to the Study of Chinese Foreign Policy*, Halifax, Nova Scotia: Centre for Foreign Policy Studies, Dalhousie University (1974).

Divine, Robert A. (ed.). *American Foreign Policy*, New York: Meridian (1960).

Gardner, Lloyd C. (ed.). *American Foreign Policy, Present to Past: A Narrative with Readings and Documents*, New York: Free Press (1974).

Gilbert, John L. (ed.). *American Foreign Policy: Prospects and Perspectives*, New York: St. Martin's Press (1973).

Gregg, Robert W., and Charles W. Kegley, Jr. (eds.). *After Vietnam: The Future of American Foreign Policy*, Garden City, N.Y.: Doubleday (1971).

Halperin, Morton H., and Arnold Kanter (eds.). *Readings in American Foreign Policy: A Bureaucratic Perspective*, Boston: Little, Brown (1973).

Hanrieder, Wolfram (ed.). *Comparative Foreign Policy: Theoretical Essays*, New York: David McKay (1971).

Higham, Robin (ed.). *Intervention or Abstention: The Dilemma of American Foreign Policy*, Lexington, Mass.: Lexington Books (1975).

Hoffmann, Erik, and Frederic Fleron (eds.). *The Conduct of Soviet Foreign Policy*, Chicago: Aldine (1971).

Ingham, Kenneth (ed.). *Foreign Relations of African States*, Hamden, Conn.: Shoestring (1974).

Irish, Marian D. (ed.). *World Pressures on American Foreign Policy*, Englewood Cliffs, N.J.: Prentice-Hall (1964).

Jacobson, Harold K. (ed.). *America's Foreign Policy*, New York: Random House (1960; 1965).

————, and William Zimmerman (eds.). *The Shaping of Foreign Policy*, New York: Atherton (1969).

Jones, Alan M., Jr. (ed.). *U.S. Foreign Policy in a Changing World: The Nixon Administration, 1969–1973*, New York: David McKay (1973).

Kegley, Charles, et al. (eds.). *International Events and the Comparative Analysis of Foreign Policy*, Columbia: University of South Carolina Press (1975).

Lederer, Ivo (ed.). *Russian Foreign Policy*, New Haven, Conn.: Yale University Press (1962).

Leifer, Michael (ed.). *Constraints and Adjustments in British Foreign Policy*, London: Allen & Unwin (1972).

London, Kurt (ed.). *The Soviet Impact on World Politics*, New York: Hawthorn (1974).

Macridis, Roy C. (ed.). *Foreign Policy in World Politics*, Englewood Cliffs, N.J.: Prentice-Hall (1958; 1962; 1967; 1972).

McKay, Vernon (ed.). *African Diplomacy: Studies in the Determinants of Foreign Policy*, New York: Praeger (1966).

Northedge, Fred S. (ed.). *The Foreign Policies of the Powers*, London: Faber & Faber (1968); New York: Free Press (1975).

Rosenau, James N. (ed.). *Domestic Sources of Foreign Policy*, New York: Free Press (1967).

———— (ed.). *Comparing Foreign Policies: Theories, Findings, and Methods*, Beverly Hills, Ca.: Sage (1974).

Rosenberg, Milton J. (ed.). *Beyond Conflict and Containment: Critical Studies of Military and Foreign Policy*, New Brunswick, N.J.: Transaction Books (1973).

Sapin, Burton (ed.). *Contemporary American Foreign and Military Foreign Policy*, Glenview, Ill.: Scott, Foresman (1970).

Sayigh, Fayiz (ed.). *The Dynamics of Neutralism in the Arab World: A Symposium*, San Francisco: Chandler (1964).

Schlesinger, Arthur M. (ed.). *Dynamics of World Power: A Documentary History of U.S. Foreign Policy, 1945–1973*, 5 vols., New York: McGraw-Hill (1973).

Seabury, Paul, and Aaron Wildavsky (eds.). *U.S. Foreign Policy: Perspectives and Proposals for the 1970s*, New York: McGraw-Hill (1969).

Snyder, Richard C., et al. (eds.). *Foreign Policy Decision-Making: An Approach to the Study of International Politics*, New York: Free Press (1962).

Speier, Hans, and W. Phillips Davison (eds.). *West German Leadership and Foreign Policy*, Evanston, Ill.: Row, Peterson (1957).

Trager, Frank N., and Philip S. Kronenberg (eds.). *National Security and American Society: Theory, Process, and Policy*, Lawrence: University Press of Kansas (1973).

Varma, S. P., and K. P. Misra (eds.). *Foreign Policies in South Asia*, Port Washington, N.Y.: Kennikat (1969).

Wilcox, Wayne A., Leo Rose, and Gavin Boyd (eds.). *Asia and the International System*, Cambridge, Mass.: Winthrop (1972).

Wilson, Ian (ed.). *China and the World Community*, Sydney, Australia: Angus & Robertson (1973).

IV. Journals and Annuals in International Politics

A. *Largely Data-Based*

Instant Research on Peace and Violence. Tampere Peace Research Institute, Tammelanpuistokatu 58 B V, 33100 Tampere 10, Finland.
Quarterly since 1971; $5 per year.
"An interdisciplinary and international journal of scientific reports in the field of peace research. The journal concentrates on actual problems and phenomena related to questions of peace and war. It deviates from the ordinary kind of scientific journals in stressing less methodological aspects and concentrating more on results obtained."
Vol. 1/1 (1971)
Raimo Väyrynen, Some Aspects of Theory and Strategy of Kidnapping
Satu Sirkka, Foreign Aid, Investments, and Economic Growth: Doctrines and Practice
Uolevi Arosalo, Structural Violence, Alienation, and Peace Action
Vol. 1/2 (1971)
Asbjorn Eide, Peace Research as Communication: How, with Whom, for What Purpose
Raimo Väyrynen and Uolevi Arosalo, Some Social Correlates of the Production of Strategic Metals
Vilho Harle, International Events Data Sources: Are They Reliable?
Vol. 1/3 (1971)
Asbjorn Eide, International Peace Academy and the Helsinki Project: The Idea and Its Execution
Johan Galtung, An IPRA Summer School?
Peter Wallensteen, Dealing with the Devil: Five African States and South Africa
Raimo Väyrynen, Bangla Desh—An Outcome of Inequality and Imperialism
Jaakko Kalela, Detente and Peace
Uolevi Arosalo, East-West Trade as a Potential Indicator of International Tension
Vol. 2/1 (1972)
Unto Vesa, Peace Research and the War in Indochina
Steven Rose, The Real Significance of CBW

Stanford Biology Study Group, The Destruction of Indochina
Malvern Lumsden, The Politics of Reconstruction in Indochina
Reino Hjerppe and Olavi E. Niitamo, Social Indicators as an Information and Cognition System of Social Conflicts
Urho Kekkonen, The Olympic Games to UNESCO

Vol. 2/2 (1972)
Yashpal Tandon, South Africa and the O.A.U.: The Dialogue on the Dialogue Issue
Steve Wilmer, Ten Years of Vain Negotiations
Helge Hveem and Ole Kristian, Holthe, EEC and the Third World
Thomas G. Hart, Contradictions and Choice in the Revolution: Whither China and How
J. P. Roos, The Nature of Welfare under Capitalism

Vol. 2/3 (1972)
Johan Galtung, Theory and Practice of Security
Raimo Väyrynen, ESC and EEC: The Incompatibles?
Evgeny Chossudovsky, Towards the ESC Conference: New Horizons for East-West Economic Co-operation
Sverre Lodgaard, Political Change and Economic Reorientation in Europe—The Role of Industrial Cooperation
Pertti Joenniemi, Force Reductions and ESC: Chances and Pitfalls

Vol. 2/4 (1972)
Ulrich Albrecht et al., Is Europe to Demilitarize? Analysis and Some Practical Suggestions

Vol. 3/1 (1973)
Tom Gronberg and Kaarle Nordenstreng, Approaching International Control of Satellite Communication
Armand Mattelart, Modern Communication Technologies and New Facets of Cultural Imperialism
Tapio Varis, European Television Exchanges and Connections with the Rest of the World
Raimo Väyrynen, Military Uses of Satellite Communication

Vol. 3/2 (1973)
Per Olav Reinton, The Green Revolution Experience
Gerd Junne, Euromoney, Multinational Corporations, and the Nation State
Solveig Hall, Who Is the Establishment Peacenik: A Study of Nobel Peace Prize Recipients
Ingrid Eide and Sverre Lodgaard, Internationalization of the Nobel Committee
Lothar Brock, Peaceful Cooperation in Europe: Some Remarks on the Task of the Scientist

Vol. 3/3 (1973)
Holger Rotkirch, Prospects for a New Law of the Sea: A Struggle for the Oceans and Their Resources
Raimo Väyrynen, Conflicts of Interests in Territorial Waters: Iceland, Ecuador and the Straits of Malacca
Claes Brundenius, The Rise and Fall of the Peruvian Fishmeal Industry

Vol. 3/4 (1973)

James Petras and Betty Petras, The Chilean Coup

Pasi Patokallio, Whither Energy Crisis?

Gunnar Adler-Karlsson, Some Roads to Humanicide

Karin Hjertonsson, A Study on the Prospects of Compliance with the Convention on Biological Weapons

Jorma K. Miettinen, Recent Developments in Tactical Nuclear Weapons and Their Bearing on Nuclear Non-Proliferation

Vol. 4/1 (1974)

Richard A. Falk, Law and Responsibility in Warfare: The Vietnam Experience

Malvern Lumsden, New Military Technology and the Erosion of International Law: The Case of the Dum-dum Bullets Today

Hans Blix, Current Efforts to Prohibit the Use of Certain Conventional Weapons

Allan Rosas, Wars of National Liberation—International or Non-International Armed Conflicts?

Pertti Joenniemi and Adam Roberts, Civil Resistance and the Law of Military Occupations

Recommendation

Books

Vol. 4/2 (1974)

Unto Vesa, The Development of Chinese Thinking on Disarmament

Raimo Väyrynen, Relations Between the Nordic Countries and the European Community: An Analysis of Main Trends

Zdenek Červenka, The Emergence and Significance of the African-Arab Solidarity

Godfried van Benthem van den Bergh, A Note on Time Demarcation in Conflict Theory

Books

Vol. 4/3 (1974)

Keith D. Suter, The Work of the ICRC in Vietnam: An Evaluation

Some Comments on Keith D. Suter's Article

James F. Petras, The U.S.–Cuban Policy Debate

Jorma K. Miettinen, Schlesinger's New Strategy and Its Implications for Europe

Ulrich Albrecht, Armaments and Inflation

Books

Vol. 4/4 (1974)

Holger Rotkirch, The UN Law of the Sea Conference after Caracas

Johan Galtung, How Can World Interests Be Better Promoted? Some ideas based on the Caracas conference

Esko Antola, The Flag of Convenience System: Freedom of the Seas for Big Capital

Raimo Väyrynen, The Struggle for Sea-bed Minerals

Books

Vol. 5/1 (1975)

René V. L. Wadlow, The Nuclear Non-Proliferation Treaty Review Conference: May 1975

Sverre Lodgaard, Reviewing the Non-Proliferation Treaty: Status and Prospects

A. Kalyadin, The Struggle for Disarmament: New Perspectives

R. R. Subramanian, Nuclear India and the NPT: Prospects for Future?

Jan Prawitz, Nuclear India and the NPT: Actions for the Future

Unto Vesa, The Revival of Proposals for Nuclear-Free Zones

Recommendations to Governments

Treaty on the Non-Proliferation of Nuclear Weapons

Books

Vol. 5/2 (1975)

Luis Herrera, Chilean Economy: Medicine Killing the Patient?

Herbert I. Schiller, Genesis of the Free Flow of Information Principles: The Imposition of Communications Domination

Henrik Plaschke, International Subcontracting: On the Migration of Labour Intensive Processing from the Center to the Periphery of Capitalism

Gert Krell, Military-Industrial Complex, Armaments Policy and the National Priorities Debate in the 92nd U.S. Senate (1971–72)

David P. Forsyth, The Work of the ICRC: A Broader View

International Interactions: A Transnational Multidisciplinary Journal. University of North Carolina, Chapel Hill, North Carolina 27514. Publishers: Gordon & Breach, Inc./Ltd., One Park Avenue South, New York 10016 or 41/42 William IV Street, London W.C. 2, England.

Quarterly since January 1974; $12 per year.

"Empirical studies and articles covering a wide range of problems in international interactions; research notes and book reviews."

Vol. 1/1 (1974)

Edward E. Azar, Introduction

A. G. Newcombe, N. S. Newcombe, and G. D. Landrus, The Development of an Inter-Nation Tensiometer

W. Feld, Multinational Corporations and Regional Integration: Some Preliminary Reflections

P. L. Beardsley, Substantive Significance vs. Quantitive Rigor in Political Inquiry: Are the Two Compatible?

P. F. Kress, On Validating Simulation: With Special Attention to Simulation of International Politics

Albert F. Eldridge and C. M. Jenks, Cue-Giving in the General Assembly: An Inductive Approach

E. A. Baloyra, Comparing Political Regimes

William Eckhardt, Toward a Science of Value

Vol. 1/2 (1974)

The Editor, Introduction

Nazli Choucri, Forecasting in International Relations: Problems and Prospects

Jurg Steiner, Why Hostility among Subcultures? An Explanatory Model and Some Applications to the European Community

Daniel Frei, Conflict Reduction by Mutual Disengagement

Research Note
Ronald J. Yalem, The Comparative Analysis of International Organizations
Book Reviews
Vol. 1/3 (1974)
Editorial Notes
Joseph S. Tulchin, Decolonizing an Informal Empire: Argentina, Great Britain, and the United States, 1930–1943
Jeffrey Hart, Structures of Influence and Cooperation-Conflict
Gary A. Hill and Peter H. Fenn, Comparing Event Flows: *The New York Times* and *The Times* of London: Conceptual Issues and Case Studies
Jack M. Schick, Crisis Studies and the Near East: The Cases of Lebanon and Cyprus
Vol. 1/4 (1974) Special Issue
Edward E. Azar, Editorial Notes
Alastair Buchan, The Emerging International System: A European Perspective
Joseph Coates, Future Societal Perspective
Norman Alcock, Reaction to Two Perspectives, the Present and the Future
Richard A. Brody, The Emerging International System: Policy Implications
William I. Cargo, American Foreign Policy: A Look Ahead
Andrew M. Scott, The Global System and the Implications of Interactions
Warren R. Phillips, Patrick T. Callahan, and Robert C. Crain, Simulated Foreign Policy Exchanges: The Rationale Underlying a Theory of Foreign Policy Interaction
Research Notes
Jack E. Vincent, The Properties of the Distance Metric in Social Field Theory
Hanna Newcombe, Guaranteed Annual Income Plan for Nations
Louis Rene Beres, On The Study Of Legal Order in Future World Systems
Marvin S. Soroos, Behavioral Science, Forecasting, and the Designing of Alternative Future Worlds
Frederic S. Pearson and Robert Baumann, Foreign Military Intervention by Large and Small Powers
Vol. 2/1 (1975)
Edward E. Azar, Introduction
Warren R. Phillips, The Theoretical Approaches in the Events of Data Movement
Alvin Richman, Issues in the Conceptualization and Measurement of Events Data
Hamid Mowlana, A Paradigm for Source Analysis in Events Data Research: Mass Media and the Problems of Validity
Russell J. Leng, The Future of Events Data Marriages: A Question of Compatibility

Research Note
P. Terrence Hopmann and Charles Walcott, The Bargaining Process in
International Arms Control Negotiations

International Studies Quarterly. Sage Publications, Inc., 275 South
Beverly Drive, Beverly Hills, California 90212.
Quarterly since March 1967: $20 per year.
Supersedes *Background: Journal of the International Studies Association*. Official publication of the International Studies Association.

"Concerned with cross-national, interdisciplinary research. . . .
Articles, discussions, and reviews are drawn from such subfields as interpolimetrics, comparative interdisciplinary studies, international organization, military affairs, foreign policy, international law, international ecology, and research utilization in the field of international studies."

Vol. 11/1 (Mar. 1967)
In Memoriam: Edgar S. Furniss, Jr.
Vernon Van Dyke, Under New Management
George I. Blanksten, Ideology and Nation-Building in the Contemporary World
Bruce M. Russett, The Ecology of Future International Politics
Irving Louis Horowitz, Social Science and Public Policy: an Examination of the Political Foundations of Modern Research
William R. Caspary, Richardson's Model of Arms Races: Description, Critique, and an Alternative Model
Reviews and Other Discussion
Claire Nader, An Invitation
Robert E. Riggs, The United Nations as an Influence on United States Policy

Vol. 11/2 (June 1967)
Andrew W. Cordier, The Professionalization of International Studies
John Gange, Are We Training Professionals in International Affairs?
Chadwick F. Alger, Internationalizing Colleges and Universities
Thomas W. Robinson, A National Interest Analysis of Sino-Soviet Relations
Urban Whitaker and Bruce Davis, The Nationalization of Ridgeway, South Carolina
Richard Butwell, International Studies and Teacher Education
Donald E. Weatherbee, Approaches to the Teaching of International Relations

Vol. 11/3 (Sept. 1967)
Kenneth N. Waltz, The Politics of Peace
P. Terry Hopmann, International Conflict and Cohesion in the Communist System
James M. Hunter, The Extent of the Legal Confines, the State-Idea, and the Zone of Function of France and Germany in the Saarland
Maurice A. East and Phillip M. Gregg, Factors Influencing Cooperation and Conflict in the International System

Leon Gordenker on Robert E. Riggs, The United Nations as an Influ-
ence on United States Policy, with rejoinder
Asa Smith, Panel on Force, Order and Justice
Laurence D. Cherkis, Panel on The Scientific Challenge
Stephen Conn, Panel on The Government Research, and the Integrity
of the Scholar
Robert W. Dean, Panel on The Role of Federal Support in Interna-
tional Education
John P. Entelis, Panel on Graduate Study in International Relations:
Problems and Prospects
Vol. 11/4 (Dec. 1967)
Stanley J. Michalak, Jr., Peacekeeping and the United Nations: The
Problem of Responsibility
Michael Haas, Bridge-Building in International Relations: A Neotradi-
tional Plea
Edgar S. Furniss, Jr., Western Alliance Development and Technologi-
cal Cooperation
Annette Baker Fox, A New Task for NATO?
Robert Jervis, The Costs of the Scientific Study of Politics: An Examina-
tion of the Stanford Content Analysis Studies
Robert C. North, Research Pluralism and the International Elephant
Vol. 12/1 (Mar. 1968)
William T. R. Fox, Science, Technology and International Politics
Herbert C. Kelman, The Use of University Resources in Foreign Policy
Research
Reviews and Other Discussion
Donald J. Puchala, The Pattern of Contemporary Regional Integration
Edwin H. Fedder, The Concept of Alliance
Ronald J. Yalem, Comment on Michael Haas, Bridge-Building in In-
ternational Relations: A Neotraditional Plea
Reports on Panel Discussions at ISA Annual Meeting
Jane Colvin (Rapporteur), Panel on Emerging Patterns in European
Security
Jasperdean C. Kobes (Rapporteur), Panel on Studies in World Affairs at
the Secondary School Level
Paul Sherman (Rapporteur), Panel on The Place of Law in Interna-
tional Studies
James Paul (Rapporteur), Panel on The Contribution of Regional
Studies to an Understanding of World Politics
Paul E. Beard (Rapporteur), Panel on The Public Impact Upon Foreign
Policy
Christopher Beal (Rapporteur), Panel on Methodology in International
Studies: A Critique
L. J. Jacques Vallet (Rapporteur), Panel on Patterns of International
Institutionalism
Vol. 12/2 (June 1968)
David A. Baldwin, Canadian-American Relations: Myth and Reality

William C. Rogers and Barney Uhlig, Small Town and Rural Midwest Foreign Policy Opinion Makers

Edmund A. Shaker, Canadian-American Relations

Vol. 13/4 (Dec. 1969)

Peter Berton, International Subsystems—A Submacro Approach to International Studies

Michael Banks, Systems Analysis and the Study of Regions

Louis J. Cantori and Steven L. Spiegel, International Regions: A Comparative Approach to Five Subordinate Systems

John H. Sigler, New Flows in the North African International Subsystem

Thomas W. Robinson, Systems Theory and the Communist System

Donald C. Hellmann, The Emergence of an East Asian International Subsystem

Vol. 14/1 (Mar. 1970)

Werner Levi, Ideology, Interests and Foreign Policy

Donald J. Puchala, The Common Market and Political Federation in Western European Public Opinion

Manus Midlarsky, Mathematical Models of Instability and a Theory of Diffusion

Andrew M. Scott, Environmental Change and Organizational Adaptation

John E. Harr, The Issue of Competence in the Department of State

Raymond Tanter, Foreign Affairs Analysis

Norman D. Palmer and E. Raymond Platig, The Government Scholar and Foreign Affairs Research

Vol. 14/2 (June 1970)

Leon V. Sigal, The Rational Policy Model and the Formosa Straits Crises

Randolph M. Siverson, International Conflict and Perceptions of Injury

C. R. Mitchell, Civil Strife and the Involvement of External Parties

Kenneth W. Terhune and Joseph M. Firestone, Global War, Limited War, and Peace

Kenneth Ray Young, Neutralism in Laos and Cambodia

Andrew M. Scott, Foreign Affairs Analysis

E. Raymond Platig, Competence in Foreign Affairs Analysis

Vol. 14/3 (Sept. 1970)

Kal J. Holsti, National Role Conceptions in the Study of Foreign Policy

Carl W. Backman, Role Theory and International Relations

Cyril E. Black, Accessibility of Government-Sponsored Research in International Studies

N. G. Onuf, International Law-in-Action and the Numbers Game

Irvin L. White, International Law-in-Action and the Numbers Game

Vol. 14/4 (Dec. 1970)

Walter C. Soderlund, An Analysis of the Guerrilla Insurgency and Coup d'Etat as Techniques of Indirect Aggression

James A. Caporaso, The Cases of Transport Integration in the European Economic Community

Robert A. Gorman, A Critical Analysis of Decision-Making Theory

William D. Coplin, The State System Exercise
Vol. 15/1 (Mar. 1971)
Jean-Jacques Salomon, Europe and the Technological Gaps
Stuart A. Scheingold, The North Atlantic Area as a Policy Arena
Glenn H. Snyder, Prisoner's Dilemma and Chicken Models in International Politics
Robert L. Pfaltzgraff, Jr., International Studies in the 1970's
Vol. 15/2 (June 1971)
J. Stephen Hoadley and Sukehiro Hasegawa, Sino-Japanese Relations 1950–1970
David W. Paul, Soviet Foreign Policy and the Invasion of Czechoslovakia
Philip E. Jacob, The Limits of Value Consensus
Elmer Plischke, Research on the Conduct of United States Foreign Relations
Vol. 15/3 (Sept. 1971)
Cal Clark, Foreign Trade as an Indicator of Political Integration in the Soviet Bloc
James E. Todd, The Law-Making Behavior of States in the United Nations as a Function of Their Location within Formal World Regions
John W. Chapman, Political Forecasting and Strategic Planning
Michael P. Sullivan, International Bargaining Behavior
Vol. 15/4 (Dec. 1971)
Stanley J. Michalak, Jr., The League of Nations and the United Nations in World Politics
Reginald Smart, The Goals and Definitions of International Education
Jack E. Vincent et al., Generating Some Empirically Based Indices for International Alliance and Regional Systems Operating in the Early 1960's
Richard J. Powers, Who Fathered Containment?
Vol. 16/1 (Mar. 1972)
John W. Burton, Resolution of Conflict
Jean-Pierre Cot, On Resolution of Conflict with Special Reference to the Cyprus Conflict
John W. Burton, Some Further Comments—In Reply to Criticism
Laura Nader, Resolution of Conflict
J. Bowyer Bell, Assassination in International Politics
Richard W. Chadwick, Theory Development Through Simulation
Vol. 16/2 (June 1972)
Paul G. Lauren, Ultimata and Coercive Diplomacy
Louis M. Terrell, Patterns of International Involvement and International Violence
Stephen A. Garrett, Foreign Policy and the American Constitution
Sheldon Appleton, Systematic Bias in U.S. Foreign Affairs Reporting
Bernard C. Cohen, Systematic Bias in U.S. Foreign Affairs Reporting
John W. Eley, Toward a Theory of Intervention

Vol. 16/3 (Sept. 1972)

Barry B. Hughes and John E. Schwarz, Dimensions of Political Integration and the Experience of the European Community

William Welch, The Possibility of an International Discipline of International Affairs

Jerone Stephens, An Appraisal of Some System Approaches in the Study of International Systems

Joanne F. Loomba, The Relationship of Images and Political Affiliations to Orientations Toward Foreign Aid for India

Edward E. Azar et al., The Problem of Source Coverage in the Use of International Events Data

John Dow et al., Computer Routines for Arraying Aggregate Data

Vol. 16/4 (Dec. 1972)

George Modelski, Multinational Business

J. Boddewyn and Ashok Kapoor, The External Relations of American Multinational Enterprises

Robert Barnes, International Oil Companies Confront Governments

John Fayerweather, Elite Attitudes Toward Multinational Firms

Jonathan F. Galloway, The Military Industrial Linkages of U.S.-Based Multinational Corporations

Fouad Ajami, Corporate Giants: Some Global Social Costs

Friedrich Von Krosigk, Marx, Universalism, and Contemporary World Business

Fouad Ajami and David Osterberg, The Multinational Corporation

Vol. 17/1 (Mar. 1973)

Ernst B. Haas and Edward Thomas Rowe, Regional Organizations in the United Nations

Kenneth A. Dahlberg, The Technological Ethic and the Spirit of International Relations

William R. Thompson, The Regional Subsystem

James N. Rosenau et al., The Adaptation of Foreign Policy Research

Vol. 17/2 (June 1973)

Michael J. Shapiro and G. Matthew Bonham, Cognitive Process and Foreign Policy Decision-Making

Charles F. Doran et al., A Test of Cross-National Event Reliability

David S. McLellan, Who Fathered Containment?

Werner Levi, Third World States

Vol. 17/3 (Sept. 1973)

Michael J. Brenner, The Problem of Innovation and the Nixon-Kissinger Foreign Policy

Thomas C. Wiegele, Decision-Making in an International Crisis

Margaret L. Cormack, American Students in India

Eng-Kung Yeh et al., The American Student in Taiwan

Vol. 17/4 (Dec. 1973)

Vernon Van Dyke, Equality and Discrimination in Education

Jack Vincent et al., Empirical Tests of Attribute, Social Field, and Status Field Theories on International Relations Data

Robert M. Jackson, Patterns of Political Interaction
Richard E. Hayes, Identifying and Measuring Changes in the Frequency of Event Data
Charles W. Hultman, Mature Creditorship and the U.S. Position in the World Economy
Vol. 18/1 (Mar. 1974)
Barbara G. Haskel, Disparities, Strategies, and Opportunity Costs
David Garnham, State Department Rigidity
Arend Lijphart, The Structure of the Theoretical Revolution in International Relations
David Krieger, A Caribbean Community for Ocean Development
Norman Furniss, Comparative Government Texts
Vol. 18/2 (June 1974)
Michael Brecher, Inputs and Decisions for War and Peace: The Israel Experience
Thomas J. Volgy, Reducing Conflict in International Politics: The Impact of Structural Variables
Michael K. O'Leary, William D. Coplin, Howard B. Shapiro, and Dale Dean, The Quest for Relevance: Quantitative International Relations Research and Government Foreign Affairs Analysis
Edward Thomas Rowe, Aid and Coups d'Etat: Aspects of the Impact of American Military Assistance Programs in the Less Developed Countries
Vol. 18/3 (Sept. 1974)
Frederic S. Pearson, Foreign Military Interventions and Domestic Disputes
R. Stephen Milne, Impulses and Obstacles to Caribbean Political Integration: Academic Theory and Guyana's Experience
Leo A. Hazlewood and Gerald T. West, Bivariate Associations, Factor Structures, and Substantive Impact: The "Source Coverage" Problem Revisited
James N. Rosenau, Assessment in International Studies: Ego Trip or Feedback?
Roger E. Kanet, Integration Theory and the Study of Eastern Europe
Vol. 18/4 (Dec. 1974)
John J. Weltman, On the Obsolescence of War: An Essay in Policy and Theory
Werner Levi, International Law in a Multicultural World
Susan Aurelia Gitelson, Why Do Small States Break Diplomatic Relations with Outside Powers? Lessons from the African Experience
Lawrence S. Finkelstein, International Organizations and Change: The Past as Prologue
Vol. 19/1 (Mar. 1975)
Marc Lindenberg, Multinational Corporations and Reinvestment Rates: The Case of the Pioneer Industry Program in Malaysia
James M. McCormick, Evaluating Models of Crisis Behavior: Some Evidence from the Middle East

Charles Lockhart, The Varying Fortunes of Incremental Commitment: An Inquiry into the Cuban and Southeast Asian Cases
Michael D. Wallace, Clusters of Nations in the Global System, 1865–1964: Some Preliminary Evidence
Joseph P. Smaldone, Comparative Government Texts Revisited: A Rejoinder to Professor Furniss
Norman Furniss, The State of Comparative Government
Vol. 19/2 (June 1975)
Kal Holsti, Editor's Report
T. Baumgartner and T. R. Burns, The Structuring of International Economic Relations
Stephen J. Andriole, Jonathan Wilkenfeld, and Gerald W. Hopple, A Framework for the Comparative Analysis of Foreign Policy Behavior
David W. Moore, Repredicting Voting Patterns in the General Assembly: A Methodological Note
Francis W. Hoole and Harvey J. Tucker, Data on International Organizations: Availability and Needs
Abraham Ben-Zvi, American Preconceptions and Policies Toward Japan, 1940–1941: A Case Study in Misperception
Vol. 19/3 (Sept. 1975)
B. Thomas Trout, Rhetoric Revisited: Political Legitimation and the Cold War
Michael B. Dolan, The Study of Regional Integration: A Quantitative Analysis of the Neo-Functionalist and Systemic Approaches
Amos Perlmutter, Crisis Management: Kissinger's Middle East Negotiations (October 1973–June 1974)
George T. Duncan and Randolph M. Siverson, Markov Chain Models for Conflict Analysis: Results from Sino-Indian Relations, 1959–1964
William D. Coplin, A Dissenting Viewpoint on Comparative Government Texts: Comments on the Smaldone-Furniss Discussion
Vol. 19/4 (Dec. 1975)
Jonathan Wilkenfeld and Judith Torney, From the Editors
Karl W. Deutsch, On Inequality and Limited Growth: Some World Political Effects
Stephen S. Kaplan, U.S. Arms Transfers to Latin America, 1945–1974: Rational Strategy, Bureaucratic Politics, and Executive Parameters
Herman M. Weil, Can Bureaucracies Be Rational Actors? Foreign Policy Decision-Making in North Vietnam
Patrick J. McGowan and Klaus-Peter Gottwald, Small State Foreign Policies: A Comparative Study of Participation, Conflict, and Political and Economic Dependence in Black Africa
Paul Marantz, Prelude to Detente: Doctrinal Change Under Khrushchev
Journal of Conflict Resolution. Political Science Department, Yale University, 124 Prospect Street, New Haven, Connecticut 06520. Publisher: Sage Publications, Inc., 275 South Beverly Drive, Beverly Hills, California 90212.

Quarterly since 1957; $12 per year.
"A serious interdisciplinary social science journal which focuses on analysis of the causes, prevention, and solution of international, domestic, and inter-personal conflicts. Draws upon the insights of political science, economics, history, social psychology, modeling and gaming techniques."

Vol. 1/1 (1957)

Quincy Wright, The Value for Conflict Resolution of a General Discipline of International Relations

Morris Janowitz, Military Elites and the Study of War

Thomas C. Schelling, Bargaining, Communication, and Limited War

Daniel J. Levinson, Authoritarian Personality and Foreign Policy

Harold Guetzkow, Isolation and Collaboration: A Partial Theory of International Relations

Ann Douglas, The Peaceful Settlement of Industrial and Intergroup Disputes

Vol. 1/2 (1957)

Jessie Bernard, Parties and Issues in Conflict

Kenneth Boulding, Organization and Conflict

Judson S. Brown, Principles of Intrapersonal Conflict

St. Clair Drake, Some Observations on Interethnic Conflict as One Type of Intergroup Conflict

Robert Dubin, Industrial Conflict and Social Welfare

Karl W. Deutsch, Mass Communications and the Loss of Freedom in National Decision-Making: A Possible Research Approach to Interstate Conflicts

Raymond W. Mack and Richard C. Snyder, The Analysis of Social Conflict—Toward an Overview and Synthesis

Vol. 1/3 (1957)

Anatol Rapoport, Lewis F. Richardson's Mathematical Theory of War

Stephen A. Richardson, Lewis Fry Richardson: A Personal Biography

Vol. 1/4 (1957)

Harold and Margaret Sprout, Environmental Factors in the Study of International Politics

George Levinger, Kurt Lewin's Approach to Conflict and Its Resolution: A Review with Some Extensions

Morris Rosenberg, Misanthropy and Attitudes toward International Affairs

Stewart E. Perry, Notes on the Role of the National: A Social-Psychological Concept for the Study of International Relations

Ralph Cassady, Jr., Taxicab Rate War: Counterpart of International Conflict

Fred A. Sondermann, A Note on Harold Guetzkow's "Isolation and Collaboration"

Vol. 2/1 (1958)

Herbert C. Kelman, Introduction to Issue on Attitudes and Communication

William A. Scott, Rationality and Nonrationality of International Attitudes

Arthur I. Gladstone and Martha A. Taylor, Threat-Related Attitudes and Reactions to Communications about International Events

Thomas F. Pettigrew, Personality and Sociocultural Factors in Intergroup Attitudes: A Cross-National Comparison

Ralph K. White, The Cold War and the Modal Philosophy

Herbert C. Kelman, Compliance, Identification, and Internalization: Three Processes of Attitude Change

Jeanne Watson and Ronald Lippitt, Cross-Cultural Experience as a Source of Attitude Change

Raymond A. Bauer, The Communicator and the Audience

M. D. Feld, Political Policy and Persuasion: The Role of Communications from Political Leaders

J. David Singer, Threat-Perception and the Armament-Tension Dilemma

Vol. 2/2 (1958)

Bernard Fensterwald, Jr., The Anatomy of American "Isolationism" and Expansionism, I

Arne Naess, A Systematization of Gandhian Ethics of Conflict Resolution

Stefan Valavanis, The Resolution of Conflict When Utilities Interact

Ralf Dahrendorf, Toward a Theory of Social Conflict

Book Reviews

Robert H. Cory, Jr.

Kenneth Thompson

Charles Boasson

Vol. 2/3 (1958) Monograph Issue

Thomas C. Schelling, The Strategy of Conflict: Prospectus for a Reorientation of Game Theory

Vol. 2/4 (1958)

Morton Deutsch, Trust and Suspicion

Bernard Fensterwald, Jr., The Anatomy of American "Isolationism" and Expansionism

Mathilda Holzman, Theories of Choice and Conflict in Psychology and Economics

Roy Pierce, Political Power, Technology, and Total War: Two French Views

Book Reviews

Kenneth Boulding

Quincy Wright

Notes

Morton A. Kaplan

William J. MacKinnon

Vol. 3/1 (1959)

Erik Rinde and Stein Rokkan, Toward an International Program of Research on the Handling of Conflicts: Introduction

Howard E. Koch, Jr., Robert C. North, and Dina A. Zinnes, Some Theoretical Notes on Geography and International Conflict

Ladis K. D. Kristof, The Origins and Evolution of Geopolitics

Richard Hartshorne, Political Geography in the Modern World

Charles Konigsberg, Climate and Society: A Review of the Literature

Rhoads Murphey, Economic Conflicts in South Asia

Emrys Jones, Problems of Partition and Segregation in Northern Ireland

John M. Dunn, American Dependence on Materials Imports: The World-Wide Resource Base

Wallace C. Magathan, Some Bases of West German Military Policy

F. Clifford German, A Tentative Evaluation of World Power

Harold and Margaret Sprout, Geography and International Politics in an Era of Revolutionary Change

Vol. 4/2 (1960)

Glenn H. Snyder, Deterrence and Power

Harvey Wheeler, The Role of Myth Systems in American-Soviet Relations

Åke Bjerstedt, "Ego-Involved World-Mindedness," Nationality Images, and Methods of Research: A Methodological Note

J. Sayer Minas, Alvin Scodel, David Marlowe, and Harve Rawson, Some Descriptive Aspects of Two-Person Non-Zero-Sum Games, Part II

Gideon Sjoberg, Contradictory Functional Requirements and Social Systems

Robert O. Blood, Jr., Resolving Family Conflicts

Book Reviews

Inis L. Claude

Edwin C. Hoyt

Theodore F. Lentz

Vol. 4/3 (1960)

Inis L. Claude, Jr., Introduction

Zbigniew Brzezinski, Communist Ideology and International Affairs

John G. Kemeny, A Philosopher Looks at Political Science

Charles A. McClelland, The Function of Theory in International Relations

Myres S. McDougal, Some Basic Theoretical Concepts about International Law: A Policy-Oriented Framework of Inquiry

Robert C. North, Howard E. Koch, Jr., and Dina A. Zinnes, The Integrative Functions of Conflict

Vol. 4/4 (1960)

Jan J. Schokking and Nels Anderson, Observations on the European Integration Process

Werner Levi, On the Causes of War and the Conditions of Peace

Ronald J. Yalem, The "Theory of Ends" of Arnold Wolfers

Daniel R. Lutzker, Internationalism as a Predictor of Cooperative Behavior

Robert R. Blake and Jane Srygley Mouton, Comprehension of Own and of Outgroup Positions under Intergroup Competition

Book Reviews

J. David Singer
George Levinger
Christian Bay
Robert I. Crane

Discussion

William Paul Livant

Vol. 5/4 (1961)

Lewis A. Coser, The Termination of Conflict
Lee E. Preston, Utility Interactions in a Two-Person World
Daniel R. Lutzker, Sex Role, Cooperation and Competition in a Two-Person, Non-Zero-Sum Game
Paul Diesing, Bargaining Strategy and Union-Management Relationships
Benjamin Ward, Majority Rule and Allocation

Book Reviews

Lincoln E. Moses
Gene Sharp
Arthur Gladstone
Lewis Alexander
George Kish
James A. Robinson
Jan F. Triska

Vol. 6/1 (1962)

Harold W. Kuhn, Game Theory and Models of Negotiation
Dean G. Pruitt, An Analysis of Responsiveness between Nations
Fred Charles Iklé, in collaboration with Nathan Leites, Political Negotiation as a Process of Modifying Utilities
John C. Harsanyi, Bargaining in Ignorance of the Opponent's Utility Function
Arnold Zellner, War and Peace: A Fantasy in Game Theory?
Ward Edwards, Utility, Subjective Probability, Their Interaction and Variance Preferences
Morton Deutsch and Robert M. Krauss, Studies of Interpersonal Bargaining

Vol. 6/2 (1962)

Paul Y. Hammond, Some Difficulties of Self-Enforcing Arms Agreements
Robert C. Angell, Defense of What?
Donald H. Kobe, A Theory of Catalytic War
William H. Blanchard, National Myth, National Character, and National Policy: A Psychological Study of the U-2 Incident
Jane Srygley Mouton and Robert R. Blake, The Influence of Competitively Vested Interests on Judgments

Vilhelm Aubert, Competition and Dissensus: Two Types of Conflict and of Conflict Resolution

Harold L. Nieburg, Uses of Violence

Vern L. Bullough, The Roman Empire vs. Persia

Vol. 7/2 (1963)

Bruce M. Russett, The Calculus of Deterrence

William J. Horvath and Caxton C. Foster, Stochastic Models of War Alliances

Inis L. Claude, Jr., United Nations Use of Military Force

Allen R. Ferguson, Tactics in a Local Crisis

Book Reviews

Fred A. Sondermann

Gene M. Lyons

Amitai Etzioni

George Totten

S. Sidney Ulmer

Roy C. Macridis

Vol. 7/3 (1963) Weapons Management in World Politics

Proceedings of the first International Arms Control Symposium, Ann Arbor, Michigan, December 1962

Edited by J. David Singer

J. David Singer, Introduction

Warner R. Schilling, Weapons, Doctrine, and Arms Control: A Case from the Good Old Days

Thomas E. Phipps, Jr., Strategy of War Limitation

John T. McNaughton, Arms Restraint in Military Decisions

Joan V. Bondurant, Paraguerrilla Strategy: A New Concept in Arms Control

Lewis Coser, Peaceful Settlements and the Dysfunctions of Secrecy

Walter Goldstein, The Peaceful Limitations of Disputes: Police Powers and System Problems

Hubert H. Humphrey, Regional Arms Control Agreements

Franklin P. Huddle, Military Aspects of Independent Initiative in Arms Control

Quincy Wright, Conditions for Successful Disarmament

Clark C. Abt, Disarmament as a Strategy

Charles A. McClelland, Unmanaged Weapons and the Calculated Control of International Politics

William C. Foster, Risk and Security in the Age of Nuclear Weapons

Victor P. Karpov, Soviet Stand on Disarmament

Robert E. Matteson, Disarmament Prospects after Cuba

Gene M. Lyons, The Problem of Compliance under Arms Control Agreements

Karl W. Deutsch, The Commitment of National Legitimacy Symbols as a Verification Technique

Thomas C. O'Sullivan, Social Inspection

Lewis C. Bohn, Whose Nuclear Test: Nonphysical Inspection and the Nuclear Test Ban

Vol. 7/4 (1963) Monograph Issue

Book Reviews

Vol. 8/1 (1964)

Joseph I. Coffey, The Soviet View of a Disarmed World

Walter C. Clemens, Jr., Ideology in Soviet Disarmament Policy

Werner Levi, On the Causes of Peace

Marc Pilisuk and Anatol Rapoport, Stepwise Disarmament and Sudden Destruction in a Two-Person Game: A Research Tool

Peter H. Merkl, European Assembly Parties and National Delegations

Book Reviews

Kenneth E. Boulding

Leon D. Epstein

Chadwick F. Alger

Robert C. Angell

Charles B. Neff

Vol. 8/2 (1964)

Alice Langley Hsieh, The Sino-Soviet Nuclear Dialogue: 1963

Lynn Turgeon, The Enigma of Soviet Defense Expenditures

Michael Barkun, Conflict Resolution through Implicit Mediation

Paul C. Rosenblatt, Origins and Effects of Group Ethnocentrism and Nationalism

James A. Schellenberg, Distributive Justice and Collaboration in Non-Zero-Sum Games

V. Edwin Bixenstine, Norman Chambers, and Kellogg V. Wilson, Effects of Asymmetry in Payoff on Behavior in a Two-Person Non-Zero-Sum Game

Book Reviews

Lawrence S. Finkelstein

Bruce M. Russett

Paul Seabury

Maurice Waters

Alvin Z. Rubinstein

Robert W. Gregg

Willard Barber

Vol. 8/3 (1964)

Edward T. Rowe, The Emerging Anti-Colonial Consensus in the United Nations

Roland L. Warren, The Conflict Intersystem and the Change Agent

Amitai Etzioni, On Self-Encapsulating Conflicts

Kenneth W. Terhune, Nationalism among Foreign and American Students: An Exploratory Study

Bernhardt Lieberman, i-Trust: A Notion of Trust in Three-Person Games and in International Affairs

J. W. Burton, "Peace Research" and "International Relations"

Book Reviews

Inis L. Claude, Jr.

William T. R. Fox

Dina Zinnes

Maurice Waters

Alton Frye

William Zimmerman

Research Note

Brendan A. Maher

Vol. 8/4 (1964) Social Values and Foreign Policy Attitudes of Soviet and American Elites

Robert C. Angell, I: A Study of Social Values: Content Analysis of Elite Media

Vera S. Dunham, I: Social Values: Insights from Soviet Literature

Robert C. Angell, I: Social Values: Comparing the Sources; Appendices

J. David Singer, II: A Study of Foreign Policy Attitudes

Robert C. Angell and J. David Singer, III: Comparing the Findings of the Two Studies

Book Reviews

Allen D. Grimshaw

Richard W. Leopold

James K. Pollock

J. Alan Winter

Vol. 9/1 (1965)

John H. Kautsky, Myth, Self-Fulfilling Prophecy, and Symbolic Reassurance in the East-West Conflict

Bryant Wedge and Cyril Muromcew, Psychological Factors in Soviet Disarmament Negotiations

Jan F. Triska and David D. Finley, Soviet-American Relations: A Multiple Symmetry Model

Clinton F. Fink, More Calculations about Deterrence

Philip S. Gallo, Jr., and Charles G. McClintock, Cooperative and Competitive Behavior in Mixed-Motive Games

Harold H. Kelley, Experimental Studies of Threats in Interpersonal Negotiations

Gerald H. Shure, Robert J. Meeker, and Earle A. Hansford, The Effectiveness of Pacifist Strategies in Bargaining Games

Book Reviews

Charles M. Rehmus

Richard A. Falk

P. J. Vatikiotis

Lloyd Jensen

Vol. 9/2 (1965)

Lloyd Jensen, Military Capabilities and Bargaining Behavior

Martin Patchen, Decision Theory in the Study of National Action: Problems and a Proposal

Kenneth J. Gergen and Kurt W. Back, Aging, Time Perspective, and Preferred Solutions to International Conflicts

David R. Inglis, The Region-by-Region System of Inspection and Disarmament

Richard J. Krickus, On the Morality of Chemical/Biological War

Edward E. Sampson and Marcelle Kardush, Age, Sex, Class, and Race Differences in Response to a Two-Person Non-Zero-Sum Game

Robert Radlow, An Experimental Study of "Cooperation" in the Prisoner's Dilemma Game

Book Reviews
Charles W. Anderson
Karl A. Lamb
Leroy N. Rieselbach
Donald A. Strickland and Kathleen Archibald
Jean Siotis
Discussion
S. D. Vestermark, Jr., Social Science as Systematic Anxiety: A Case Study in the Civil Defense Dialogue

Vol. 9/3 (1965)
Wolfram F. Hanrieder, The International System: Bipolar or Multibloc?
Arnold M. Kuzmak, Technological Change and Stable Deterrence
Joel T. Campbell and Leila S. Cain, Public Opinion and the Outbreak of War
Comments on Campbell-Cain Article
Clark C. Abt, National Opinion and Military Security: Research Problems
William Eckhardt, War Propaganda, Welfare Values, and Political Ideologies
Stuart Oskamp and Daniel Perlman, Factors Affecting Cooperation in a Prisoner's Dilemma Game
Book Reviews
William H. Riker
Samuel H. Barnes
Warner R. Schilling
Lawrence Scheinman
Discussion
Arthur I. Waskow, Social Science and Civil Defense: Problems in the Study of an Unprecedented Future
Research Note
M. Jane Stroup, Problems of Research on Social Conflict in the Area of International Relations

Vol. 9/4 (1965)
Morton Gorden and Daniel Lerner, The Setting for European Arms Controls: Political and Strategic Choices of European Elites
Quincy Wright, The Escalation of International Conflicts
John R. Raser, Weapons Design and Arms Control: The Polaris Example
Robert B. McKersie, Charles R. Perry, and Richard E. Walton, Intra-organizational Bargaining in Labor Negotiations
Elliott McGinnies, Some Reactions of Japanese University Students to Persuasive Communications
Marc Pilisuk, Paul Potter, Anatol Rapoport, and J. Alan Winter, War Hawks and Peace Doves: Alternate Resolutions of Experimental Conflicts
Book Reviews
James N. Rosenau
Alan R. Beals

Richard W. Van Wagenen
Edgar S. Furniss, Jr.
Communication
J. David Singer, Negotiation by Proxy
Vol. 10/1 (1966)
Catherine S. Manno, Majority Decisions and Minority Responses in the UN General Assembly
Sheldon W. Simon, The Asian States and the ILO: New Problems in International Consensus
Raymond Tanter, Dimensions of Conflict Behavior within and between Nations, 1958–60
Rudolph J. Rummel, Dimensions of Conflict Behavior within Nations, 1946–59
William Erbe, Interest in a Peace Organization
Frederick J. Todd, Kenneth R. Hammond, and Marilyn M. Wilkins, Differential Effects of Ambiguous and Exact Feedback on Two-Person Conflict and Compromise
Charles G. McClintock and S. P. McNeel, Reward Level and Game Playing Behavior
Vol. 10/2 (1966)
Frank Klingberg, Predicting the Termination of War: Battle Casualties and Population Losses
George H. Quester, On the Identification of Real and Pretended Communist Military Doctrine
Paul Ekman, Edward R. Tufte, Kathleen Archibald, and Richard A. Brody, Coping with Cuba: Divergent Policy Preferences of State Political Leaders
Jerome Laulicht and N. Z. Alcock, The Support of Peace Research
Z. Pylyshyn, N. Agnew, and J. Illingworth, Comparison in Individuals and Pairs as Participants in a Mixed-Motive Game
Stuart Oskamp and D. Perlman, Effects of Friendship and Disliking on Cooperation in a Mixed-Motive Game
Book Reviews
Fred A. Sondermann
Cecil V. Crabb, Jr.
Edward H. Buehrig
Vol. 10/3 (1966)
Ivo K. and Rosalind L. Feierabend, Aggressive Behaviors within Politics, 1948–62
Kal J. Holsti, Resolving International Conflicts: A Taxonomy of Behavior and Some Figures on Procedures
Wolfram F. Hanrieder, International Organizations and International Systems
Richard N. Rosecrance, Bipolarity, Multipolarity, and the Future
Ralph M. Goldman, A Theory of Conflict Processes and Organizational Offices
Lillian Randolph, A Suggested Model of International Negotiations
L. G. Morehous, One-Play, Two-Play, Five-Play, and Ten-Play Runs of Prisoner's Dilemma

Anatol Rapoport and P. S. Dale, The "End" and "Start" Effects in Iterated Prisoner's Dilemma
Book Reviews
John R. Raser
B. G. Bechhoefer
Communication
C. D. Sullivan
Vol. 10/4 (1966)
Brent Rutherford, Psychopathology, Decision-Making, and Political Involvement
B. M. Blechman, The Quantitative Evaluation of Foreign Policy Alternatives
Gerald Marwell, Conflict over Proposed Group Actions: A Typology of Cleavage
Alfred O. Hero, Jr., The American Public and the UN, 1954–1966
V. E. Bixenstine and H. Blundell, Control of Choice Exerted by Structural Factors in Two-Person, Non-Zero-Sum Games
V. E. Bixenstine, Clifford A. Levitt, and Kellogg V. Wilson, Collaboration among Six Persons in a Prisoner's Dilemma Game
R. Radlow and M. F. Weidner, Unenforced Commitments in Non-Constant-Sum Games
F. T. Dolbear and L. B. Lave, Risk Orientation as a Predictor in Prisoner's Dilemma
Book Reviews
Melvin Small
William Zimmerman
Vol. 11/1 (1967)
Leopold Pospisil, Legal Levels and Multiplicity of Legal Systems in Human Societies
Harold D. Lasswell and Richard Arens, The Role of Sanction in Conflict Resolution
Vilhelm Aubert, Courts and Conflict Resolution
Jerome H. Skolnick, Social Control in the Adversary System
David J. Danelski, Conflict and Its Resolution in the Supreme Court
Robert Axelrod, Conflict of Interest: An Axiomatic Approach
Anatol Rapoport, A Note on the Index of Cooperation for Prisoner's Dilemma
T. Harford and L. Solomon, Reformed Sinner and Lapsed Saint Strategies in the Prisoner's Dilemma Game
Marc Pilisuk et al., Boredom vs. Cognitive Reappraisal in the Development of Cooperative Strategy
Book Review
R. Roger Majak
Communications
Peter Bondanella
R. Norman Junker
Jim McNab
Wayne Mixon
J. P. Whitson

Communication
Berkley B. Eddins

Vol. 12/1 (1968)

Theodore Caplow and Kurt Finsterbusch, France and Other Countries: A Study of International Interaction

Roland Robertson, Strategic Relations between National Societies: A Sociological Analysis

Thomas C. Schelling, Game Theory and the Study of Ethical Systems

Daniel Druckman, Ethnocentrism in the Inter-Nation Simulation

Edward D. Hoedemaker, Distrust and Aggression: An Interpersonal-International Analogy

Martin Shubik, On the Study of Disarmament and Escalation

John Thibaut, The Development of Contractual Norms in Bargaining: Replication and Variation

Book Reviews
Jessie Bernard
Ronald Inglehart

Communication
Joseph W. Eaton

Vol. 12/2 (1968)

Stephen G. Xydis, The UN General Assembly as an Instrument of Greek Policy: Cyprus, 1954–58

Robert A. Bernstein and Peter D. Weldon, A Structural Approach to the Analysis of International Relations

Frank H. Denton and Warren Phillips, Some Patterns in the History of Violence

Allan Mazur, A Nonrational Approach to Theories of Conflict and Coalitions

James L. Phillips and Lawrence Nitz, Social Contacts in a Three-Person "Political Convention" Situation

David A. Summers, Conflict, Compromise, and Belief Change in a Decision-Making Task

James P. Gahagan and James T. Tedeschi, Strategy and the Credibility of Promises in the Prisoner's Dilemma Game

William M. Knapp and Jerome E. Podell, Mental Patients, Prisoners, and Students with Simulated Partners in a Mixed-Motive Game

Book Reviews
S. Sidney Ulmer
Melvin Small
Dina A. Zinnes

Vol. 12/3 (1968)

Ali A. Mazrui, Anti-Militarism and Political Militancy in Tanzania

Bruce M. Russett, Components of an Operational Theory of International Alliance Formation

Albert Wohlstetter, Theory and Opposed-Systems Design

Margaret G. Hermann and Nathan Kogan, Negotiation in Leader and Delegate Groups

Vol. 13/3 (1969)

Jurg Steiner, Nonviolent Conflict Resolution in Democratic Systems: Switzerland

I. A. Litvak and C. J. Maule, Conflict Resolution and Extraterritoriality

John Delamater, Daniel Katz, and Herbert C. Kelman, On the Nature of National Involvement: A Preliminary Study

Stephen A. Cobb, Defense Spending and Foreign Policy in the House of Representatives

Donnel Wallace and Paul Rothaus, Communication, Group Loyalty and Trust in the PD Game

Lawrence H. Nitz and James L. Phillips, The Effects of Divisibility of Payoff on Confederate Behavior

Vol. 13/4 (1969)

Richard E. Gift, Trading in a Threat System: The U.S.-Soviet Case

Dorothy Wertz, Conflict Resolution in the Medieval Morality Plays

Doris A. Graber, Perceptions of Middle East Conflict in the UN, 1953–1965

Robert J. Meeker and Gerald H. Shure, Pacifist Bargaining Tactics: Some Outsider Influences

Jack E. Vincent and William M. Knapp, The Effect of Mediation on the Perceived Firmness of the Opponent

Vol. 14/1 (1970)

R. C. Raack, When Plans Fail: Small Group Behavior and Decision-Making in the Conspiracy of 1808 in Germany

Gunther Luschen, Cooperation, Association, and Contest

Edmund S. Glenn et al., A Cognitive Interaction Model to Analyze Culture Conflict in International Relations

John D. Mitchell, Cross-cutting Memberships, Integration and the International System

James T. Tedeschi, Thomas Bonoma, and Noel Novinson, Behavior of a Threatener: Retaliation vs. Fixed Opportunity Costs

J. R. Emshoff and Russell L. Ackoff, Explanatory Models of Interactive Choice Behavior

Carol J. Orwant and Jack E. Orwant, A Comparison of Interpreted and Abstract Versions of Mixed-Motive Games

Yoshitaka Umeoka, A 2 × 2 Non-constant-sum Game with a Coordination Problem

Joseph D. Ben-Dak, Time for Reorientation: A Review of Recent Research on the Arab-Israeli Conflict

Joel W. Goldstein, The Psychology of Conflict and International Relations: A Course Plan and Bibliography

Vol. 14/2 (1970)

George Modelski, The World's Foreign Ministers: A Political Elite

Martin Shubik, Game Theory, Behavior and the Paradox of the Prisoner's Dilemma: Three Solutions

David W. Conrath, Experience as a Factor in Experimental Gaming Behavior

Kenneth W. Terhune, From National Character to National Behavior:
A Reformulation
H. Merrill Jackson, Social Progress and Mental Health
Anatol Rapoport, Can Peace Research Be Applied?
Vol. 14/3 (1970)
Ole R. Holsti, Individual Differences in Definition of the Situation
Ernst F. Mueller, Attitudes Towards Westbound Refugees in the East
German Press
Norman Z. Alcock and Alan G. Newcombe, The Perception of National Power
James A. Schellenberg, County Seat Wars: A Preliminary Analysis
Herbert W. Kee and Robert E. Knox, Conceptual and Methodological
Considerations in the Study of Trust and Suspicion
Morton Deutsch and Roy J. Lewicki, Locking-in Effects during a Game
of Chicken
Phillip Bonacich, Putting the Dilemma back into Prisoner's Dilemma
Martin Patchen, Models of Cooperation and Conflict: A Critical Review
Milton Bloombaum, Doing Smallest Space Analysis
Vol. 14/4 (1970)
Edward T. Rowe, Human Rights Issues in the UN General Assembly
Allen S. Whiting, In Memoriam: Quincy Wright, 1890–1970—A Symposium
William T. R. Fox, The Truth Shall Make You Free: One Student's
Appreciation of Quincy Wright
Robert C. Angell, Quincy Wright: A Personal Memoir
Inis L. Claude, Jr., The Heritage of Quincy Wright
Percy E. Corbett, Quincy Wright's Contribution to International Law
Abdul Majid Abbass, The Personal Impact of a Great Teacher
Karl W. Deutsch, Quincy Wright's Contribution to the Study of War: A
Preface to the Second Edition
Kenneth W. Thompson, Policy and Theory in Quincy Wright's International Relations
Robert C. North, Wright on War
Harold K. Jacobson, Quincy Wright's Study of the Mandates System
Frank L. Klingberg, Historical Periods, Trends and Cycles in International Relations
Raymond Tanter and James N. Rosenau, Field and Environmental
Approaches to World Politics: Implications for Data Archives
J. David Singer, From A Study of War to Peace Research: Some Criteria
and Strategies
Clinton F. Fink and Christopher Wright, Quincy Wright on War and
Peace: A Statistical Overview and Selected Bibliography
Vol. 15/1 (1971)
Roger W. Benjamin and Lewis J. Edinger, Conditions for Military Control Over Foreign Policy Decisions in Major States: A Historical Exploration
Lincoln P. Bloomfield and Robert Beattie, Computers and Policy-Making: The CASCON Experiment

George Kent, The Application of Peace Studies

W. Basil McDermott, Thinking about Herman Kahn

David A. Baldwin, Thinking About Threats

Marc Pilisuk, Stewart Kiritz, and Stuart Clampitt, Undoing Deadlocks of Distrust: Hip Berkeley Students and the ROTC

Ronald L. Michelini, Effects of Prior Interaction, Contact, Strategy, and Expectation of Meeting on Game Behavior and Sentiment

Bruce John Morrison et al., The Effect of Electrical Shock and Warning on Cooperation in a Non-Zero-Sum Game

Bernhardt Lieberman, Not an Artifact

Vol. 15/2 (1971)

Henry Bain, Nigel Howard, and Thomas L. Saaty, Using the Analysis of Options Technique to Analyze a Community Conflict

David A. Baldwin, The Costs of Power

V. Edwin Bixenstine and Jacquelyn W. Gaebelein, Strategies of Real Others in Eliciting Cooperative Choice in a Prisoner's Dilemma Game

Warner Wilson, Reciprocation and Other Techniques for Inducing Cooperation in the Prisoner's Dilemma Game

James T. Tedeschi et al., A Paradigm for the Study of Coercive Power

Stuart Oskamp, Effects of Programmed Strategies on Cooperation in the Prisoner's Dilemma and Other Mixed-Motive Games

Richard Ofshe, The Effectiveness of Pacifist Strategies: A Theoretical Approach

Vol. 15/3 (1971)

Edward Saraydar, A Certainty-Equivalent Model of Bargaining

G. Matthew Bonham, Stimulating International Disarmament Negotiations

William Welch, Soviet Expansionism and Its Assessment

Louis M. Terrell, Societal Stress, Political Instability and Levels of Military Effort

Donald G. Morrison and Hugh Michael Stevenson, Political Instability in Independent Black Africa: More Dimensions of Conflict Behavior within Nations

Jerome M. Chertkoff, Coalition Formation as a Function of Differences in Resources

Michael Lupfer et al., Risk Taking in Cooperative and Competitive Dyads

John S. Gillis and George T. Woods, The 16PF as an Indicator of Performance in the Prisoner's Dilemma Game

Charles L. Gruder, Relationships with Opponent and Partner in Mixed-Motive Bargaining

Vol. 15/4 (1971)

Alan Dowty, Foreign-Linked Factionalism as a Historical Pattern

Douglas G. Hartle and Richard M. Bird, The Demand for Local Political Autonomy: An Individualistic Theory

David Osterberg and Fouad Ajami, The Multinational Corporation: Expanding the Frontiers of World Politics

David Baldwin, Inter-Nation Influence Revisited

Jack E. Vincent and Edward W. Schwerin, Ratios of Force and Escalation in a Game Situation

Paul G. Swingle and Brian MacLean, The Effect of Illusory Power in Non-Zero-Sum Games

Daniel Druckman, The Influence of the Situation in Interparty Conflict

Vol. 16/1 (Mar. 1972)

L. L. Farrar, Jr., The Limits of Choice: July 1914 Reconsidered

Ralph H. Turner, Integrative Beliefs in Group Crisis

Arthur S. Banks, Patterns of Domestic Conflict: 1919–39 and 1946–66

Oran R. Young, Intermediaries' Additional Thoughts on Third Parties

Ronald J. Fisher, Third Party Consultation: A Method for the Study and Resolution of Conflict

Richard Tropper, The Consequences of Investment in the Process of Conflict

John Cheney et al., The Effects of Communicating Threats and Promises upon the Bargaining Process

R. E. Overstreet, Social Exchange in a Three-Person Game

Vol. 16/2 (June 1972)

Joseph D. Ben-Dak and Edward E. Azar, Research Perspectives on the Arab-Israeli Conflict: Introduction to a Symposium

Jonathan Wilkenfeld et al., Conflict Interactions in the Middle East, 1949–1967

Barry M. Blechman, The Impact of Israel's Reprisals on Behavior of the Bordering Arab Nations Directed at Israel

Edward E. Azar, Conflict Escalation and Conflict Reduction in an International Crisis: Suez, 1956

Randolph M. Siverson, The Evaluation of Self, Allies, and Enemies in the 1956 Suez Crisis

Robert Burrowes and Douglas Muzzio, The Road to the Six Day War: Aspects of an Enumerative History of Four Arab States and Israel, 1965–1967

Saad E. M. Ibraham, Arab Images of the United States and the Soviet Union Before and After the June War of 1967

John E. Hofman, Readiness for Social Relations between Arabs and Jews in Israel

Alan Dowty, The Application of International Guarantees to the Egypt-Israel Conflict

Benjamin Beit-Hallahmi, Some Psychosocial and Cultural Factors in the Arab-Israel Conflict: A Review of the Literature

Joseph D. Ben-Dak, Some Directions for Research Toward Peaceful Arab-Israel Relations: Analysis of Past Events and Gaming Simulation of the Future

Vol. 16/3 (Sept. 1972)

William Zimmerman, The Transformation of the Modern Multistate System: The Exhaustion of Communist Alternatives

John J. Ray, Militarism, Authoritarianism, Neuroticism, and Antisocial Behavior

William Eckhardt, Attitudes of Canadian Peace Groups

Charles F. Hermann, Margaret G. Hermann, and Robert A. Cantor, Counterattack or Delay: Characteristics Influencing Decision Makers' Responses to the Simulation of an Unidentified Attack

Stuart Oskamp, Comparison of Sequential and Simultaneous Responding, Matrix, and Strategy Variables in a Prisoner's Dilemma Game

Review Section

Joseph M. Firestone, Continuities in the Theory of Violence

Peter Flora, A New Stage of Political Arithmetic

Vol. 18/2 (June 1974)

James E. Alcock, Cooperation, Competition, and the Effects of Time Pressure in Canada and India

T. Edward Westen and James J. Buckley, Toward an Explanation of Experimentally Obtained Outcomes to a Simple, Majority Rule Game

Leonard W. Doob and William J. Foltz, The Impact of a Workshop upon Grass-Roots Leaders in Belfast

G. H. Boehringer, V. Zeruolis, J. Bayley, and K. Boehringer, Stirling: The Destructive Application of Group Techniques to a Conflict

Daniel I. Alevy, Barbara B. Bunker, Leonard W. Doob, William J. Foltz, Nancy French, Edward B. Klein, and James C. Miller, Rationale, Research, and Role Relations in the Stirling Workshop

Review Section

Stephen D. Nelson, Nature/Nurture Revisited I: A Review of the Biological Bases of Conflict

Harvey Starr, The Quantitative International Relations Scholar as Surfer: Riding the "Fourth Wave"

Vol. 18/3 (Sept. 1974)

Editorial Comments

Allen H. Stix, Chlordiazepoxide (Librium): The Effects of a Minor Tranquilizer on Strategic Choice Behavior in the Prisoner's Dilemma

Manus I. Midlarsky, Power, Uncertainty, and the Onset of International Violence

Frederic S. Pearson, Geographic Proximity and Foreign Military Intervention

D. W. Carment, Effects of Sex Role in a Maximizing Difference Game: A Replication in Canada

Charles L. Gruder, Cost and Dependency as Determinants of Helping and Exploitation

Dov Friedlander and Calvin Goldscheider, Peace and the Demographic Future of Israel

Fred M. Gottheil, An Economic Assessment of the Military Burden in the Middle East: 1960–1980

Review Section

Andrew Mack, Theories of Imperialism: The European Perspective

Robert L. Harlow, Conflict Reduction in Environmental Policy

Vol. 18/4 (Dec. 1974)

Kendall Moll, International Conflict as a Decision System

Eva Etzioni-Halevy, Patterns of Conflict Generation and Conflict "Absorption": The Cases of Israeli Labor and Ethnic Conflicts

Norman Frohlich, Thomas Hunt, Joe Oppenheimer, and R. Harrison Wagner, Individual Contributions for Collective Goods: Alternative Models

Todd Sandler and Jon Cauley, On the Economic Theory of Alliances

Thomas J. Volgy and Jon E. Quistgaard, Learning About the Value of Global Cooperation: Role-Taking in the United Nations as a Predictor of World Mindedness

Vol. 19/3 (Sept. 1975)

Michael Stohl, War and Domestic Political Violence: The Case of the United States 1890–1970

T. Baumgartner, W. Buckley, and T. Burns, Relational Control: The Human Structuring of Cooperation and Conflict

Norman Schofield, A Game Theoretic Analysis of Olson's Game of Collective Action

Bruce D. Fitzgerald, Self-Interest or Altruism: Corrections and Extensions

Norman Frohlich, Comments in Reply

Marc Pilisuk and Emmanuel Uren, Deriving a Language for Interaction Sequences

Henry Hamburger, Melvin Guyer, and John Fox, Group Size and Cooperation

Jean M. Bartunek, Alan A. Benton, and Christopher B. Keys, Third Party Intervention and the Bargaining Behavior of Group Representatives

Review Section

Gustav Ranis, Equity and Growth: New Dimensions of Development

Vol. 19/4 (Dec. 1975)

Hans Rattinger, Armaments, Detente, and Bureaucracy: The Case of the Arms Race in Europe

Steven J. Brams, Newcomb's Problem and Prisoners' Dilemma

Anatol Rapoport, Comment on Brams's Discussion of Newcomb's Paradox

Miroslav Nincic, Determinants of Third World Hostility Toward the United States: An Exploratory Analysis

Nancy S. Smith, Charles R. Vernon, and Robert D. Tarte, Random Strategies and Sex Differences in the Prisoner's Dilemma Game

Anatol Rapoport, Comments on "Random Strategies and Sex Differences"

Sanford L. Braver and Van Rohrer, When Martyrdom Pays: The Effects of Information Concerning the Opponents' Past Game Behavior

Anatol Rapoport, Comments on "When Martyrdom Pays"

Stephen P. McNeel and Edward C. Reid, Attitude Similarity, Social Goals, and Cooperation

J. Lynn England, Linear Learning Models for Two-Party Negotiations

Stephen S. Kaplan, The Use of Military Force Abroad by the United States Since 1798: An Annotated Bibliography of Unclassified Lists of Incidents Prepared by the U.S. Government

Review Section
Lewis Lipsitz and Herbert M. Kritzer, Unconventional Approaches to Conflict Resolution: Erikson and Sharp on Nonviolence
Stephen D. Nelson, Nature/Nurture Revisited II: Social, Political, and Technological Implications of Biological Approaches to Human Conflict
Editor's Acknowledgement
Index

Journal of Peace Research. Universitetsforlaget, P. O. Box 307, Oslo 3, Norway, or P. O. Box 142, Boston, Massachusetts 02113. Editorial Office: P. O. Box 5052, Oslo 3, Norway. Quarterly since 1964; $6 per year.

"The journal is an interdisciplinary and international publication of scientific reports in the field of peace research with the emphasis on ways and means of resolving conflicts rather than on empirical or theoretical works."

Vol. 1/1 (1964)
An Editorial
Arne Martin Klausen, Technical Assistance and Social Conflict
Ingrid Eide Galtung, Technical Assistance and Public Opinion
Johan Galtung, Summit Meetings and International Relations
Paul Smoker, Fear in the Arms Race: A Mathematical Study

Vol. 1/2 (1964)
Paul Smoker, Sino-Indian Relations: A Study of Trade, Communication and Defence
Mari Holmboe Ruge, Technical Assistance and Parliamentary Debates
Johan Galtung, A Structural Theory of Aggression
Per Maurseth, Balance-of-Power Thinking from the Renaissance to the French Revolution
Erland Brun Hansen and J. W. Ulrich, Some Problems of Nuclear Power Dynamics
I. Glagolev and M. Goryainov, Research Communication: Some Problems of Disarmament Research

Vol. 1/3–4 (1964)
Papers presented at the meetings of the Peace Research Society (International), Ghent, 18–19 July 1964
Guest Editors: Walter Isard and Julian Wolpert
Wassily Leontief, Disarmament, Foreign Aid and Economic Growth
Josef Sebestyén, Comments on Leontief's Paper
Ole R. Holsti, Richard A. Brody, and Robert C. North, Affect and Action in International Reaction Models
John W. Dyckman, Some Regional Development Issues in Defense Program Shifts
Igor Glagolev, Concerning the Reduction of Military Expenditures
Johan Galtung, Foreign Policy Opinion as a Function of Social Position
Bart Landheer, The Image of World Society and the Function of Armaments
Walter Isard and Julian Wolpert, Notes on Social Science Principles for World Law and Order

Vol. 2/1 (1965)
Peter Cooper, The Development of the Concept of War
J. David Singer and Hirohide Hinomoto, Inspecting for Weapons Production: A Modest Computer Simulation
Einar Östgaard, Factors Influencing the Flow of News
Johan Galtung and Mari Holmboe Ruge, The Structure of Foreign News
Anders Boserup, Research Communication: On a Theory of Nuclear War
Paul Smoker, Research Communication: On Mathematical Models in Arms Races
Vol. 2/2 (1965)
Johan Galtung and Mari Holmboe Ruge, Patterns of Diplomacy
Amitai Etzioni, Strategic Models for a De-polarizing World
Jerome Laulicht, Public Opinion and Foreign Policy Decisions
Paul Smoker, Trade, Defence and the Richardson Theory of Arms Races: A Seven Nation Study
W. F. Duisenberg, The Economic Consequences of Disarmament in the Netherlands
A. C. Nunn, Research Communication: The Arming of an International Police
Erland Brun Hansen and Jörgen Wilian Ulrich, A Rejoinder
Vol. 2/3 (1965)
Giuliano Pontara, The Rejection of Violence in Gandhian Ethics of Conflict Resolution
John R. Raser, Learning and Affect in International Politics
Johan Galtung, On the Meaning of Nonviolence
Ingrid Eide Galtung, The Impact of Study Abroad
Kenneth W. Terhune, Nationalistic Aspiration, Loyalty, and Internationalism
Theodore F. Lentz, Research Communication: Japan vs. USA: A Comparative Public Opinion Study
Vol. 2/4 (1965)
Milan Šahović, International Control of the Uses of Nuclear Energy
Michael Haas, Societal Approaches to the Study of War
Sivert Langholm, Violent Conflict Resolution and the Loser's Reaction
Johan Galtung, Institutionalized Conflict Resolution
Alan Coddington, Policies Advocated in Conflict Situations by British Newspapers
Vol. 3/1 (1966)
J. David Singer and Melvin Small, Formal Alliances, 1815–1939
Tom Broch and Johan Galtung, Belligerence Among the Primitives
Nils H. Halle, Social Position and Foreign Policy Attitudes
Bo Ohlström, Information and Propaganda
Murray L. Weidenbaum and Ben Chieu-Liu, Research Communication: Effect of Disarmament on Income Distribution
Vol. 3/2 (1966)
Emile Benoit and Harold Lubell, World Defense Expenditures
Berenice Carroll, Germany Disarmed and Rearming, 1925–1935

Asbjørn Eide, Peace-keeping and Enforcement by Regional Organizations

Johan Galtung, East-West Interaction Patterns

Lars Porsholt, On Methods of Conflict Prevention

Malvern Lumsden, Research Communication: Research on International Peace-keeping Forces

Vol. 3/3 (1966)

Rudolph J. Rummel, Some Dimensions in the Foreign Behavior of Nations

Simon Schwartzman and Manuel Mora y Araujo, The Images of International Stratification in Latin America

Alain Joxe, Analyse d'un Système d'Objectifs Nationaux

Malvern Lumsden, Perception and Information in Strategic Thinking

Atle Grahl-Madsen, The European Tradition of Asylum and the Development of Refugee Law

Vol. 3/4 (1966)

John R. Raser, Deterrence Research

Anders Boserup and Claus Iversen, Demonstrations as a Source of Change

George R. Pitman, Jr., A Calculus of Military Stability

Ingrid Eide Galtung, The Status of the Technical Assistance Expert

Yasumasa Kuroda, Research Communication: Peace-War Orientation in a Japanese Community

Mari Holmboe Ruge, Research Communication: "Are You a Member of a Peace Organization?"

Vol. 4/1 (1967)

Papers prepared by the Peace Research Centre, Lancaster
Guest editors: Paul Smoker and Robin Jenkins

John MacRae and Paul Smoker, A Vietnam Simulation

Michael Nicholson, Tariff Wars and a Model of Conflict

Alan Coddington, Game Theory, Bargaining Theory, and Strategic Reasoning

Robin Jenkins, Who Are These Marchers?

Paul Smoker, Nation State Escalation and International Integration

Peter Abell and Robin Jenkins, Research Communication: Perception and Structural Balance of Part of the International System of Nations

Vol. 4/2 (1967)

Bruce M. Russett, Pearl Harbor: Deterrence Theory and Decision Theory

Hans and Shulamith Kreitler, Crucial Dimensions of the Attitude towards National and Supra-national Ideals

Gutorm Gjessing, Ecology and Peace Research

Fredrik Hoffmann, The Functions of Economic Sanctions

Johan Galtung, Two Approaches to Disarmament

Rudolph J. Rummel, Research Communication: Some Attributes and Behavioral Patterns of Nations

Vol. 4/3 (1967)

Manus Midlarsky and Raymond Tanter, Toward a Theory of Political Instability in Latin America

Egil Fossum, Factors Influencing the Occurrence of Military Coups d'Etat in Latin America

Jean-Luc Vellut, Smaller States and the Problem of War and Peace: Some Consequences of the Emergence of Smaller States in Africa

Dina A. Zinnes, An Analytical Study of the Balance of Power Theories

Malvern Lumsden, Social Position and Cognitive Style in Strategic Thinking

Vol. 4/4 (1967)

Johan Galtung, On the Future of the International System

Per Olav Reinton, International Structure and International Integration: The Case of Latin America

Nils Petter Gleditsch, Trends in World Airline Patterns

Vol. 5/1 (1968)

Karel Kára, On the Marxist Theory of War and Peace

Charles Boasson, The Place of International Law in Peace Research

Charles H. Grey and Glenn W. Gregory, Military Spending and Senate Voting

Jonathan Wilkenfeld, Domestic and Foreign Conflict Behavior of Nations

Alaor S. Passos, Developmental Tension and Political Instability

Steven J. Brams, Research Communication: A Note on the Cosmopolitanism of World Regions

Vol. 5/2 (1968)

Chihiro Hosoya, Miscalculations in Deterrent Policy: Japanese–U.S. Relations, 1938–1941

Louis C. Goldberg, Ghetto Riots and Others

Stahis S. Panagides, Communal Conflict and Economic Considerations: The Case of Cyprus

Helge Hveem, Foreign Policy Thinking in the Elite and the General Population

Trond Ålvik, The Development of Views on Conflict, War, and Peace Among School Children

Toyomasa Fusé, Religion, War, and the Institutional Dilemma

Utz-Peter Reich, Research Communication: Conflict of Interest: A Pragmatic Approach

Vol. 5/3 (1968)

Herman Schmid, Politics and Peace Research

Mats Friberg and Dan Jonsson, A Simple War and Armament Game

Peter Wallensteen, Characteristics of Economic Sanctions

Leif Rosell, Children's Views of War and Peace

Håkan Wiberg, Social Position and Peace Philosophy

Eva Stina Bengtsson, Research Communication: Some Political Perspectives of Academic Reserve Officers

Vol. 5/4 (1968)
Karl Nandrup Dahl, The Rôle of I.L.O. Standards in the Global Integration Process
Istvàn Kende, Peaceful Co-existence: Its Interpretation and Misinterpretation
Mohammed Ahsen Chaudri, Peace Research and the Developing Countries
Johan Galtung, A Structural Theory of Integration
Vahakn N. Dadrian, Kant's Concepts of "Human Nature" and "Rationality": Two Arch Determinants of an Envisioned "Eternal Peace"

Vol. 6/1 (1969)
Terry Nardin and Neal E. Cutler, Reliability and Validity of Some Patterns of International Interaction in an Internation Simulation
R. T. Green and G. Santori, A Cross Cultural Study of Hostility and Aggression
Raymond F. Smith, On the Structure of Foreign News: A Comparison of the New York Times and the Indian White Papers
Bruce M. Russett and W. Curtis Lamb, Global Patterns of Diplomatic Exchange, 1963–64
Pirkko Niemalä, Sirkku Honka-Hallila, and Aila Järvikoski, Research Communication: A Study in Intergroup Perception Stereotypy
Discussion
Gudmund Hernes, On Rank Disequilibrium and Military Coups d'Etat
Egil Fossum, Reply to Gudmund Hernes
Johan Galtung, Reply to Gudmund Hernes
Book Notes

Vol. 6/2 (1969)
Ulf Himmelstrand, Tribalism, Nationalism, Rank-Equilibration, and Social Structure
Norman Z. Alcock and Keith Lowe, The Vietnam War as a Richardson Process
Ståle Seierstad, A Statistical Study of Political Determinants for Economic Growth
William Eckhardt, The Factor of Militarism
Takeshi Ishida, Beyond the Traditional Concept of Peace in Different Cultures
Jonathan Wilkenfeld, Research Communication: Some Further Findings Regarding the Domestic and Foreign Conflict Behavior of Nations
Knud S. Larsen, Gary Schwendiman, and David V. Stimpson, Research Communication: Change in Attitude Towards Negroes Resulting From Exposure to Congruent and Non-Congruent Attitudinal Objects
Book Notes

Vol. 6/3 (1969)
Johan Galtung, Violence, Peace, and Peace Research
Richard W. Chadwick, An Inductive, Empirical Analysis of Intra- and International Behavior, Aimed at a Partial Extension of Inter-Nation Simulation Theory

Donald von Eschen, Jerome Kirk, and Maurice Pinard, The Disintegration of the Negro Non-Violent Movement

Kurt Jacobsen, Sponsorships in the United Nations

Melvin Small and J. David Singer, Formal Alliances, 1816–1965: An Extension of the Basic Data

Book Notes

Vol. 6/4 (1969)

Berenice A. Carroll, Introduction: History and Peace Research

Berenice A. Carroll, How Wars End: An Analysis of Some Current Hypotheses

Ronald P. Legon, The Peace of Nicias

J. Lee Schneidman, Ending the War of the Sicilian Vespers

Richard B. Morris, Ending the American Revolution: Lessons for Our Time

J. A. White, Portsmouth 1905: Peace or Truce?

Raymond O'Connor, Victory in Modern War

F. Hilary Conroy, The Conference on Peace Research in History: A Memoir

Sandi E. Cooper, Recent Developments in the Teaching of Peace History and Related Areas in North America

Book Notes

Vol. 7/1 (1970)

James A. Stegenga, UN Peace-Keeping: The Cyprus Venture

Egil Fossum, Political Development and Strategies for Change

Neal E. Cutler, Generational Succession as a Source of Foreign Policy Attitudes: A Cohort Analysis of American Opinion, 1946–66

Helge Hveem, "Blame" as International Behavior

Knud S. Larsen and Gary Schwendiman, Research Communication: Perceived Aggression Training as a Predictor of Two Assessments of Authoritarianism

Book Notes

Books Received

Vol. 7/2 (1970)

Harry R. Targ, Children's Developing Orientations to International Politics

Magnus Haavelsrud, Views on War and Peace Among Students in West Berlin Public Schools

Richard W. Chadwick, A Partial Model of National Political-Economic Systems: Evaluation by Causal Inference

Jack E. Vincent, Research Communication: An Analysis of Caucusing Group Activity at the United Nations

William R. Thompson, Research Communication: The Arab Sub-System and the Feudal Pattern of Interaction: 1965

Book Notes

Books Received

List of Publications

Vol. 7/3 (1970)

Eduardo Archetti, Egil Fossum, and Per Olav Reinton, Agrarian Structure and Peasant Autonomy

Sverre Lodgaard, Industrial Cooperation, Consumption Patterns, and Division of Labor in the East-West Setting
Book Notes
Books Received
Vol. 11/1 (1974)
Asbjørn Eide, International Law, Dominance and the Use of Force
Bishwa B. Chatterjee, Search for an Appropriate Game Model for Gandhian Satyagraha
William Eckhardt, A Conformity Theory of Aggression
Review Article
Fouad Ajami, On Nasser and His Legacy
Research Communication
Stein Ringen, Fruits of the UN: The Distribution of Development Aid
Claud R. Sutcliffe, Palestinian Refugee Resettlement: Lessons from the East Ghor Canal Project
Discussion
R. W. Davis, Palestinian Arab Sovereignty and Peace in the Middle East: A Reassessment
Book Notes
Books Received
Vol. 11/2 (1974)
Joan E. Garcés, World Equilibrium, Crisis and Militarization of Chile
Ekkehart Krippendorff, Chile, Violence and Peace Research
Deodato Rivera, Let Us Face Chile, Yes: But Which Chile?
Bo Wirmark, Nonviolent Methods and the American Civil Rights Movement 1955–1965
Ronald J. Terchek, Protest and Bargaining
Karl Erik Rosengren, International News: Methods, Data and Theory
Johan Galtung, A Rejoinder
Book Notes
Vol. 11/3 (1974)
Robert B. Stauffer, The Political Economy of a Coup: Transnational Linkages and Philippine Political Response
Tim Ingold, Entrepreneur and Protagonist: Two Faces of a Political Career
Elise Boulding, The Measurement of Cultural Potentials for Trans-nationalism
Partha Chatterjee, The Equilibrium Theory of Arms Races: Some Extensions
Jerry L. Weaver, Arms Transfers to Latin America: A Note on the Contagion Effect
Tom Burns and Walter Buckley, The Prisoner's Dilemma Game as a System of Social Domination
Jeffrey Hart, Symmetry and Polarization in the European International System, 1870–1879: A Methodological Study
Research Communication
David Statt, The Influence of National Power on the Child's View of the World

Geoff Mercer, Adolescent Views of War and Peace—Another Look
Books Received
Book Notes
Vol. 11/4 (1974)
David Holloway, Technology and Political Decision in Soviet Armaments Policy
Tord Høivik, The Development of Romania: A Cohort Study
Amalendu B. Guha, Rumania as a Development Model
Sverre Lodgaard, On the Relationship between East-West Economic Cooperation and Political Change in Eastern Europe
Research Communication
Hossein Askari and Vittorio Corbo, Economic Implications of Military Expenditures in the Middle East
D. G. Morrison and H. M. Stevenson, Social Complexity, Economic Development and Military Coups d'Etat: Convergence and Divergence of Empirical Tests of Theory in Latin America, Asia, and Africa
Book Notes
Books Received
Vol. 12/1 (1975)
Thomas G. Weiss, The Tradition of Philosophical Anarchism and Future Directions in World Policy
Adam Roberts, Civil Resistance to Military Coups
Ottar Hellevik, Nils Petter Gleditsch, and Kristen Ringdal, The Common Market Issue in Norway: A Conflict between Center and Periphery
William Eckhardt, Primitive Militarism
Silviu Brucan, The Systemic Power
N. G. Onuf, Peace Research Parochialism
Asbjørn Eide, Global and Parochial Perspectives in International Studies and Peace Research
Books Received
Book Notes
Vol. 12/2 (1975) Special Issue: Peace Research in Switzerland
Daniel Frei, Editor's Preface
Peter Heintz, Conformist and Non-Conformist Behavior of Developed Nations
Dieter Ruloff, The Dynamics of Cooperation and Conflict between Nations—A Mathematical Model and Some Results
John C. Lambelet, Do Arms Races Lead to War? Some Preliminary Thoughts
Urs Luterbacher, Bipolarity and Generational Factors in Major Power Military Activity 1900–1965
Michel Bassand, The Jura Problem
Jean Pierre Allamand and Gérard de Rham, Elements for the Analysis of the Sets of Values in Switzerland
Vol. 12/3 (1975)
Johan Galtung, Security and Cooperation: A Skeptical Contribution

Journal of Peace Science: An International Journal of the Scientific Study of Conflict and Conflict Management. Department of Peace Science, University of Pennsylvania, 3718 Locust Street, Philadelphia, Pennsylvania 19104. Irregularly since 1973.

"Papers that lead to clearer understanding of conflict and its resolution, and which display a novel underlying theoretical structure, offer methodological advances in the study of peace science, or serve to clarify or to advance established results within the field."

A Roundtable on Foreign Aid
Bruno Frey, Weapon Exports and Aid to Developing Countries
Martin Bronfenbrenner, Historical-Institutional Doubts on the Frey Thesis
Bruce D. Fitzgerald, Notes on the Grants Economy of Foreign Aid
Roger M. Krause, Daniel Druckman, Richard Rozelle, and Robert Mahoney, Components of Value and Representation in Coalition Formation
David L. Wagner, Ronald T. Perkins, and Rein Taagepera, Complete Solution to Richardson's Arms Race Equations
Walter Isard and Panagis Liossatos, Social Injustice and Economic Development Revisited

Reviews
Boulding on Rapoport
Starr on Blainey

Peace Research: A Monthly Journal of Original Research on the Problem of War. Canadian Peace Research Institute, 119 Thomas Street, Oakville, Ontario, Canada.
Editorial Office: 25 Dundana Avenue, Dundas, Ontario L9H 4E5, Canada.
Monthly since 1969; $3 per year.
"Very condensed reports of results of empirical peace research, or theoretical peace research that can be tested empirically."

Peace Science Society (International) Papers. The Peace Science Society (International), Department of Peace Science, University of Pennsylvania, Philadelphia, Pennsylvania 19104.
Annually since 1964; $5 per year.
Formerly known as *Peace Research Society (International) Papers.* Composed primarily of papers presented at PSS(I) Conferences, reporting ongoing research.

Vol. 1 (1964)
Robert C. North, Richard A. Brody, and Ole R. Holsti, Some Empirical Data on the Conflict Spiral
Walter Isard and Eugene W. Schooler, An Economic Analysis of Local and Regional Impacts of Reduction of Military Expenditures
Igor Glagolev, Comments on Isard and Schooler
Emile Benoit, Comments on Isard and Schooler and on North, Brody, and Holsti
Marc Pilisuk and Anatol Rapoport, A Non-zero-sum Game Model of Some Disarmament Problems
Rudolph J. Rummel, Testing Some Possible Predicators of Conflict Behavior Within and Between Nations
Daniel Katz, Herbert Kelman, and Richard Flacks, The National Role: Some Hypotheses about the Relation of Individuals to Nation in America Today
Sheldon G. Levy and Robert Hefner, Multidimensional Scaling of International Attitudes

Vol. 2 (1965)

Wassily Leontief, Disarmament, Foreign Aid and Economic Development

Josef Sebestyén, Comments on Leontief's Paper

Ole R. Holsti, Richard A. Brody, and Robert C. North, Measuring Affect and Action in International Reaction Models: Empirical Materials from the 1962 Cuban Crisis

John W. Dyckman, Some Regional Development Issues in Defense Program Shifts

Igor Glagolev, Concerning the Reduction of Military Expenditures

Johan Galtung, Foreign Policy Opinion as a Function of Social Position

Walter Isard and Julian Wolpert, Notes on Social Science Principles for World Law and Order

Bart Landheer, The Image of World Society and the Function of Armaments

Vol. 3 (1965)

Kenneth E. Boulding and Alan Gleason, War as an Investment: The Case of Japan

Walter Isard and Stanislaw Czamanski, Techniques for Estimating Local and Regional Multiplier Effects of Changes in the Level of Major Governmental Programs

William A. Gamson and Andre Modigliani, Soviet Responses to Western Foreign Policy, 1946–1953

Ole R. Holsti, Perceptions of Time and Alternatives as Factors in Crisis Decision-Making

Jerome Laulicht and John Paul, An Analysis of Canadian Foreign Policy Attitudes

Thomas A. Reiner, Spatial Criteria for Programs to Offset Military Cutbacks

Raymond Tanter, Dimensions of Conflict Behavior Within Nations, 1955–60: Turmoil and Internal War

Robert C. Angell, An Analysis of Trends in International Organizations

Hayward R. Alker, Jr., The Politics of Supranationalism in the United Nations

Vol. 4 (1966)

M. Megee, Factor Analysis: A Method to Delineate World Regions

A. Szalai, Cohesion Indices for Regional Determination

M. Chatterji, Local Impact of Disarmament, Foreign Aid Programs and Development of Poor World Regions: A Critique of the Leontief and Other Growth Models

Igor Glagolev, Economic and Social Consequences of Disarmament

Walter Isard and T. E. Smith, Practical Applications of Game Theoretical Approaches to Arms Reduction (and to Goal Determinations among Regional Planning Authorities)

W. Warntz, World Population Potential Analysis and International Crises

Rudolph J. Rummel, Social Field Theory and Foreign Conflict

Paul Smoker, The Arms Race as a Mathematical Model (a Contribution from Physics and Mathematics)

P. Cooper, Towards a Model of Political-Moral Development (a Contribution from Psychology)

Jerzy Sawicki, Perspectives on Peace Research

Vol. 5 (1966)

Walter Isard and Stanislaw Czamanski, A Model for the Projection of Regional Industrial Structure, Land Use Patterns and Conversion Potentialities

Murray L. Weidenbaum, Shifting the Composition of Government Spending: Implications for the Regional Distribution of Income

Gerald J. Karaska, Interregional Flows of Defense-Space Awards

Emile Benoit, Comments on Papers by Weidenbaum and by Karaska

Dean G. Pruitt, Reward Structure and Its Effect on Cooperation

Anatol Rapoport, Additional Experimental Findings on Conflict and Games

Marc Pilisuk, Timing and Integrity of Inspection in Arms Reduction Games

J. David Singer and Melvin Small, National Alliance Commitments and War Involvement, 1815–1945

Chadwick F. Alger, Interaction and Negotiation in a Committee of the United Nations General Assembly

John R. Raser, Personal Characteristics of Political Decision-Makers: A Literature Review

Roger L. Sisson and Russell L. Ackoff, Toward a Theory of the Dynamics of Conflict

Lloyd Jensen, American Foreign Policy Elites and the Prediction of International Events

Vol. 6 (1966)

Kenneth E. Boulding, Arms Limitation and Integrative Activity as Elements in the Establishment of Stable Peace

Anatol Rapoport and Melvin Guyer, A Taxonomy of 2 × 2 Games

L. N. Karpov, Frontier Regions and Disarmament

Tamas Bacskai, The Armament Race and the Developing Countries

Stig Lindholm, Aspects on Goals and Values in Swedish Foreign Policy Making

Walter C. Clemens, Jr., Underlying Factors in Soviet Arms Control Policy: Problems of Systematic Analysis

Horst Zimmermann and Hans D. Klingemann, The Regional Impact of Defense Purchases in the Federal Republic of Germany

Gunnar Adler-Karlsson, Functional Socialism—A Concept for the Analysis of Convergence of National Economies

Davis B. Bobrow and Allen R. Wilcox, Dimensions of Defense Opinion: The American Public

Steven J. Brams, Trade in the North Atlantic Area: An Approach to the Analysis of Transformations in a System

Vol. 7 (1967)

Walter Isard, Peter Isard, Mark Barchas, and Richard Epps, On a General Political-Social-Economic Equilibrium Theory Oriented to Cooperative Solutions and Conflict Resolution

Eugene Smolensky, Comments on the Paper by Isard, Isard, Barchas, and Epps

Richard A. Brody, Alexandra H. Benham, and Jeffrey S. Milstein, Hostile International Communication, Arms Production, and Perception of Threat: A Simulation Study

Paul Smoker, The Arms Race as an Open and Closed System

J. G. Dash, Comments on the Paper by Smoker

Jerome Herniter, Anthony Williams, and Julian Wolpert, Learning to Cooperate

Raoul Naroll, Imperial Cycles and World Order

Murray Wolfson, Comment on the Paper by Naroll

John D. Nystuen, Boundary Shapes and Boundary Problems

Ryszard Domanski, Comments on Paper by Nystuen

Andrew P. Vayda, Research on the Functions of Primitive War

Robert Hefner, Sheldon G. Levy, and H. Lester Warner, A Survey of Internationally Relevant Attitudes and Behavior

Vol. 8 (1968)

Walter Isard and Tony Smith, On Social Decision Procedures for Conflict Situations

Davis B. Bobrow and Neal E. Cutler, Time-Oriented Explanations of National Security Beliefs: Cohort, Life-Stage and Situation

Anders Boserup and Claus Iversen, Rank Analysis of a Polarized Community: A Case Study from Northern Ireland

Jerzy Sawicki, Calling to Action a U.N. Force

Jerome Herniter and Julian Wolpert, Coalition Structures in the Three-Person Non-Zero-Sum Game

Gerald J. Karaska, The Spatial Impacts of Defense-Space Procurement: An Analysis of Subcontracting Patterns in the United States

Theodore C. Pontzen, A Comprehensive Model of Socio-Economic Development at all Levels

Vol. 9 (1969)

Kenneth E. Boulding, Requirements for a Social Systems Analysis of the Dynamics of the World War Industry

William A. Gamson and Andre Modigliani, Some Aspects of Soviet-Western Conflict

William R. Caspary, United States Public Opinion during the Onset of the Cold War

Nigel Howard, A Method for Metagame Analysis of Political Problems

Terry Nardin, Communication and the Effects of Threats in Strategic Interaction

Ithiel de Sola Pool, Village Violence and International Violence

David W. Conrath, Subject Game Experience and Its Role in Games of Conflict

Murray Wolfson, A Mathematical Model of the Cold War
Robert C. North and Nazli Choucri, Background Conditions to the
   Outbreak of the First World War
Vol. 10 (1969)
Preface
Walter Isard, Introduction and Overview
   Village and Social-Political Structure: Implications for
      Viable Government in South Vietnam
Ithiel de Sola Pool, Further Thoughts on Rural Pacification and In-
   surgency
Samuel L. Popkin, Village Authority Patterns in Vietnam
Ralph K. White, Attitudes of the South Vietnamese
David C. Schwartz, A Critique of Pool's "Further Thoughts on Rural
   Pacification and Insurgency"
   Attitudes of the United States Public: Significance for
      U.S. Strategies and Alternatives
John P. Robinson and Solomon G. Jacobson, American Public Opinion
   About Vietnam
Philip Brickman, Phillip Shaver, and Peter Archibald, American Tactics
   and Goals in Vietnam as Perceived by Social Scientists
   The Big Power Confrontation: Relevance for
      the Resolution of the Conflict
Robert Strausz-Hupé, Vietnam: An Arena of the Big Powers
   Analytic Models: Possible Solutions, Procedures for
      Reaching Agreement, and Statistical Predictions
Allan E. Goodman, Diplomatic and Strategic Outcomes of the Conflict
Nigel Howard, Metagame Analysis of Vietnam Policy
Thomas C. Schelling, Notes on Policies, Games, Metagames, and
   Vietnam
Walter Isard, The Veto-Incremax Procedure: Potential for Vietnam
   Conflict Resolution
Jeffrey S. Milstein and William C. Mitchell, Dynamics of the Vietnam
   Conflict: A Quantitative Analysis and Predictive Computer Simula-
   tion
Vol. 11 (1969)
Walter Isard, Toward a More Adequate General Regional Theory and
   Approach to Conflict Resolution
George Kent, Determinants of Bargaining Outcomes
David C. Schwartz, From Political Theory to Peace Policy: Notes on a
   More Structured Peace Research Process
Per Olav Reinton, Inequality in International Systems of Nations
Diane S. Clemens, The Structure of Negotiations: Dynamics and In-
   teraction Patterns of the Crimean Conference
Davis B. Bobrow, Ecology of International Games: Requirement for a
   Model of the International System
Patrick Doreian, Interaction under Conditions of Crisis: Applications of
   Graph Theory to International Relations

Gerald H. Shure and Robert J. Meeker, Bargaining Processes in Experimental Territorial Conflict Situations

Nils Petter Gleditsch, The International Airline Network: A Test of the Zipf and Stouffer Hypotheses

Vol. 12 (1970)

W. Curtis Lamb and Bruce M. Russett, Politics in the Emerging Regions

Nazli Choucri and Robert C. North, The Determinants of International Violence

Michael Haas, Communication Factors in Decision Making

Manas Chatterji, A Model of Resolution of Conflict between India and Pakistan

Roger Fisher, Effective Influence of Decisions in an International Setting

James R. Emshoff and Russell L. Ackoff, Prediction, Explanation, and Control of Conflict

Jeffrey S. Milstein and William Charles Mitchell, Computer Simulation of International Processes: The Vietnam War and the Pre-World War I Naval Race

Vol. 13 (1970)

William R. Caspary, Dimensions of Attitudes on International Conflict: Internationalism and Military Offensive Action

Alan G. Newcombe, Towards the Development of an Inter-Nation Tensiometer

Pertti Joenniemi, An Analysis of the Economic Consequences of Disarmament in Finland

Jerzy Sawicki, UN Reactions to Unauthorized Use of Force in International Relations

Kenneth E. Boulding, The Balance of Peace

Anders Boserup, Power in a Post-Colonial Setting: The Why and Whither of Religious Confrontation in Ulster

Alan Dowty, Conflict in War Potential Politics: An Approach to Historical Macroanalysis

Morris Davis, On the Applicability of the Notion of Self-Restraint

Gordon Hilton, The 1914 Studies—A Re-Assessment of the Evidence and Some Further Thoughts

Vol. 14 (1970)

Daniel Katz, Herbert C. Kelman, and Vasso Vassiliou, A Comparative Approach to the Study of Nationalism

Stephen A. Salmore and Charles Hermann, The Effect of Size, Development and Accountability on Foreign Policy

George Modelski, The Foreign Ministers as a World Elite

Sheldon G. Levy, Assassination—Levels, Motivation, and Attitudes

Robert H. Stroup and Richard E. Gift, Employment Patterns and Employment Alternatives in Rural South Vietnam

George Kent, Foreign Policy Analysis: Middle East

Maurice A. East, Rank-Dependent Interaction and Mobility: Two Aspects of International Stratification
Walter Isard and Tony E. Smith, On Political Conflict Resolution in Policy Spaces
Michael F. Dacey, A Probability Model for the Rise and Decline of States
Ole Jess Olsen and Ib Martin Jarvad, The Vietnam Conference Papers, A Case Study of a Failure of Peace Research

Vol. 15 (1971)
Preface
Walter Isard and Julian Wolpert, Introduction and Overview
Jeffrey Milstein, Soviet and American Influences on the Arab-Israeli Arms Race: A Quantitative Analysis
Nazli Choucri, Defense Budgets and the Middle East Conflict: A Commentary
Walter Isard and Tony E. Smith, The Major Power Confrontation in the Middle East: Some Analysis of Short-Run, Middle-Run and Long-Run Considerations
Norman Z. Alcock, An Empirical Measure of Internation Threat: Some Preliminary Implications for the Middle East Conflict
Frederic Pearson, Interaction in an International Political Subsystem: The "Middle East," 1963-64
George Kent, Perceptions of Foreign Policies: Middle East
Edward E. Azar, The Dimensionality of Violent Conflict: A Quantitative Analysis

Vol. 16 (1971)
Kenneth E. Boulding and Tapan Mukerjee, Unprofitable Empire: Britain in India, 1800-1967, A Critique of the Hobson-Lenin Thesis on Imperialism
Richard Van Atta and R. J. Rummel, Testing Field Theory on the 1963 Behavior Space of Nations
Ekkehart Krippendorff, The State as a Focus of Peace Research
Roderick Ogley, Investigating the Effects of Threats
Paul Smoker, Anarchism, Peace and Control: Some Ideas for Future Experiment

Vol. 17 (1971)
Walter Isard, Relativistic Perceptions of Time and Space: Implications for Conflict Resolution
Thomas L. Saaty, Mathematical Structures Applicable to Multi-Party Conflict
Warren R. Phillips, The Dynamics of Behavioral Action and Reaction in International Conflict
William C. Mitchell, Simulating Armaments Behavior of Competing Nations
Steven Rosen, Cost-Limits for Preferences in Foreign Policy Issue Areas
Sheldon G. Levy, Political Assassination and the Theory of Reduced Alternatives

Volker Rittberger, International Organization and Integration within Regional Settings: A Preliminary Analysis

Vol. 18 (1972)

Walter Isard and Panagis Liossatos, A Small Nation—Two Big Powers Model

Edward P. Levine, Mediation in International Politics: A Universe and Some Observations

George Modelski, War and the Great Powers

Morris Davis, The Structuring of International Communications about the Nigeria-Biafra War

John Gerard Ruggie, The Structure of International Organization: Contingency, Complexity, and Post-Modern Form

Norman J. Schofield, A Topological Model of International Relations

Robert Axelrod, Psycho-Algebra: A Mathematical Theory of Cognition and Choice with an Application to the British Eastern Committee in 1918

Vol. 19 (1972)

Walter Isard and Panagis Liossatos, A General Equilibrium System for Nations: The Case of Many Small Nations and One Big Power

Robert P. Strauss, An Adaptive Expectations Model of the East-West Arms Race

Nigel Howard, The Arab-Israeli Conflict: A Metagame Analysis Done in 1970

Allen K. Philbrick and Robert Harold Brown, Cosmos and International Hierarchies of Functions

Anatol Rapoport, Various Conceptions of Peace Research

John H. Sigler, Cooperation and Conflict in U.S.-Soviet-Chinese Relations, 1966–71: A Quantitative Analysis

Vol. 20 (1973)

Klaus Jürgen Gantzel, Armament Dynamics in the East-West Conflict: An Arms Race?

Raymond Tanter and William C. Potter, Modelling Alliance Behavior: East-West Conflict Over Berlin

Murray Wolfson, A Dynamic Model of Present World Conflict

Erich Weede, Nation-Environment Relations as Determinants of Hostilities among Nations

Vol. 21 (1973)

J. David Singer, The Peace Researcher and Foreign Policy Prediction

Nazli Choucri, Applications of Econometric Analysis to Forecasting in International Relations

Jong Ryool Lee and Jeffrey S. Milstein, A Political Economy of the Vietnam War, 1965–1972

Allen K. Philbrick, Present and Future Spatial Structure of International Organization

Alan Newcombe and James Wert, The Use of an Inter-Nation Tensiometer for the Prediction of War

Vol. 22 (1974)

John C. Lambelet, The Anglo-German Dreadnought Race, 1905–1914

Robert Burrowes and José Garriga-Picó, The Road to the Six Day War:
Relational Analysis of Conflict and Cooperation
Roderick Ogley and David Thomas, New Hypotheses in Game Experiments
Bruno S. Frey, An Insurance System for Peace

Vol. 23 (1974)
Karl W. Deutsch, Imperialism and Neocolonialism
Edward Azar, James Bennett, and Thomas Sloan, Steps Toward Forecasting International Interactions
James Lee Ray, Status Inconsistency and War Involvement in Europe, 1816–1970
Herb Addo, Structural Basis of International Communication
Alfred H. Bloom, Cross-cultural Investigation of the Moral Bases of Political Reasoning
Arthur A. Stein, Balance-of-Payments Policy in the Kennedy Administration
Kevin R. Cox and John A. Agnew, Optimal and Non-optimal Territorial Partitions: A Possible Approach toward Conflict
Walter Isard, World Environmental Conflicts: Some Relevant Analytical Frameworks
Stephen Gale, Comments on Territorial Partitions and Environmental Conflicts

Vol. 24 (1975)
Nigel Howard, Examples of a Dynamic Theory of Games
John C. Lambelet, A Numerical Model of the Anglo-German Dreadnought Race
From the Second Vienna Conference
Erich Weede, World Order in the Fifties and Sixties: Dependence, Deterrence, and Limited Peace
From the Fourth Chicago Conference
Bruce D. Fitzgerald, Voluntarism, Conscription, and the Likelihood of War
Walter Isard, Notes on an Evolutionary Theoretic Approach to World Organization

Proceedings of the International Peace Research Association. Assen, the Netherlands: Koninklijke VanGorcum & Company.
Biannually since 1966.
"Reports of the biannual conference of the International Peace Research Association; articles demonstrating the wide range of peace research, and the different methods of approach to the problem. Represented by peace researchers from 25 countries."

Inaugural Conference, Vol. 1 (1966)
Kenneth Boulding, Integrative Aspects of the International System
Paul Smoker, A Preliminary Empirical Study of an International Integration Sub-System
Simon Schwartzman, International Development and International Feudalism: The Latin American Case
Anatol Rapoport, Two Views on Conflict: The Cataclysmic and the Strategic Models

F. C. Spits, War and Revolution

Jaap Nobel, Competition and Co-operation in International Politics as a Bargaining Problem

Bart Landheer, Peace as an Engineering Problem: Possible Stabilization of the Threat System

John Raser and Wayman J. Crow, A Simulation Study of Deterrence Theories

Jerzy Sawicki, The UN Charter and the Type of Military Force of the United Nations Organization

Malvern Lumsden, Field Research of Conflict: First Results from an Empirical Study of Cyprus

Ingrid Eide Galtung, Are International Civil Servants International? A Case Study of UN Experts in Latin America

Johan Galtung, Attitudes towards Different Forms of Disarmament: A Study of Norwegian Public Opinion

Michaelo Adamovic, Economic Aspects of Disarmament

Gideon Rosenbluth, The Effect of Disarmament on Research and Development in Canada

Tadashi Kawata, The Growing Defense Industry of Japan: An Essay on Disarmament and the Economy

T. K. N. Unnithan, Towards a Sociology of Non-Violence

Iwao Munahata, Socialization towards Humanity

Mari Holmboe-Ruge, Present Trends in Peace Research

Marion Mushkat, Observations on Certain Modern Approaches to the Study of International Relations

Anatol Rapoport, Comments on a Plan for Peace Research

Second Conference, Vol. 1 (1968)

Johan Galtung, Entropy and the General Theory of Peace

Miroslav Soukup, František Charvát, and Jaroslav Kučera, Toward a General Social Systems Theory of Dependence: Introduction of Entropy of Behavior

Theodore Pontzen, The Missing Link: A Technology of Peace

Theodore F. Lentz, Towards a Technological Orientation for Peace Research

Gaston Bouthoul, L'Apport de la Polémologie à la Solution des Conflits

Michael H. Banks, A. J. R. Groom, and A. N. Oppenheim, International Crisis Gaming—The CONEX Experience

Robin Jenkins and John MacRae, Religion, Conflict and Polarisation in Northern Ireland

Robin Jenkins, Perception in Crises

Léo Hamon, Les Facteurs de Guerre, Essai Classement et Esquisse

Malvern Lumsden, Cyprus: A Case Study in Strategic Analysis

Kinhide Mushakoji, Negotiation between the West and the Non-West

J. D. Newnham, Arab-Israeli Relations: A Pilot Study of International Attitudes

Paul Smoker, A Time Series Analysis of Sino-Indian Relations

Alain Joxe, L'Escalade et les Limites du Réel

André Glucksmann, Décomposition du Concept d'Escalade

Ib Martin Jarvad, Power versus Equality

Kurt Jacobsen, Some Aspects of UN Voting Patterns
Ottar Hellevik, Recruitment to the Position of Foreign Policy Specialists
in the Norwegian Parliament
Mari Holmboe Ruge, Factors Affecting the Structure of Diplomacy:
The Case of Norway
Jerome Laulicht, Comparative Studies of Foreign Policy Opinions

Second Conference, Vol. 2 (1968)

Bert V. A. Röling, An Introduction to the Problem of Poverty, De-
velopment and Peace
Sugata Dasgupta, Peacelessness and Maldevelopment
Manuel Mora y Araujo, Structural Tension, Sociopolitical Conflict and
Economic Development: A Cross-National Study
Michael Haas, Societal Asymmetries and World Peace
Niels Lindberg, The Conflict Theory and Economic Depressions with
Some Views on Various Political Aspects of an Anti-Depression Pro-
gramme as Supplementary to Armament Cuts
Pradip Sarbadhikari, Domestic Conflicts and Foreign Policy: Aspects of
the Indian Situation
O. Bassir, Human Malnutrition, Poverty and Conflict Generation
Tadashi Kawata, "International Solidarity" and Economic Inequality
G. R. Tamarin and D. Ben-Zwi, "Man's Most Dangerous Myth"—
Today
Håkan Wiberg, Recent Trends in the Theory of Race Conflicts
Péter Vas-Zoltan, "Poverty"—Technical Development—Armament
Geoffrey Kemp, Arms Transfers to "Developing Countries"
Egil Fossum, Some Attributes of the Latin American Military Coup
Per Olav Reinton, Cognitive and Evaluative Elements in Latin Ameri-
can Integration Programs
Vojin Dimitrijević, Private Political Activity Aimed at Effects Abroad
M. Mushkat, Poverty, Conflict and the Concepts of Intervention and
Non-Intervention in International Law
Ingrid Eide Galtung, Attitudes to Technical Assistance
Quincy Wright, Intervention and Civil Strife
Omni Wiherheimo, Raising the Standard of Living in the Developing
Countries: Some Principles for the Analysis of the Problem

Third Conference, Vol. 1 (1970)

Bert V. A. Röling, Introduction
Kenneth E. Boulding, The Philosophy of Peace Research
Herman Schmid, Peace Research as a Technology for Pacification
Johan Galtung, Confrontation versus Debate
Lars Dencik, Peace Research: Pacification or Revolution?
Ole Jess Olsen and Ib Martin Jarvad, The Political Functions of Social
Research—With Special Reference to Peace and Conflict Research
Johan Galtung, Feudal Systems, Structural Violence and the Structural
Theory of Revolutions
Bert V. A. Röling, Subjectivity in Peace Research
Charles Boasson, The Nature and Possible Philosophies of Peace Re-
search

Godfried van Benthem van den Bergh, Science and Reason in Peace Research

Marion Mushkat, The Small States and Research into Aspects of War and Peace

Johan Galtung, Towards a World Peace Academy: A Proposal

Third Conference, Vol. 2 (1970)

Nils Petter Gleditsch, Rank and Interaction: A General Theory with Some Applications to the International System

Kurt Jacobsen, Some Behavioral Characteristics in the United Nations as a Function of Rank

Hanna Newcombe, Michael Ross, and Alan G. Newcombe, United Nations Voting Pattern

Kjell Skjelsbæk, Development of the Systems of International Organisations: A Diachronic Study

J. David Singer, The Outcome of Arms Races: A Policy Problem and a Research Approach

Andrew Mack, "Sticks and Carrots": Theoretical Assumption Underlying Current Work on Civilian Defense Strategies

Olaf Hasselager, The Relevance of International Law to Civilian Defence

Daniel Frei, Conditions Affecting the Effectiveness of Small State Mediative Functions

Jørgen Rasmussen, Economic Impact of the Rhodesia Sanctions

Per Olav Reinton, Peace through Conflict? On the Future of the Nation-State

B. Landheer, The Situational Model in the Analysis of International Relations

Third Conference, Vol. 3 (1970)

Anders Boserup, Power in a Post-Colonial Setting: The Why and Whither of Religious Confrontation in Ulster

Malvern Lumsden, A Test of Cognitive Balance Theory in a Field Situation: A Factor-analytic Study of Perceptions in the Cyprus Conflict

Gordon Hilton, A Closed and Open Model, Analysis of Perceptions in Crisis

Peter Ernstrøm, Individual Versus Collective Conflict Behaviour: A Study of Industrial Conflict in Sweden

A. N. Oppenheim and J. C. R. Baley, Productivity and Conflict

Robin Jenkins, Ethnic Conflict and Class Consciousness: A Case Study from Belgium

Georges R. Tamarin, Dialectics of Prestige and Human Coexistence

Elia T. Zurick, The Child's Orientation to International Conflict and the United Nations: A Review of the Literature and an Analysis of a Canadian Sample

Yasumasa Tanaka, Attitudes-Expectation: Conflict in Japanese Attitudes Toward Nuclear Arms

Niels Lindberg, Strategic Targets for Conflict Prevention

Mari Holmboe Ruge, Small-Power vs Big-Power Perspective on Foreign Policy: A Comparative Analysis of Behaviour in Norwegian and US Simulation Experiments

Peter Boskma and Hylke Tromp, A Report on Explorative Experiments with Simulation Models of International Relations and on the Effects of Participation

Fourth Conference, Vol. 1 (1974)

Norman Alcock, C. Young, and E. Kielly, Arms Race Regularities

U. Arosalo, Alliances—Coercion or Mutual Support

G. van Benthem van den Bergh, The Structure of Development

N. Bozic, On the Polymorphism of War in Our Era

G. Darnton, The Concept "Peace"

William Eckhardt, A Brief Review of the Radical Critique of Peace Research

E. daSilva, "Current Situation" and Dynamic Processes: Brazil

P. Everts, Peace and Conflict Research 1965–1971: A Preliminary Analysis of Trends and Developments

Johan Galtung, On Peace Education

H. Hveem, Peace Research—Historical Development and Future Perspective

J. Mates, The Role of Peace Research and Peace Teaching

K. Mushakoji, Structures for Peace in the North-South Perspective

M. Mushkat, Modern African Nationalism

Anatol Rapoport, Problems of Peace Research

P. O. Reinton, Tarzan and the Division of Labor

H. Schmid, Working Notes on Populism

Kjell Skjelsbæk, Young Believers in a World State

Abstracts of most of the other papers presented in Bled are appended to the volume.

Fifth Conference, Vol. 1 (1975) [published by the Asian Printing Works, Sonarpura, Váranasi, India, with the assistance of UNESCO]

M. Rafiq Khan, Editor's Note

Peace Education

Narayan Desai, The Gandhian Concept of Peace Education

Jaime Diaz, Reflections on Adult Education for Justice and Peace in Latin America (A Synthesis)

Håkan Wiberg, The Prospects of Peace

Abstracts

Betty Reardon and Charles Rivera, Approaches to Peace Education

Charles Chatfield, Peace Education as Orientation at Gustavus Adolphus and Wittenberg

Charles Chatfield, Restructuring Reality: Gandhi's Image in the United States

Anatol Pikas, The Concept of Positive Peace Meets Educational Necessities

Elmer Framvig, Education and Emancipation: The Role of the Educator as the De-manipulator

Ashakant Nimbark, War and Peace in a Sociology Curriculum

Raghubir S. Basi, A Program in Peaceful Change: The Kent State Profile

Ernst Gund, International Comprehensive School
Pierre Deleu and Alfred Vermandel, Teacher Education: A Key to the
Problem of Conflict and Education
Magnus Haavelsrud, Formal Education and the Quest for Peace
Economic Growth and Violence
Ulrich Albrecht, Peter Lock, Dieter Ernst, and Herbert Wulf, Arma-
ments and Underdevelopment
Amritananda Das, Foundations of a Theory of Maldevelopment
Rekha Mukherjee, Maldevelopment and Peacelessness: A Social Work
Viewpoint
Ernst Feder, Six Plausible Theses about the Peasants' Perspectives in
the Developing World
Abstracts
Catherine Houghton, The Language Factor in Peaceful National De-
velopment
The International System
Helge Hveem, Anti-Domination Struggle: A Problem Inventory
Chadwick F. Alger and David Hoovler, The Feudal Structure of System
of International Organisations
Dieter Senghaas, Peace Research and the Third World
Kurt P. Tudyka, Peace Research and Multinational Corporations
Elise Boulding, Transnational Networks and National Conflict Levels
R. Ko-Chih Tung, International Structure, Inter- and Intra-state Vio-
lence: A Causal Model Analysis of Change
Marek Thee, Detente and Security in the Aftermath of the Fourth
Middle East War: The International System Revisited
Svante Iger, Some Notes on the Concept of Economic Dependence
Ole Kristian Holthe, External Domination and Peripheral Development
Pasi Patokallio, United States, Japanese and European Community
Energy Strategies: An Empirical Study
Abstracts
Amalendu Guha, U.S. Economic Warfare against the Developing Con-
tinents
H. P. Handrikx, Some Coments on the Prospects of the World Univer-
sity (United Nations University)
B. B. Chatterjee, Search for an Appropriate Game Model for Gandhian
Satyagraha
I. N. Tewary, Prescriptive Control of International Conflict
Theories of Conflict and Case Studies
Alan G. Newcombe, Gernot Koehler, and James Wert, The Predictions
of War Using an Internation Tensiometer
Martin Janicke, The Comparative Analysis of Political Systems in
Terms of Crisis
Bo Wirmark, The Buddhist in Vietnam: An Alternative View of the War
H. J. Krysmanski, H. Huelsmann, and J. Brinkmann, Theory and Con-
flict
M. Aram, Nagaland Peace Mission: A Case in Creative Conflict Resolu-
tion

Michael Stohl, Relationship between Foreign and Domestic Conflict: A Theoretical and Methodological Assessment

Rune D. Jorgensen, Social Mobilisation, Class Alliances and Class Conflict in Latin America

Paul Wehr, Some Thoughts on Conflict Education

Nils Petter Gleditsch and J. David Singer, Distance and International War, 1816–1965

Unto Vesa, The Politics of Peace Education—The Case of Finland
Abstracts

Adam Curle, Problems of Peace Education

Takeshi Ishida, The Significance of Nonviolent Direct Action

L. P. Singh, The U.N. and Conflicts in Southern Africa: Structural Violence and International Public Policy

Sage International Yearbook of Foreign Policy Studies. Department of Political Science, Syracuse University, Syracuse, New York 13210. Publisher: Sage Publications, Inc., 275 South Beverly Drive, Beverly Hills, California 90212.

Annually since 1973; $12.50 per year.

"The fundamental assumption of this series is that the analysis of foreign policy should be grounded in the empirical tradition of the social sciences—rather than the largely descriptive or prescriptive scholarship of the past. The *Yearbook* will encourage systematic studies of the causes and consequences of foreign policy behavior that develop the field of foreign policy analysis through theoretical, comparative, logical, quantitative, normative, mathematical and qualitative forms of analysis."

Vol. 1 (1973)

Patrick J. McGowan, Introduction
Controversies

Michael Haas, On the Scope and Methods of Foreign Policy Studies
Theories

G. Matthew Bonham and Michael J. Shapiro, Simulation in the Development of a Theory of Foreign Policy Decision-Making

William D. Coplin, Stephen L. Mills, and Michael K. O'Leary, The PRINCE Concepts and the Study of Foreign Policy
Findings

Martin Abravanel and Barry Hughes, The Relationship Between Public Opinion and Governmental Foreign Policy. A Cross-National Study

Stephen Cobb, The Impact of Defense Spending on Senatorial Voting Behavior: A Study of Foreign Policy Feedback

John W. Eley and John H. Petersen, Economic Interests and American Foreign Policy Allocations, 1960–69

Raymond W. Copson, Foreign Policy Conflict Among African States, 1964–69

James G. Kean and Patrick J. McGowan, National Attributes and Foreign Policy Participation: A Path Analysis
Appraisals

Richard L. Merritt, Public Opinion and Foreign Policy in West Germany

Karl W. Deutsch and Dieter Senghaas, The Steps to War: A Survey of System Levels, Decision Stages, and Research Results

Vol. 2 (1974)
Patrick J. McGowan, Preface
Controversies
Vithal Rajan, Variations on a Theme by Richardson
Theories
Michael Brecher, Research Findings and Theory-Building in Foreign Policy Behavior
Stuart J. Thorson, Adaptation and Foreign Policy Theory
Findings
Peter Hansen, Adaptive Behavior of Small States: The Case of Denmark and the European Community
David Howard Davis, State Department Structure and Foreign Policy Decision Rules
Russell J. Leng with Robert A. Goodsell, Behavioral Indicators of War Proneness in Bilateral Conflicts
Warren R. Phillips and Robert C. Crain, Dynamic Foreign Policy Interactions: Reciprocity and Uncertainty in Foreign Policy
Methods
Joseph D. Ben-Dak and Kurt Finsterbusch, Bayesian Analysis: Applications for the Study of Foreign Behavior
Appraisals
Charles W. Kegley, Jr., Stephen A. Salmore, and David J. Rosen, Convergences in the Measurement of Interstate Behavior
Bibliography
Stewart S. Johnson, Bibliography of Recent Foreign Policy Studies, 1972–1973

Vol. 3 (1975)
Patrick J. McGowan, Preface
Theories
Abraham R. Wagner, A Rational Choice Model of Aggression: The Case of the Six Day War
Findings
Elijah Ben-Zion Kaminsky, The French Chief Executive and Foreign Policy
David H. Johns, Diplomatic Activity, Power, and Integration in Africa
John S. Odell, The Hostility of U.S. External Behavior: An Exploration
Craig Liske, Changing Patterns of Partisanship in Senate Voting on Defense and Foreign Policy, 1946–1969
Jonathan Wilkenfeld, A Time-Series Perspective on Conflict Behavior in the Middle East
Replications
Leo Hazlewood, Diversion Mechanisms and Encapsulation Processes: The Domestic Conflict–Foreign Conflict Hypothesis Reconsidered
James N. Rosenau and George H. Ramsey, Jr., External and Internal Typologies of Foreign Policy Behavior: Testing the Stability of an Intriguing Set of Findings

Appraisals
Sophia Peterson, Research on Research: Events Data Studies, 1961–1972
Bibliography
Helen E. Purkitt, Bibliography of Recent Foreign Policy Studies, 1973–1974

B. Largely Traditional

Armed Forces and Society: An Interdisciplinary Journal. Inter-University Seminar on Armed Forces and Society, Box 46 Social Science Building, University of Chicago, Chicago, Illinois 60637. Quarterly since Fall 1974.
"Devoted to research, analysis and policy papers on military organization, civil-military relations, arms control, peace keeping and conflict management, it will be international in scope with a strong emphasis on comparative and interdisciplinary writing."

Confluence: An International Forum. Summer School of Arts and Sciences and of Education, Harvard University, Cambridge, Massachusetts 02138.
Quarterly, 1952–1959.
"Contributions by scholars from all over the world who are interested in the meeting of West and East."

Cooperation and Conflict. Utrikespolitiska Institutet, Sveavaegen 166, 11346 Stockholm, Sweden, or Box 142, Boston, Massachusetts 02113.
Semiannually since 1965.
Nordic studies in international politics; book reviews, cumulative index every two years.

India Quarterly: A Journal of International Affairs. Indian Council of World Affairs, Sapru Hosse, Barakhamba Road, New Delhi 1, India.
Quarterly since 1945.
Indian politics, international relations, especially concerning Asian countries. 10–15 critical book reviews; problems; bibliography of Indian publications in the social science field.

Indian Yearbook of International Affairs. Indian Study of International Affairs, University of Madras, Madras 5, India.
Annually since 1952.
Law and international relations; documents; critical book reviews.

International Affairs. All-Union Society "Znaniye," 14 Gorokhovsky Pereulok, Moscow K-64, USSR.

Monthly since 1955.
Articles on international affairs. Sections include Our Guest Commentator, Ideology and Foreign Policy, Background Facts, International Commentary, Reviews, Facts and Figures, and Documents.

International Affairs. Polish Institute of International Affairs, "Ars Polona," Krakowskie Przedmiescie 7, Warsaw, Poland.
Monthly since 1963.
Discusses the legal, political, economic, and historical aspects of international problems; contains archival documents, book reviews, a bibliography of books and articles on international relations, a chronology of major international events.

International Affairs. Royal Institute of International Affairs, Chatham House, St. James's Square, London S.W. 1, England.
Quarterly since 1931.
National and international studies; 170 book reviews.

International Journal. Canadian Institute of International Affairs, 230 Bloor Street West, Toronto 5, Canada.
Quarterly since 1946.
International questions, Canadian foreign policy, affairs of the British Commonwealth, book reviews, books received.

International Relations. David Davies Memorial Institute of International Studies, Thorney House, Smith Square, London S.W. 1, England.
6 per year since 1954.
History and theory of international relations, book reviews.

International Studies. Indian School of International Studies, New Delhi, India.
Publisher: Asia Publishing House, Bombay 1, India.
Quarterly since 1959.
Problems of international politics. Articles and reports on existing sources and documents on problems of international politics.

The Jerusalem Journal of International Relations. Hebrew University, Givat Ram, Jerusalem, Israel.
Quarterly since 1974.
"It will strive to reflect the global significance of the Middle East. . . . An important function of the Journal will be to act as a medium for the exchange of research findings and views between Israeli scholars and the international scientific community."

Journal of Common Market Studies. Journals Department, Basil Blackwell & Wott Ltd., 108 Cowley Road, Oxford OX4 1JF, England.
Quarterly since 1962.
"Integration studies with efforts to improve theoretical understanding of the integration process."

Journal of International Affairs. School of International Affairs, Columbia University, 409 W. 117 Street, New York, New York 10027.
Semiannually since 1947.
Supersedes *Columbia Journal of International Affairs.*
Each issue is devoted to a given international, political, or economic problem; includes news reports, critical book reviews, and list of books received.

Journal of Political and Military Sociology. Northern Illinois University, DeKalb, Illinois 60115.
Semiannually since 1973.
Deals with the vital social, political, economic, and military issues.

Peace and Change. California State College, Sonoma, 1801 E. Cotati Avenue, Rohnert Park, California 94928.
Quarterly since 1972.
A forum for communicating current thought and research; transnational in character, placing emphasis on the historical and humanistic dimensions of peace studies.

SAIS Review. School of Advanced International Studies, Johns Hopkins University, 1740 Massachusetts Avenue N.W., Washington, D.C. 20036.
Quarterly since 1957.
Presents current thought on the theoretical and practical aspects of international relations as well as news items regarding the school.

World Politics. Princeton University Press, Princeton, New Jersey 08540.
Editorial Office: Corwin Hall, Princeton, New Jersey 08540.
Quarterly since 1948.
"Journal of international relations. Articles present the results of original scholarly research which have a broad theoretical impact in history, geography, economics, international relations, military affairs, foreign policy, sociology, and political theory [editorial statement]. Review articles."

World Studies. School of International Relations, University of Southern California, Los Angeles, California 90007.
3 per year since 1974.
"A new journal concerned with the more rapid dissemination of new work in the area of international studies. It is especially interested in encouraging the submission of student manuscripts, both graduate and undergraduate."

The Yearbook of World Affairs. London Institute of World Affairs.
Editorial Office: Institute of World Affairs, Thorne House, 4–8 Endsleigh Gardens, London W.C. 1H OEH, England.
Publisher: Stevens & Sons, London.
Annually since 1947.

"An invaluable collection of research articles covering important theoretical and practical topics in international relations, emphasizing political, institutional, and economic problems."

C. Largely Policy Analysis

Alternatives: A Journal of World Policy. Centre for the Study of Developing Societies, 29 Rajpur Road, Delhi 6, India.
Quarterly since March 1975.
"The Journal will be normative and policy oriented and not merely confined to presentation of empirical findings. It will deal with the problems of growing gaps between the Third World and the industrially advanced countries in both economic welfare and political power."

Atlas: Magazine of the World Press. World Press Company, 1180 Avenue of the Americas, New York, New York 10036.
Monthly since 1960.
English translations and excerpts from over 600 foreign newspapers, magazines, and books.

Australian Outlook. Australian Institute of International Affairs, 252 Swanston Street, Melbourne, Australia.
3 per year since 1947.
International affairs, particularly in the Far East and Southeast Asia. Worldwide economic and political developments; 12 critical reviews.

Bulletin of Peace Proposals. International Peace Research Institute, P. O. Box 307, Oslo 3, Norway, or Box 142, Boston, Massachusetts 02113.
Quarterly since 1970.
Science and social problems as well as current and general conflict situations in the contemporary world.

Co-existence. Box 429, Pickering, Ontario, Canada.
Semiannually since 1964.
Comparative economic, sociological, and political studies in the light of peaceful co-existence; statistics.

Foreign Affairs. Council on Foreign Relations, 58 East 68th Street, New York, New York 10021.
Quarterly since 1922.
International politics, current national and international problems, diplomacy, international economy. Annotated bibliography of recent books and official documents.

Foreign Policy. Foreign Policy Association, 345 East 46th Street, New York, New York 10017.
Quarterly since 1971.

"Published in order to bring together the best minds of this generation, to debate and help reformulate America's role in the world. It has already become the most relevant and provocative magazine of its kind in the U.S."

Foreign Policy Bulletin. Foreign Policy Association, 345 E. 46th Street, New York, New York 10017.
Semimonthly since 1921.
Contains articles by specialists on international relations and chronicles current international events.

Foreign Service Journal. American Foreign Service Association, 1742 G Street, Washington, D.C. 20006.
Monthly since 1924.
Articles on life and work in the foreign service of the U.S. and on diplomacy and foreign policy. Not an official publication.

International Conciliation. Carnegie Endowment for International Peace, United Nations Plaza, East 46th Street, New York, New York 10017.
5 per year since 1907.
One or two studies on a given international question (political, economic, cultural) or reports on the activities of an international organization.

International Problems [Baayot Benlumiyot]. Israeli Institute of International Affairs, 2 Pinkser Street, Tel Aviv; P. O. Box 17027, Tel Aviv, Israel.
Quarterly since 1963.
International problems; notes; book reviews. Articles in English, French, and Hebrew.

Japan Annual of International Affairs. Japanese Institute of International Affairs, No. 2, 2-chome, Kasumigaseki, Chiyoda-ku, Tokyo, Japan.
Annually since 1961.
Japanese foreign policy and economy, economic development, international relations, reports on societies, diplomatic report.

Korean Journal of International Law [Kuk jae beup hak hoeu none tchang]. Korean Association of International Law, 24 Sokong-dong, Choong-ku, Seoul, Korea.
Quarterly since 1957.
"Studies in public and private international law; studies on the powers' foreign policy, especially U.S. policy towards Korea and Japanese policy; international affairs; problems of collective security within the UNO; list of books received; critical book review."

Lo Spettatore Internazionale [English version]. Instituto Affari Internazionali, Viale Mazzini 88, 00195, Rome, Italy.
Quarterly since 1965.

Maral: A Political Fortnightly. Surag Bhan Gupta, 11 South Avenue, New Delhi 11, India.
Quarterly since 1959.
Problems of international politics; debates on international problems; documents; book reviews.

Orbis. Foreign Policy Research Institute, University of Pennsylvania, 133 S. 36th Street, Room 102, Philadelphia, Pennsylvania 19174.
Quarterly since 1957.
"Important issues, events, and trends in international relations, with emphasis on problems in U.S. foreign policy, country and area studies, and analyses of communist strategy, arms control, technology, and military affairs. Occasional articles on theory and methodology in international relations."

Policy Sciences. Elsevier Publishing Co., Box 211, Amsterdam, the Netherlands.
Quarterly since 1972.
"Theoretical and analytical studies of the methods, content, rationality, and problems of the policy sciences. Features case histories; aim is to provide a forum for papers combining the behavioral and decision sciences and developing a new interdisciplinary activity."

Review of International Affairs. P. O. Box 413, 11001 Belgrade, Yugoslavia.
Semimonthly since 1949.
"A reliable and indispensable source of information on Yugoslav views relating to current international developments as well as political, economic and social trends in Yugoslavia today."

The Round Table: The Commonwealth Journal of International Affairs. 18 Northumberland Avenue, London W.C. 2N 5AP, England.
Quarterly since 1910.

Survival. The International Institute for Strategic Studies, 18 Adam Street, London W.C. 2N 6AL, England.
Bimonthly since 1959.
Reprints of articles in periodicals and statements of official policy concerning defense and disarmament problems published in various countries, including Soviet Russia and Red China. Book reviews.

War/Peace Report. Center for War/Peace Studies, 218 East 18th Street, New York, New York 10003.
Monthly since 1961.
Fact and opinion on progress toward a world of peace.

World Affairs. American Peace Society, Suite 302, 4000 Albemarle Street N.W., Washington, D.C. 20016.
Quarterly since 1837.
Oldest journal of international affairs in the U.S. International relations, law and organization, foreign policy, comparative politics, theory, and diplomatic history.

The World Today. Royal Institute of International Affairs, Press Road,
  Neasden, London N.W. 10 ODD, England.
  Monthly since 1945.
    Deals with international problems; includes articles on internal political
    and economic conditions in individual countries.

V. Special Series in International Politics

Adelphi Papers, Research Publications Services, Victoria Hall, East Greenwich, London S.E. 10, England (1963–).

American-Asian Educational Exchange Monograph Series, Institute of Far Eastern Studies, Seton Hall University, South Orange, N.J. 07079 (1968–).

Conflict Studies, Institute for the Study of Conflict, 17 Northumberland Avenue, London W.C. 2N 5BJ, England (1970–).

Headline Series, Foreign Policy Association, 345 East 46th Street, New York 10017 (1935–).

International Conciliation, Carnegie Endowment for International Peace, New York (1907–).

Jerusalem Papers on Peace Problems, Leonard Davis Institute for International Relations, Hebrew University of Jerusalem, Israel (1974–).

Monograph Series, Department of International Relations, Lehigh University, Bethlehem, Pa. 18016 (1973–).

Monograph Series in World Affairs, Social Science Foundation and Graduate School of International Studies, University of Denver, Denver, Col. 80210 (1963–).

National Strategy Information Center, Monograph Series, 130 East 67th Street, New York 10021 (1962–).

Occasional Papers in International Affairs, Center for International Affairs, 6 Divinity Avenue, Cambridge, Mass. 02138 (1961–1974). Superseded by *Harvard Studies in International Affairs* (1974–).

Peace Research Reviews, 25 Dundana Avenue, Dundas, Ontario L9H 4E5, Canada (1968–).

Sage Professional Papers in International Studies, Beverly Hills, Ca.: Sage (1972–).

Security Studies Papers, Security Studies Project, University of California, Los Angeles 90024 (1965–).

Southern California Arms Control and Foreign Policy Seminar, 1700 Main Street, Santa Monica, Ca. 90406 (1971–).

Studies in International Affairs Series, Institute of International Studies, University of South Carolina Press, Columbia 29208 (1974–).

War, Revolution, and Peacekeeping, Beverly Hills, Ca.: Sage Research Progress Series (1973–).

The Washington Papers, Beverly Hills, Ca.: Sage Papers (1972–).

The Yearbook of World Policy, New York: Praeger (1957–).

VI. Abstracts and Book Reviews

Background on World Politics. Center for Foreign Service Studies, Baylor University, Waco, Texas 76703.
Quarterly, 1957–1962.
Superseded by *Background: Journal of the International Studies Association*.
"Serving the generalists by condensing the specialists." Digests of articles from American and foreign periodicals specializing in military, scientific, economic, political, and social developments relating to national policy-making processes.

Background: Journal of the International Studies Association. University of California, Los Angeles 90024.
Quarterly, 1962–1966.
Superseded by *International Studies Quarterly*.
"Articles and essays which survey and appraise 'the state of the field' in particular aspects or specializations, which introduce or suggest clearly new concepts, conceptual frameworks, models, or theoretical constructions, or which explore the relationships between fields and disciplines in international studies."

Book Review Digest. New York: H. W. Wilson.
Annually since 1905.

Current Thought on Peace and War: A Semiannual Digest of Literature and Research in Progress on the Problems of World Order and Conflict. White Plains, N.Y.
Semiannually, 1960–1967.

Dissertation Abstracts: Abstracts of Dissertations and Monographs in Microfilm. Ann Arbor: University of Michigan Microfilms.
Monthly since 1938.

Historical Abstracts 1775–1945: A Quarterly of Abstracts of Historical Articles Appearing Currently in Periodicals the World Over. Vienna and New York.
Annually since 1955.

169

International Political Science Abstracts. Basil Blackwell, 4 Broad Street, Oxford, England.
Quarterly since 1950.
  Periodicals in political science and other social sciences are the source.

Jones, Susan D., and J. David Singer. *Beyond Conjecture in International Politics,* Itasca, Ill.: Peacock (1972).

McGowan, Patrick J., and Howard B. Shapiro. *The Comparative Study of Foreign Policy: A Survey of Scientific Findings,* Beverly Hills, Ca.: Sage (1973).

Peace Research Abstracts Journal. Canadian Peace Research Institute, 119 Thomas Street, Oakville, Ontario, Canada (1964–).

Perspective. Government/Politics/International Affairs, 4000 Albemarle Street N.W., Suite 302, Washington, D.C. 20016 (1972–).

The Political Science Reviewer. P. O. Box 52, Hampden-Sydney College, Hampden-Sydney, Virginia 23943.
Annually since 1970.
  "An annual review, featuring article-length reviews of the leading political science textbooks, the great classics, and recent studies in law and politics."

VII. Data Sources and Handbooks

A. Approaches

International Encyclopedia of the Social Sciences, New York: Macmillan and Free Press (1968).

Lorwin, Val R., and Jacob Price (eds.). *The Dimensions of the Past: Materials, Problems, and Opportunities for Quantitative Work in History*, New Haven, Conn.: Yale University Press (1972).

Moor, Carol, and Waldo Chamberlin. *How to Use United Nations Documents*, New York: New York University Press (1952).

Morgenstern, Oskar. *On the Accuracy of Economic Observations*, rev. ed., Princeton, N.J.: Princeton University Press (1963).

Munton, Donald, and Philip Burgess. "An Inventory of Archived and Fugitive International Data," Columbus, Ohio: Behavioral Sciences Laboratory Research Report No. 39-P (1971).

Murdock, George P. *An Outline of Cultural Materials*, 4th ed., New Haven, Conn.: Yale University Press (1961).

Park, Tong-when. "A Guide to Data Sources in International Relations: Annotated Bibliography with Lists of Variables," Evanston, Ill.: Northwestern University, mimeographed (1968).

B. Attribute Data (Ecological Phenomena)

Almanac of Current World Leaders, Los Angeles: Llewellyn (1958–).

Almanach de Gotha: Annual of Statistics, Gotha, Germany: Justus Perthes (1764–1940).

Angel, Juvenal L. *Directory of International Agencies*, New York: Simon & Schuster (1970).

Balance of Payments Yearbook, Washington, D.C.: International Monetary Fund, United Nations (1946/47–).

Banks, Arthur S. *Cross-Polity Time-Series Data*, Cambridge, Mass.: MIT Press (1971).

_____, and Robert B. Textor (eds.). A *Cross-Polity Survey*, Cambridge, Mass.: MIT Press (1963).

Beyer, Siegfried. *Guide to the Soviet Navy*, Annapolis: U.S. Naval Institute (1970).

Bidwell, Robin. *Bidwell's Guide to Government Ministers*, 3 vols., London: Frank Cass (1974).

Boyd, Andrew. *An Atlas of World Affairs*, 4th ed., New York: Praeger (1962).

Brassey's Annual: The Armed Forces Yearbook, New York: Praeger; Macmillan (1886–1972).

Commodity Trade Statistics According to the Standard International Trade Classification, New York: U.N. Statistical Office (1951–).

Davies, Howell (ed.). *South American Handbook, 1955–1956*, New York: H. W. Wilson (1955).

Demographic Yearbook, New York: U.N. Publications (1948–).

Doane, Robert. *World Balance Sheet*, New York: Harper (1957–).

Dougall, Richardson, and Mary Patricia Chapman. *United States Chief of Mission, 1778–1973*, Washington, D.C.: Department of State (1973).

Dupuy, Trevor N., et al. (eds.). *The Almanac of World Military Power*, Harrisburg, Pa.: Stackpole (1970).

Economic Survey of Europe, New York: U.N. Economic Commission for Europe (1947–).

European Year Book, The Hague: Nijhoff (1955–).

Fielder, William R. A *Rationale: Holt Data Bank System*, New York: Holt, Rinehart & Winston (1971).

The Foreign Office List and Diplomatic and Consular Yearbook, 160 vols., London: Harrison (1806–1966).

Ginsburg, Norton S. *Atlas of Economic Development*, Chicago: University of Chicago Press (1961).

Industrial Statistics 1900–1962, Paris: Organisation for Economic Co-operation and Development (1964).

International Financial Statistics, Washington, D.C.: International Monetary Fund, United Nations (1948–).

Jameson, John Franklin. A *Provisional List of Printed Lists of Ambassadors and other Diplomatic Representatives*, Paris: Presses universitaires de France (1928).

Jane, Fred T. (ed.). *Jane's All the World's Aircraft*, New York: McGraw-Hill (1919-).

————. *Jane's Fighting Ships*, New York: Arco (1898-).

Jane's Weapon Systems [comp. Ron Pretty and Denis Archer], New York: McGraw-Hill (1970-1972).

Main Economic Indicators 1955-1971, Paris: Organisation for Economic Co-operation and Development (1973).

Mallory, Walter H. *Political Handbook of the World: Parliaments, Parties, and Press as of January 1, 1962*, New York: Harper (1962).

Martell, Paul, and Grace P. Hayes. *World Military Leaders*, New York: Bowker (1974).

Mickiewicz, Ellen (ed.). *Handbook of Soviet Social Science Data*, New York: Free Press (1973).

Mitchell, Brian R. *European Historical Statistics*, New York: Columbia University Press (1975).

Mulhall, Michael G. *The Dictionary of Statistics*, London: G. Routledge & Sons (1899-).

Myers, Denys Peter. *List of Arbitration Treaties, Pacts, to Which Pairs of Nations are Parties*, World Peace Foundation Pamphlet Series 2/1, Boston (1911).

Network of World Trade, Geneva: League of Nations Publications (1942).

Patterton, W. J. *International Businessmen's Who's Who*, London: Burke's Peerage (1967; 1970).

Political Handbook and Atlas of the World, New York: Harper & Row (1964).

Production Yearbook, New York: Food and Agriculture Organization of the U.N. (1948-).

Reference Handbook of the Armed Forces of the World, Washington, D.C.: Robert C. Sellers & Associates (1966-).

The Report on World Affairs 1919-1973, London: World Microfilms Publications (1919-).

Rummel, Rudolph J. *Dimensions of Nations*, Beverly Hills, Ca.: Sage (1972).

Russett, Bruce M., et al. *World Handbook of Political and Social Indicators*, New Haven, Conn.: Yale University Press (1964).

SIPRI Yearbook of World Armaments and Disarmament, Stockholm, Sweden: Almqvist & Wiksell; New York: Humanities Press; London: Gerald Duckworth (1968-1969; 1969-1970).

174   ATTRIBUTE DATA

Statistical Abstract of Latin America, Los Angeles: University of California Press (1955–).

Statistical Yearbook, New York: U.N. Statistical Office (1948–).

Statistical Yearbook, Paris: UNESCO (1963–).

Strategic Survey. The International Institute for Strategic Studies, 18 Adam Street, London W.C. 2N 6AL, England (1971–).

Sworalowski, Witold S. (ed.). *World Communism: A Handbook, 1918–1965*, Stanford, Ca.: Hoover Institution Press (1973).

Taylor, Charles, and Michael Hudson. *World Handbook of Political and Social Indicators*, 2d ed., New Haven, Conn.: Yale University Press (1972).

Teng, Catherine (comp.). *Synopses of United Nations Cases in the Field of Peace and Security, 1946–1967*, New York: Carnegie Endowment for International Peace (1968).

Trade Yearbook, Rome: Food and Agriculture Organization of the U.N. (1958–).

Treaties and Alliances of the World: A Survey of International Treaties in Force and Communities of States, London: Keesing's (1968); New York: Scribner's (1969).

United Nations Demographic Yearbook, New York: U.N. Statistical Office (1948–).

United Nations Yearbook of International Trade Statistics, New York: U.N. Statistical Office (1950–).

Verzijl, J. H. W. *The Jurisprudence of the World Court*, vol. 1, *The Permanent Court of International Justice, 1922–1940*, Leyden: Sijthoff (1965); vol. 2, *The International Court of Justice, 1947–1965* (1966).

Vincent, Jack E. *The Handbook of International Relations*, New York: Barron's (1969; 1974).

_____. *Handbook of the United Nations*, New York: Barron's (1969; 1974).

World Energy Supplies, New York: U.N. Statistical Office (1929–).

World Guide to Trade Associations: Part 1, Europe, New York: Bowker (1973).

World Guide to Trade Associations: Part 2, Africa, New York: Bowker (1973).

The Worldmark Encyclopedia of the Nations, 5 vols., New York: Harper & Row (1963).

World Military Expenditures, Washington, D.C.: U.S. Arms Control and Disarmament Agency (1964–).

The World's Telephones: Telephone Statistics of the World; Telephone and Telegraph Statistics of the World, New York: American Telephone and Telegraph Company (Jan. 1, 1914, 1921, 1926, 1939, 1948, 1953).

Woytinski, Wladimir, and Emma S. Woytinski. *World Population and Production: Trends and Outlook*, New York: Twentieth Century Fund (1953).

––––––. *World Commerce and Governments: Trends and Outlook*, New York: Twentieth Century Fund (1955).

Yearbook of International Organizations, Brussels: Union of International Associations (1948–).

Yearbook of International Statistics, New York: U.N. Statistical Office (1950–).

Yearbook of Labour Statistics, Geneva: International Labor Office, United Nations (1935/36–).

Yearbook of National Accounts Statistics, New York: U.N. Statistical Office (1957–).

Yearbook of the United Nations, Geneva: U.N. Publications (1970–).

C. Diplomatic, Political, and Military Events Data (Behavioral Phenomena)

Annual of Power and Conflict: A Survey of Political Violence and International Influence, London: Institute for the Study of Conflict (1972–).

Annual Register of World Events, London: Longmans (1758–).

Annual Review of United Nations Affairs, New York: Graduate Program of International Studies, New York University (1949–).

Arbitrations and Diplomatic Settlements of the United States, 1794–1914, Washington, D.C.: Carnegie Endowment for International Peace (1914).

Arnold-Baker, C., and Anthony Dent. *Everyman's Dictionary of Dates*, New York: Dutton (1954).

Britannica Book of the Year, Chicago: Encyclopedia Britannica (1938–).

Chamberlin, Waldo, et al. (eds.). *A Chronology and Fact Book of the United Nations, 1941–1969*, Dobbs Ferry, N.Y.: Oceana (1959; 1964; 1970).

"Chronology of Year's Events," *World Almanac and Book of Facts*, Cleveland, Ohio: Newspaper Enterprise Association (1868–).

Collier's Year Book, New York: Crowell-Collier & Son (1939–).

Deadline Data on World Affairs, Greenwich, Conn.: DMS Inc. (1956–).

Donelan, M. D., and M. J. Grieve. *International Disputes: Case Histories 1945–1970*, New York: St. Martin's Press (1973).

Drachkovitch, Milorad M., and Branko Lazitch. *The Comintern: Historical Highlights*, Stanford, Ca.: Hoover Institution Press (1967).

Dupuy, R. Ernest, and Trevor N. Dupuy. *The Encyclopedia of Military History from 3500 B.C. to the Present*, New York: Harper & Row (1970).

Facts on File: Weekly World News Digest with Cumulative Index, New York: Person's Index, Facts on File, Inc. (1940–).

Harbottle, Thomas B. *Dictionary of Battles from the Earliest Date to the Present Time*, London: Sonneschein (1904).

Keesing's Contemporary Archives: Weekly Diary of World Events with Index Continually Kept Up-to-Date, London: Keesing's (1931–).

Keller, Helen Rex. *A Dictionary of Dates*, New York: Macmillan (1934).

Langer, William L. (ed.). *An Encyclopedia of World History*, Boston: Houghton Mifflin (1940; 1948; 1952; 1968; 1972).

The New International Year Book: A Compendium of the World's Progress for the Year, New York: Funk & Wagnalls (1932–).

The New York Times Index, New York: New York Times (1851–).

Nordheim, Erik V., and Pamela Wilcox. "Major Events of the Nuclear Age: A Chronology to Assist in the Analysis of American Public Opinion," Oak Ridge, Tenn.: Oak Ridge National Laboratory Civil Defense Research Project (1967).

Palmer, A. W. *A Dictionary of Modern History, 1789–1945*, Baltimore: Penguin (1962).

Putnam, George, and George Haven Putnam (comps.). *Dictionary of Events: A Handbook of Universal History*, New York: Grosset & Dunlap (1890).

Rohn, Peter H. *World Treaty Index*, 5 vols., Santa Barbara: ABC–Clio (1975).

_____. *Treaty Profiles*, Santa Barbara: ABC–Clio (forthcoming).

Singer, J. David, and Melvin Small. *The Wages of War, 1816–1965: A Statistical Handbook*, New York: Wiley (1972).

SIPRI Yearbook of World Armaments and Disarmament, Stockholm: International Research Institute (1973–1974).

Sorokin, Pitirim A. *Social and Cultural Dynamics*, vol. 3, *Fluctuation of Social Relationships, War and Revolution*, New York: American (1937).

Stuyt, Alexander M. *Survey of International Arbitrations, 1794–1970*, Dobbs Ferry, N.Y.: Oceana (1972).

Survey of International Affairs, New York: Oxford University Press (1925–).

Survey of International Affairs: Consolidated Index to the Survey of International Affairs, 1920–1938 [comp. E. M. P. Ditman], London: Oxford University Press (1967).

Toynbee, Arnold. *Survey of International Affairs, 1939–1946: The War and the Neutrals*, New York: Oxford University Press (1956).

The United States in World Affairs, New York: Harper & Bros. (1932–).

Williams, Neville. *Chronology of the Modern World: 1763 to the Present Time*, New York: David McKay (1967).

Yearbook of International Congress Proceedings, Brussels: Union of International Associations (1970).

Yearbook on International Communist Affairs, Stanford, Ca.: Hoover Institution Press (1966–).

D. Collections of Documents

British Foreign Policy: Some Relevant Documents, January 1950–April 1955, London and New York: Royal Institute of International Affairs (1955).

Brockway, Thomas P. *Basic Documents in U.S. Foreign Policy*, Princeton, N.J.: Van Nostrand (1957; 1968).

Burr, Robert N., and Roland D. Hussey. *Documents of Inter-American Cooperation*, vol. 1, *1810–1881*, Philadelphia: University of Pennsylvania Press (1955).

Communist Perspective: A Handbook of Communist Doctrinal Statements in the Original Russian and English, Washington, D.C.: External Research Staff, Office of Intelligence Research (1955).

Degras, Jane (ed.). *The Communist International, 1919–1943: Documents*, vol. 1, *1919–1922*, New York: Oxford University Press (1956).⁻

The Documents of the League of Nations, New Haven, Conn.: Research Publications (1973).

Documents on American Foreign Relations, Boston: World Peace Foundation (1938–).

Documents on Foreign Policy, Canberra: Australian Government Publishing Service (1974).

Documents on International Affairs, London: Royal Institute of International Affairs (1929–).

Grenville, John S. *Major International Treaties 1914–1973: History and Guide with Texts*, New York: Stein & Day (1974).

Historic Documents: An Annual Series. Congressional Quarterly Inc., 1414 22nd Street N.W., Washington, D.C. 20037.

Hudson, Manley (ed.). *International Legislation: A Collection of the Texts of Multipartite International Instruments of General Interest, 1919–1940*, 9 vols., Washington, D.C.: Carnegie Endowment (1931–1950).

Peaslee, Amos J. *International Governmental Organizations*, The Hague: Nijhoff (1956; 1961; 1974).

Plischke, Elmer (ed.). *International Relations: Basic Documents*, Princeton, N.J.: Van Nostrand (1953; 1962).

Renoux, Yvette. *Glossary of International Treaties*, Amsterdam: Elsevier (1970).

Schlesinger, Arthur M. *Major Documents of American Foreign Policy since 1945*, New York: Chelsea House (1970).

Temperley, Harold William Vazeille. *A Century of Diplomatic Blue Books, 1814–1914*, Cambridge: At the University Press (1938).

Watt, D. C., et al. (eds.). *Documents on International Affairs 1963*, New York: Oxford University Press (1973).

VIII. Bibliographies of International Politics

Aggarwal, Lalit K. *Peace Science: A Bibliography*, Philadelphia: Department of Peace Science, University of Pennsylvania (1974).

Annotated Bibliography on Disarmament and Military Questions, Geneva: League of Nations Publications (1931).

Aufricht, Hans. *General Bibliography on International Organizations and Post-War Reconstruction*, New York: Commission to Study the Organization of Peace (1942).

————. *Guide to League of Nations Publications*, New York: Columbia University Press (1951).

Ball, Joyce. *Foreign Statistical Documents: A Bibliography of General, International Trade, and Agricultural Statistics*, Stanford, Ca.: Hoover Institution Press (1967).

Beardsley, Seymour W., and Alvin G. Edgell. *Human Relations in International Affairs: A Guide to Significant Interpretation and Research*, Washington, D.C.: Public Affairs Press (1956).

Bemis, Samuel F., and Grace Griffin. *Guide to the Diplomatic History of the United States, 1775–1921*, Washington, D.C.: Government Printing Office (1935).

Bestermann, Theodore. *World Bibliography of Bibliographies*, 4 vols., 3d ed., Geneva: Societas Bibliographica (1955–1956).

Blumberg, Harry H. "An Annotated Bibliography of Serials Concerned with the Non-Violent Protest Movement," *Sociological Abstracts* 17 (July–Aug. 1959): 21–50.

Boardman, Robert. *Britain and the International System, 1945–1973: A Guide to the Literature*, Halifax, Nova Scotia: Centre for Foreign Policy Studies, Dalhousie University (1974).

Boehm, Eric H. *Bibliographies on International Relations and World Affairs: An Annotated Directory*, Santa Barbara: ABC–Clio (1965).

179

Breycha-Vauthier, A. C. von. *Sources of Information: A Handbook on the Publications of the League of Nations*, New York: Columbia University Press (1939).

Brimmer, Brenda, et al. *A Guide to the Use of United Nations Documents*, Dobbs Ferry, N.Y.: Oceana (1962).

Brock, Clifton. *The Literature of Political Science: A Guide for Students, Librarians, and Teachers*, New York: Bowker (1969).

Brodie, Fawn. *Peace Aims and Post War Planning: A Bibliography*, Boston: World Peace Foundation (1942).

Brown, Everett S. *Manual of Government Publications, United States and Foreign*, New York: Johnson Reprint Co. (1950).

Brown, J. Cudd, and Michael Rieg. *Administration of United States Foreign Affairs: A Bibliography*, University Park, Pa.: Pattee Library (1968).

Burchfield, Laverne. *Student's Guide to Materials in Political Science*, New York: Holt (1935).

Burt, Richard, and Geoffrey Kemp. *Congressional Hearings on American Defense Policy: An Annotated Bibliography*, Lawrence: University Press of Kansas (1973).

Carter, April, et al. *Non-Violent Action: Theory and Practice, A Selected Bibliography*, London: Housmans (1966).

Chamberlin, Waldo, and Hartley Clark. "Materials for Undergraduate Study of the United Nations," *American Political Science Review* 49 (Mar. 1954): 204–211.

Civil Defense, 1960–1967: A Bibliographic Survey, Washington, D.C.: Government Printing Office (1967).

Clark, G. Kitson. *Guide for Research Students Working on Historical Subjects*, London: Cambridge University Press (1958).

Clemens, Walter C., Jr. *Soviet Disarmament Policy, 1917–1963: An Annotated Bibliography*, Stanford, Ca.: Hoover Institution Press (1968).

Collart, Yves. *Disarmament: A Study Guide and Bibliography on the Efforts of the United Nations*, The Hague: Nijhoff (1958).

Comprehensive Dissertation Index, 1861–, Ann Arbor, Mich.: Xerox University Microfilms (1973–).

Condit, D. M., et al. *A Counterinsurgency Bibliography*, Washington, D.C.: American University Press (1963).

Conover, Helen F. *Non-Self-Governing Areas with Special Emphasis on Mandates and Trusteeships: A Selected List of References*, Washington, D.C.: Library of Congress (1947).

———. *A Guide to Bibliographic Tools for Research in Foreign Affairs*, 2d ed., Washington, D.C.: Library of Congress (1958).

Conscientious Objection to War: A Selected Bibliography, Philadelphia: Central Committee for Conscientious Objectors (1950).

Cook, Blanche W. *A Bibliography on Peace Research in History*, Santa Barbara: ABC–Clio (1969).

———, et al. *The Garland Library of War and Peace*, New York: Garland (1971).

Crawford, Elizabeth T. *The Social Sciences in International and Military Policy: An Analytic Bibliography*, Washington, D.C.: Bureau of Social Science Research (1965).

Danielson, Wayne A., and G. C. Wilhoit, Jr. *A Computerized Bibliography of Mass Communication Research*, New York: Magazine Publishers Association (1967).

Davis, E. Jeffries, and E. G. R. Taylor. *Guide to Periodicals and Bibliographies Dealing with Geography, Archeology and History*, London: Historical Association (1938).

DeGrazia, Alfred. *The Universal Reference System: Political Science, Government and Public Policy Series*, vol. 1, *International Affairs*, New York: Universal Reference System (1965).

Deutsch, Karl W. *An Interdisciplinary Bibliography on Nationalism, 1935–1953*, Cambridge, Mass.: MIT Press (1956).

Dexter, Byron. *The Foreign Affairs 50-Year Bibliography: New Evaluations of Significant Books on International Relations, 1920–1970*, New York: Bowker (1972).

Dimitrov, Th. D. *Documents of International Organisations: A Bibliographic Handbook*, London: International University Publications (1973).

Directory of Periodicals Published by International Organizations, 3d ed., Brussels: Union of International Associations (1969).

Ditmas, E. M. R. *Consolidated Index to the Survey of International Affairs, 1920–1938, and Documents on International Affairs, 1928–1938*, London: Oxford University Press (1967).

Documents Index: United Nations and Specialized Agencies Documents and Publications, ST/LIB/SERE/1–67 (Jan. 1950–Oct. 1954).

Douma, J. *Bibliographical List of Official and Unofficial Publications Concerning the Court of International Justice*, The Hague: Permanent Court of International Justice (1926).

———. *Bibliography on the International Court Including the Permanent Court, 1918–1964*, Leyden: Sijthoff (1966).

Driver, Edwin D. *World Population Policy: An Annotated Bibliography*, Lexington, Mass.: Lexington Books (1971).

Engel, Trude. *Bibliography on Peace Research in History*, Urbana, Ill.: Conference on Peace Research in History (1964).

Five Foot Shelf of Pacifist Literature, Philadelphia: Pacifist Research Bureau (1942).

Five Year Index to ABC POL SCI, Santa Barbara: ABC–Clio (1974).

Foreign Affairs Bibliography: A Selected and Annotated List of Books on International Relations, 1919–1962, New York: Harper & Bros. (1933–1955); New York: Bowker (1964).

Foreign Affairs Research: A Directory of Governmental Resources, Washington, D.C.: Government Printing Office (1967).

Geiger, Kent. *National Development: An Annotated, Evaluated Bibliography of the Most Important Articles on National Development*, Metuchen, N.J.: Scarecrow (1969).

Gould, Wesley L., and Michael Barkun (eds.). *Social Science Literature: A Bibliography for International Law*, Princeton, N.J.: Princeton University Press (1972).

Gray, Charles H., et al. *A Bibliography of Peace Research*, Eugene, Ore.: General Research Analysis Methods (1968).

Greenwood, John, et al. *American Defense Policy since 1945: A Preliminary Bibliography*, Lawrence: University Press of Kansas (1973).

Guide to Microforms in Print 1974, Washington, D.C.: Microcard Editions Books (1974).

Guide to Reprints, Englewood, Col.: Microcard Editions Books (1974).

Haas, Michael. *International Organization: An Interdisciplinary Bibliography*, Stanford, Ca.: Hoover Institution Press (1972).

Hammond, Thomas T. *Soviet Foreign Relations and World Communism: A Selected Annotated Bibliography of 7,000 Books in 30 Languages*, Princeton, N.J.: Princeton University Press (1965).

Hamori, Laszlo. *Bibliography on Federalism*, Geneva: League of Nations Library (1940).

Hansen, Donald, and Herschel Parsons. *Mass Communication: A Research Bibliography*, Santa Barbara: Glendessary (1968).

Harmon, Robert B. *Political Science: A Bibliographical Guide to the Literature*, Metuchen, N.J.: Scarecrow (1965; supplement 1972).

_____. *The Art and Practice of Diplomacy: A Selected and Annotated Guide*, Metuchen, N.J.: Scarecrow (1971).

Hicks, Frederick C. "International Organization: An Annotated Reading List," *International Conciliation* 124 (Jan. 1919): 67–115.

Holler, Frederick L. *Information Sources of Political Science: International Relations and Organizations, Comparative and Area Studies of Politics*, vol. 4, Santa Barbara: ABC–Clio (1974).

International Bibliography of Political Science, Paris: UNESCO (1952–).

International Politics: A Selective Monthly Bibliography, Washington, D.C.: Department of State (1956–1961).

Kanet, Roger. *Soviet and East European Foreign Policy: A Bibliography of English- and Russian-Language Publications 1967–1971*, Santa Barbara: ABC–Clio (1974).

Kenworthy, Leonard S. *Free and Inexpensive Materials on World Affairs*, Washington, D.C.: Public Affairs Press (1954).

Kuehl, Warren F. *Dissertations in History: An Index to Dissertations Completed in History Departments of United States and Canada Universities, 1873–1960*, Lexington: University of Kentucky Press (1965).

Lang, Kurt. *Military Institutions and the Sociology of War: A Review of the Literature with Annotated Bibliography*, Beverly Hills, Ca.: Sage (1972).

Langer, William L., and Hamilton F. Armstrong (eds.). *Foreign Affairs Bibliography: A Selected and Annotated List of Books on International Affairs, 1919–1932*, New York: Russell & Russell (1960).

Legault, Albert. *Peace-Keeping Operations: A Bibliography*, Paris: International Information Center on Peace-Keeping Operations (1967).

Mason, John Brown. *Research Resources*, vol. 1, *International Relations and Recent History*, Santa Barbara: ABC–Clio (1968).

———. *Research Resources: Annotated Guides to the Social Sciences*, Santa Barbara: ABC–Clio (1968).

Matthews, Mary Alice. *The Peace Movement: A Select List of References on National and International Organizations for the Advancement of Peace*, New York: Carnegie Endowment (1940).

Meulen, Jacob. *Bibliography of the Peace Movement before 1899*, The Hague: Nijhoff (1936).

Miller, William R. *Bibliography of Books on War, Pacifism, Nonviolence and Related Studies*, Nyack, N.Y.: Fellowship of Reconciliation (1961).

Moody, Margaret. *Catalog of International Law and Relations*, 20 vols., Dobbs Ferry, N.Y.: Oceana (1965–1967).

Mowlana, Hamid. *International Communication: A Selected Bibliography*, Dubuque, Iowa: Kendall/Hunt (1972).

Nafziger, Ralph Otto. *International News and the Press: An Annotated Bibliography*, New York: H. W. Wilson (1940).

Newspapers in Microform: Foreign Countries, 1948–1972, Washington, D.C.: Library of Congress, Card Division, Navy Yard Annex (1974).

Page, Donald M. *Bibliography of Works on Canadian Foreign Relations, 1945–1970*, Toronto: Canadian Institute of International Affairs (1973).

Palmer, Robert J. (comp.). *Foreign Affairs 50-Year Index* [for vols. 1–50, 1922–1972], New York: Bowker (1973).

Plischke, Elmer. *American Foreign Relations: A Bibliography of Official Sources*, College Park: University of Maryland Press (1955).

_____. *American Diplomacy: A Bibliography of Biographies, Autobiographies, and Commentaries*, College Park: University of Maryland Press (1957).

Pogany, Andras H. and Hortenzia L. *Political Science and International Relations: Books Recommended for Use of American Catholic College and University Libraries*, Metuchen, N.J.: Scarecrow (1967).

Prosad, Devi. *Non-Violence and Peacemaking: A Bibliography*, London: Commonweal Trust for War Resisters International (1963).

A *Quarterly Bibliography with Abstracts and Annotations*, vol. 1, Washington, D.C.: Arms Control and Disarmament Agency (Winter 1964–65).

Ragatz, Lowell J. *The Literature of European Imperialism, 1815–1939*, Washington, D.C.: P. Pearlman (1944).

Reno, Edward A. *League of Nations Documents, 1919–1946: A Descriptive Guide and Key to the Microfilm Collection*, New Haven, Conn.: Research Publications (1973).

Robinson, Jacob. *International Law and Organization: General Sources of Information*, Leyden: Sijthoff (1967).

Rogers, W. C. *International Administration: A Bibliography*, Chicago: Public Administration Service (1945).

Rudzinski, A. *A Selected Bibliography on International Organization*, New York: Carnegie (1953).

Schmeckebier, Laurence F., and Roy B. Eastin. *Government Publications and Their Use*, Washington, D.C.: Brookings Institution (1969).

Schutter, B. de. *Bibliography on International Criminal Law*, Leyden: Sijthoff (1972).

Social Science and Humanities Index, New York: H. W. Wilson (1907–1974). Superseded by *Social Science Index*, New York: H. W. Wilson (1974–).

Social Sciences Citation Index, Philadelphia: Institute for Scientific Information (1970–).

Speeckaert, Georges P. *International Institutions and International Organizations: A Select Bibliography*, Brussels: Union of International Associations (1956).

————. *Select Bibliography on International Organizations, 1885–1964*, Brussels: Union of International Associations (1965).

To End War: An Annotated Bibliography and 1968 Literature Catalogue, Berkeley, Ca.: World without War Council (1968).

Trask, David, et al. *A Bibliography of United States-Latin American Relations since 1810: A Selected List*, Lincoln: University of Nebraska Press (1968).

United Nations: List of Treaty Collections, New York: United Nations (1956).

Vogel, Robert. *A Breviate of British Diplomatic Blue Books, 1919–1939*, Montreal: McGill University Press (1963).

Wall, Linwood, and Brenda Brimmer. *Guide to the Use of United Nations Documents*, Dobbs Ferry, N.Y.: Oceana (1962).

Watkins, James T., and J. William Robinson (eds.). *General International Organization: A Source Book*, Princeton, N.J.: Van Nostrand (1956).

Wilcox, Francis O., and Thorsten V. Kalijarvi (eds.). *Recent American Foreign Policy: Basic Documents 1941–1951*, New York: Appleton (1952).

Williams, Stillman P. *Toward a Genuine World Security System: An Annotated Bibliography for Layman and Scholar*, Washington, D.C.: United World Federalists (1964).

Willoughby, George. *Select Bibliography on the History of the American Peace Movement*, Philadelphia: American Friends Service Committee (1967).

Wilson, Larman C. *The Teaching of International Law: An Assessment and Bibliography*, Tucson: Institute of Government Research, University of Arizona (1973).

Winchell, Constance. *Guide to Reference Books*, 8th ed., Chicago: American Library Association (1967).

Winton, Harry N. M. *Publications of the United Nations System: A Reference Guide*, New York: Bowker (1972).

Wynar, Lubomyr R. *Guide to Reference Materials in Political Science: A Selective Bibliography*, 2 vols., Denver, Col.: Libraries Unlimited (1968).

Xerox: Comprehensive Disseration Index, Ann Arbor, Mich.: University Microfilms (1973).

Zawodny, Janusz K. *Guide to the Study of International Relations*, San Francisco: Chandler (1966).

Ziegler, Janet. *World War II: A Bibliography of Books in English, 1945–1965*, Stanford, Ca.: Hoover Institution Press (1971).

Author Index

Author Index

189

The Study of International Politics was composed in 10-point Electra and Electra display by Holmes Composition Service, San Jose, California. Printing and binding by Edwards Brothers, Inc., Ann Arbor, Michigan, using a 55-pound EB Book Natural for text stock. Binding is smyth sewn with head and footbands, using Kivar 6 with cambric finish, printed in PMS 299 blue and process black, .080 binders boards, and plain white endsheets. Copy editing and text design: Barbara Phillips; proofreading, Paulette Wamego; cover design: Raymond Glass.